D0389708

More Praise for *Bright Not Broken*

"In this vitally important book, written in clear and vivid terms, the authors have succeeded admirably in explaining—to parents and professionals alike—the urgency of identifying and supporting a child's giftedness in the face of the obvious difficulties of living with disabilities, as well as the dangers of relying exclusively on the categorical approach to childhood disorders."

—**Adam Feinstein**, editor, *Looking Up;* author, *A History of Autism: Conversations with the Pioneers*

"Diane Kennedy and Rebecca Banks, with the support of Temple Grandin, have created a book to make the journey easier for parents, professionals, and anyone who cares about a twice-exceptional child. Parents, I expect you will buy many copies of this book to pass on to your children's teachers."

—**Brian Hughes**, parent and university trustee, MIT

"Kennedy and Banks have done it again! This wonderfully informative book is a must-read for parents, mental health professionals, and educators who work with exceptional children. It is exceptionally well written and speaks to everyone who works with and loves an exceptional child. Highly recommended!"

—**Donald Gallo**, PhD, clinical psychologist; author, *Diagnosing Autism Spectrum Disorders*

"The authors integrate and explain lucidly findings from the best scientific literature on ADHD and autism. *Bright Not Broken* has the power to change perspectives among professionals and laypersons alike. Exceedingly impressive ... a monumental work."

—**Steven Thurber**, PhD, ABPP, Minnesota Child and Adolescent Behavioral Health Services

"*Bright Not Broken* is a unique resource for parents and professionals who seek to understand children's behaviors. The authors are to be applauded for their clear-thinking approach to the jungle of DSM labels—a must-read for the open-minded!"

—**Lydia Furman**, MD, Rainbow Babies and Children's Hospital, Cleveland, Ohio

"*Bright Not Broken* is an outstanding analysis of the flaws in the educational and psychiatric approaches to children's challenges. Reading it gave me excellent insight into some of my more challenging cases and has had a profound impact on my personal and professional life."

—**Ruth Goldberg**, PhD, clinical and school psychologist and mother of three 2e children

"*Bright Not Broken* is a much-needed book presenting a holistic approach to those with autism and ADHD. For too long professionals have overemphasized the deficit model and ignored the talents that persons with autism and ADHD have. This book provides a much-needed corrective view, which is not alone balanced but reduces stigma. I can fully recommend the book to parents, professionals, and all those who have contact with these unique persons."

—**Michael Fitzgerald**, MD, Henry Marsh Professor of Child and Adolescent Psychiatry, Trinity College, Dublin

"A bright kid with learning disabilities sounds like an oxymoron to many—yet there are millions of brilliant children who struggle daily at school. This comprehensive guide shows how to give these kids the support they need to thrive in a one-size-fits-all education system."

—**Whitney Hoffman**, producer, LDPodcast.com

Bright Not Broken

Gifted Kids, ADHD, and Autism

Diane M. Kennedy
and Rebecca S. Banks

with Temple Grandin

JOSSEY-BASS
A Wiley Imprint
www.josseybass.com

Published by Jossey-Bass
A Wiley Imprint
989 Market Street, San Francisco, CA 94103-1741—www.josseybass.com

Jossey-Bass books and products are available through most bookstores. To contact Jossey-Bass directly call our Customer Care Department within the U.S. at 800-956-7739, outside the U.S. at 317-572-3986, or fax 317-572-4002.

Wiley also publishes its books in a variety of electronic formats and by print-on-demand. Not all content that is available in standard print versions of this book may appear or be packaged in all book formats. If you have purchased a version of this book that did not include media that is referenced by or accompanies a standard print version, you may request this media by visiting http://booksupport.wiley.com. For more information about Wiley products, visit us www.wiley.com.

Library of Congress Cataloging-in-Publication Data

Kennedy, Diane M.
Bright not broken : gifted kids, ADHD, and autism / Diane M. Kennedy, Rebecca S. Banks with Temple Grandin. — 1
p. cm.
Includes bibliographical references and index.
ISBN 978-0-470-62332-9 (cloth); ISBN 978-1-118-10181-0 (ebk.); ISBN 978-1-118-10182-7 (ebk.); ISBN 978-1-118-10183-4 (ebk.)
1. Children with disabilities—Care. 2. Gifted children—Care. 3. Exceptional children—Care. 4. Families. I. Banks, Rebecca S. II. Grandin, Temple. III. Title.
RJ137.K46 2011
649'.1528—dc23

2011021317

Printed in the United States of America
FIRST EDITION
HB Printing 10 9 8 7 6 5 4 3 2 1

For our children and grandchildren

Live as children of light (for the fruit of the light consists in all goodness, righteousness, and truth)

—Ephesians 5:8–9

Contents

Part II: Why They're Stuck

Part III: How to Help Them

About the Authors

Diane M. Kennedy, coauthor of the groundbreaking book *The ADHD-Autism Connection* (2002), is a longtime advocate for individuals with Asperger's syndrome. She is a national speaker and trainer for parents and professionals on autism spectrum disorders, ADHD, and giftedness. She is the proud mother of three twice-exceptional sons.

Rebecca S. Banks, MA, coauthor of *The ADHD-Autism Connection,* is a veteran university and public school educator. She is an experienced national speaker and trainer for parents and professionals on autism spectrum disorders, ADHD, and giftedness. A longtime advocate, she is the proud mother of two twice-exceptional children.

About the Contributor

Temple Grandin, PhD, is a professor, prolific author, and one of the most accomplished and renowned adults with autism in the world. She is the subject of the award-winning HBO movie *Temple Grandin* and has been named one of *Time* magazine's top 100 individuals in 2010.

Authors' Note

Although Temple Grandin has consulted with us on all aspects of this book, there are points in the text where her insights are best presented in her words, rather than from a collaborator's perspective. At these points, we have italicized Temple's comments and information to indicate that she is speaking directly to the reader.

For the purposes of our book, the terms *gifted* and *giftedness* refer to children who have the potential to perform creatively, intellectually, physically, or academically at levels well above what would be expected for their age group. Yet, like children with developmental or learning disabilities, they have very specific learning needs that must be identified and met in order for them to reach their full potential.

Likewise, we use the acronym HFA/AS to refer to children at the higher-IQ end of the autism spectrum, those with average to above-average intelligence. These children are usually diagnosed with Pervasive Developmental Disorder-Not Otherwise Specified (PDD-NOS) or Asperger's syndrome (AS). Where appropriate for our discussion, we will make it clear when information is particularly relevant for one diagnosis or another. Though used widely, high-functioning autism (HFA) is an unofficial diagnosis.

For the purposes of consistency, we use the masculine pronoun *he* to refer to all children, male and female.

Preface

Temple Grandin

When Diane and Rebecca contacted me about collaborating on a book about giftedness and disabilities, I was excited. I have long believed that the fields of giftedness, autism, and related disabilities need to share information. Professional literature needs to address the presence of giftedness in individuals with disabilities, especially Asperger's syndrome and high-functioning autism. In fact, giftedness combined with disabilities is an area that in my opinion has been underserved for too long. I have spoken at a few gifted conferences and have had the opportunity to share important information about how autism and giftedness have much in common.

At the many different kinds of meetings I have attended for autism, giftedness, ADHD, dyslexia, and troubled youth, I see the same kinds of kids. Although these young people may be similar, when they have different labels they are subjected to totally different ways of being treated. Each label has its own set of books, professionals, and philosophy. One of the biggest indicators that each label group stays in its own little sphere is that the books its members are reading are almost all totally different. About 95 percent of the books are unique to each label. Which "label community" the child gets assigned to can greatly affect the path he or she goes down because the label affects people's expectations.

Some of the views on giftedness and disabilities presented in this book may be novel, but they are necessary. *Bright Not*

Broken endeavors to share valuable information from the gifted field with parents and professionals in the field of disabilities. I believe strongly that this discussion is necessary to provide a comprehensive perspective on the problems facing our gifted kids who are stuck in labels, and to bring the fields of giftedness and disabilities together to focus on children's special talents, not on labels. This is why I agreed to be a contributor to this book.

One of the most troubling situations I find myself in is when I am approached by a child who introduces himself to me as a person with autism—in other words, the child is identifying himself by his autism instead of his area of interest. I personally prefer being thought of as a doctor of animal science first and as a person with autism second. This is the way our kids should be taught to see themselves, too—by their abilities, not their disabilities.

Today I am seeing too many kids who have less severe symptoms than I had, going nowhere. One of the reasons this is happening is that there are not high enough expectations for them. Some parents have adopted a "handicapped" mentality and rely too much on medication to control their children. They think "Oh, poor little Joey. He can't do this because he has ADHD (or autism or some other disorder)." I have seen smart, fully verbal twelve-year-olds who have never learned how to purchase a meal in a restaurant because it was always done for them.

Bright Not Broken provides parents and professionals a good overview of the problems facing our kids who are gifted and labeled as ADHD, ODD, Asperger's syndrome, or learning disabled. It explains who these kids are, the labels they carry, and how giftedness is not recognized or developed enough. It explores why these kids are stuck, while also critically questioning the diagnostic system and the labels it gives to children. Finally, it explains how to help develop the special abilities of kids and how to help them reach their potential. It concludes with a provocative chapter on future directions in disabilities, diagnosis, and education to stimulate dialogue among these fields about the importance of developing abilities instead of focusing on weaknesses. By helping these bright not broken children achieve their full potential, all of society will benefit.

Introduction

Diane M. Kennedy and Rebecca S. Banks

You probably picked up this book because you are the parent, teacher, or extended family member of a child whom others may view as broken—whose behavior is often out of control, who has problems making and keeping friends, who is uncooperative and headstrong, and who is underachieving even though *you* know he is bright. Chances are, this child belongs to a unique group of children known as twice-exceptional (2e) learners.

Twice exceptional is a relatively recent term that refers to children who have dual "exceptionalities"—that is, exceptional gifts (creative, academic, intellectual, or physical abilities) along with a learning or developmental disability like ADHD or an autism spectrum disorder. This perplexing mix of strengths and weaknesses often causes 2e children to "fall through the cracks" academically and socially. In many cases, a child's disability masks his giftedness, causing parents, educators, and other adults in the child's life to focus on his weaknesses rather than on developing his talents. In other cases, a child's giftedness can mask his disability, meaning that he won't receive the interventions or special education services that could help him manage and possibly overcome his disability.

It is imperative that we find and nurture the gifts in *all* our kids, 2e or not, not only for their own happiness but also for the good of society. Yet our gifted children—the Isaac Newtons and Albert

Einsteins of tomorrow—are our best hope for solving the myriad problems humanity faces. It is therefore crucial that parents and teachers of 2e kids be able to identify and support these children's giftedness in the face of the obvious difficulties of living with disabilities. This approach follows what is known as the whole child model, and it addresses both exceptionalities—the gift and the disability. (We'll be covering the whole child model in detail in Part Three, "How to Help Them.") By focusing on the whole child rather than on one exceptionality, parents and educators can strengthen and develop a child's innate giftedness while also intervening to support the deficits. With the whole child approach, adults can help 2e children recognize and develop their own talents and realize their unique potential.

We are honored to work with Temple Grandin on this project. To us she is the ultimate example of being bright not broken. Temple has dedicated her life to helping others understand autism from the inside out. By sharing her life experiences, including her struggles with autism and her extraordinary achievements, she has been able to help millions of individuals with autism spectrum disorders and related conditions worldwide find success by developing their talents. Her accomplishments are nothing short of amazing. She was named one of *Time* magazine's top influential people of 2010. An HBO biopic spotlighting her life and her accomplishments in the male-dominated world of animal science won seven Emmy Awards. And several of her books have reached the *New York Times* best-seller list. Because of her outstanding achievements as a gifted woman with autism, it is easy to understand why Temple shares several of our key concerns and insights into why 2e children are stuck, the dangers that face them, and how to help them.

There are a number of excellent books in the field of education that advocate for the importance of identifying giftedness and educating the whole child. Some authors before us have recognized that gifted children are frequently misdiagnosed with Attention-Deficit/Hyperactivity Disorder (ADHD) and, less commonly, with a high-functioning autism spectrum disorder, such as Asperger's syndrome (AS) or Pervasive Developmental Disorder-Not Otherwise Specified (PDD-NOS). However, no one yet has addressed the fact that this widespread misdiagnosis and confusion point to a much larger problem with our diagnostic system itself—and that this problem traps 2e students in two of the largest systems in our society. In *Bright Not Broken,* we explore the dysfunctional interaction between our mental health and education systems to shed light on why 2e children so often fall through the cracks. We also examine why so many of these children (and their parents) remain trapped in an endless cycle of chasing labels and interventions while our education system fails to recognize and develop their giftedness.

Two of us are mothers of 2e children; we wrote this book in large part to help other parents advocate for their own 2e children. Parents, we hope *Bright Not Broken* helps you understand why your child is stuck in a web of misdiagnosis and misunderstanding because of a flawed diagnostic system that distorts the way you and others see him. In addition, we hope that the book helps you understand why our education system too often fails to meet the needs of either your child's disability or his giftedness. We also offer you encouragement and resources to help you work around these systems to develop your child's unique talents as you minimize his deficits. Ultimately, we hope that armed with a new perspective, you will see your child as bright not broken and will understand how best to help him achieve his full potential.

Because 2e children come from an exceptional gene pool, you may, as we have, recognize qualities of yourself in this book as you learn about your child. We encourage you to use the appropriate resources given in the Additional Resources section to seek support for your own exceptionalities.

2e Moms on a Mission

We (Diane and Rebecca) began our journey into the relatively obscure world of dual exceptionalities with our struggles to see our own children as bright not broken—disabled and mislabeled. As mothers who have spent the last twenty years in the disabilities arena, we have listened as parents from around the world shared their yearning to see their children's giftedness recognized along with their disabilities. As moms, we, too, privately grieved how so much of our children's potential had been subsumed by the emphasis on their disabilities.

Diane's Story

As the mother of three wonderfully different 2e sons, I have lived with a unique mix of abilities and challenges. But it was my youngest son's challenges that set me on the journey leading to this book. I was stunned to learn when Sam was four that his overall IQ measured over 140, placing him in the highly gifted range. I had always known that Sam was *scary* smart. He was intensely passionate, curious, and *very* persistent, especially when he wanted to know how things worked. His gruelingly insistent line of questioning about his latest area of interest could last for days, even weeks. Like many 2e children, he's endured more than his share of suffering because of academic underachievement, peer rejection, bullying, and even judgment by adults who thought he was too smart to be autistic and too autistic to be smart. Through his teen years, Sam's pervasive social anxiety limited his confidence and reminded him how much he didn't fit in. But thankfully, as a young adult, Sam intuitively realized that to survive and to thrive, he had to make the most of his gifts. Tired of being defeated, he adopted the bright not broken philosophy. He embraced his mechanical abilities and love of muscle cars, using his area of strength to earn respect and acceptance among his peers. He's now pursuing a college degree and has joined a fraternity.

Likewise, working in their areas of giftedness, my other two sons are leading productive, fulfilling lives serving their country and raising their own families.

Rebecca's Story

Having two 2e children whose passionate intensities filled my days with drama and my nights with worry has been a delightful roller coaster ride of discovery. I learned through my son, Graham, that a bright, engaging child in a gifted academic program can suddenly be leveled by a hidden disability. Like Diane, I have witnessed how social anxiety can compel even the most wonderfully sensitive child to compromise himself just to fit in. After watching my son struggle to regain his identity in the face of academic failure, peer rejection, and being labeled as lazy, defiant, and unreliable, I have witnessed firsthand the restorative power of the whole child approach. Always a highly creative and artistic child, Graham began working in the culinary arts and is now locally recognized and respected for his exceptional talents in food design. I also learned through my daughter, Erin, that a child with more obvious learning impairments can be extremely bright. Her unwavering determination to succeed despite her ongoing challenges has taught me the meaning of resilience. Now, as a young adult, she uses her remarkable leadership abilities to serve her campus community through her areas of strength.

Although parents respond very differently when they discover their child is gifted, all want to see their child reach his full potential. For us, the awareness that our children were blessed with gifts brought with it an awesome sense of responsibility to help our children discover and cultivate their talents. Yet the focus on our children's giftedness slipped farther away as we were faced with the ins and outs of dealing daily with the more pressing needs of their disabilities.

Although we both found volumes of information on how to intervene in our children's disabilities through advocacy and education, at that time there were limited resources available for recognizing and developing their giftedness. So we followed the advice we were given and focused on shoring up our children's deficits. Our goal was to help our kids navigate the world despite their differences, believing that once we found the right answers to explain their disabilities, we could then focus on developing the significant gifts we intuitively knew each possessed.

Providence brought us together, and our work culminated in the 2002 publication of the internationally acclaimed book *The ADHD-Autism Connection*. Naively, we believed that by introducing parents to the comprehensive, more scientifically based understanding and explanations for their children's deficits or impairments that the field of autism provides, parents could use this information to protect themselves and their children from the "alphabet soup of labels" that usually begins with an ADHD diagnosis. We had hoped that by allowing parents to see their children through the lens of autism, they could save precious time seeking the "right" label and instead focus on developing their children's strengths. In short, we were trying to save parents from chasing labels to explain each emerging symptom in lieu of understanding the true nature of the deficits affecting their children.

Now, nearly ten years after the publication of our first book, we have found the missing pieces in our quest to help our children realize their full potential: we have discovered the world of 2e learners. The more we educated ourselves on giftedness and the whole child model, the more we recognized that *this* is how most parents want to see their 2e children. We're happy to report that as young adults, our children are no longer trapped by their disabilities and are now focusing on their areas of special interest and their abilities. As a result, they have each discovered a deep sense of purpose and achievement.

The 2e Mission Grows

Although it took us nearly a decade to discover the valuable information provided by the 2e field, we embraced its explanations with a renewed sense of purpose for ourselves and for the parents and educators we seek to serve. Yet we realized that given the overwhelming amount of literature on disabilities, parents and teachers of 2e children were unlikely to chance across this important information as long as it remained embedded primarily in the field of gifted education.

As we researched and developed our message, we centered our information around three main questions: Who are 2e children? Why do they get trapped by their disabilities? How can we help them recognize and develop their gifts?

Who They Are

As we attended gifted education conferences, contacted experts, and read countless articles, we realized that 2e kids are some of the most misunderstood children in both the world of disabilities and the field of education. Commonly, parents, clinicians, teachers, and therapists observe certain behaviors they interpret as laziness, lack of intelligence, apathy, or defiance and judge the child's character based on these factors. However, often these behaviors obscure a true picture of the hidden deficits, disabilities, and gifts that are unique to the child. At the same time, mental health professionals are frequently limited in their understanding of the emotional characteristics and needs of bright children, and educators are often unaware of how the interplay between intelligence and disability impacts 2e children.

In a climate of such misunderstanding and frustration, we are excited to help other adults give a name to the challenges these children face—a name that is not all about being broken or disabled but one that allows them to recognize these children's gifts while providing support for the difficulties: twice exceptional.

In Part One, "Who They Are," we'll discuss the concept of 2e in more detail, to help you recognize a 2e child and understand the diagnoses of ADHD, autism, and related conditions.

Why They're Stuck

Two of the largest systems in our culture too frequently trap 2e children: our mental health system and our education system.

The Mental Health System

One reason 2e children are stuck in the mental health system is that too many of the behaviors, deficits, and characteristics of autism and giftedness are being mislabeled as ADHD, opening the door to a whole host of negatively charged labels, including Oppositional Defiant Disorder (ODD) and Conduct Disorder (CD). These disorders, along with Bipolar Disorder, are increasingly diagnosed in preschoolers and are being treated with powerful atypical antipsychotics, anticonvulsants, stimulants, and antidepressants, not only singly but, even more alarmingly, in combination. The three of us stand in total agreement that until these conditions are better explained and their origins better understood, we decry the practice of prescribing psychoactive medications, especially antipsychotics, to children, whose brains are at critical stages of development.

Medication should only be used as a last resort, after all other therapies have been exhausted. Medication should *never* be the first course of treatment, particularly for behavioral disorders. We do agree that in *older* populations, such medications as stimulants and certain antidepressants can be effective tools, provided they are used cautiously, conservatively, and judiciously. Medications should be used only in cases where the benefits clearly and obviously outweigh the risks.[1]

At the same time, we must examine why the mental health system perpetuates this misdiagnosis, misunderstanding, and overmedicating of our children's gifts, deficits, and behaviors. What is it that allows so many 2e children to be trapped in the diagnosis of a behavioral disorder (such as ADHD) that attaches additional labels to explain their other symptoms, leads to treatment with strong psychoactive medications, and too often prohibits an accurate identification of hidden impairments, causing countless parents to spend years chasing labels and trying ineffective treatments?

The overriding answer to why 2e children are trapped by the mental health field is that our diagnostic system itself — the foundation of which is the *Diagnostic and Statistical Manual of Mental Disorders* (DSM) — is fundamentally flawed. As you will see in Chapter Five, this system is mired in controversy at the highest levels of psychiatry, where debates rage about the system's usefulness and validity, especially at the clinical level where diagnoses are made. The "demonizing polarization"[2] of top-level psychiatrists testifies to the fierce civil war going on about the DSM system and its fundamental design, which is based on categories that separate disorders from one another through narrowly defined sets of symptoms. In fact, exclusive reliance on the categorical system has been described as "one of the greatest mistakes of psychiatry research in the 20th century."[3]

We believe strongly that the public at large, but especially parents of 2e children diagnosed with ADHD or autism, should be made aware of the controversies surrounding the DSM. With their children's futures at stake, parents are the premier stakeholders in the DSM system and rely on the professionals who use it.

Another reason 2e children are stuck is that, because of the DSM, the current paradigm of autism misses a large portion of the true autism population. Although estimates suggest that a majority of individuals with autism may be high functioning, the focus in the autism field continues to be on those with severe cognitive impairments. Because of this emphasis on low-functioning autism, the highest-functioning population, which includes 2e children, remains misdiagnosed and misunderstood. (More on this in Chapter Seven.)

The Education System

Too often, the extraordinary creativity and potential in 2e children remains unrecognized and undeveloped by our current system of education. With the focus on proficiency and standards brought about by legislation such as No Child Left Behind (NCLB), the emphasis in education is on the lowest-performing students, including those with learning and developmental disabilities. A primary goal in public education is to bring these students *up* to proficiency. Unfortunately, success is thus equated with meeting proficiency standards, so once this goal is met, the child is defined as "achieving." However, the interplay between high IQ and disability in 2e students makes it very difficult to identify one, let alone both, exceptionalities. Consequently, 2e students' gifted potential too often remains untapped.

Because 2e students are of two worlds in education, so to speak—the world of disabilities and the world of gifted and talented—it is likely that one or more of their educational needs will be unmet by the current education system. Federal legislation requires that each child receive a free and appropriate public education (FAPE), but the definition of appropriate is complex for the 2e student. On the one hand, such laws as the Individuals with Disabilities Educational Act of 2004 have improved the educational supports for children identified as learning or developmentally disabled. On the other hand, the paltry resources devoted to identifying and educating gifted and talented students, as well as to hiring teachers to teach them, underscore the extent to which gifted education remains a low priority in the U.S. education system. As a result, 2e children are much more likely to be recognized as learning disabled rather than as gifted and to receive supports for only their special education needs, while their creativity and potential wither with each passing year.

In Part Two, "Why They're Stuck," we'll explore our mental health and education systems in greater detail, to help shed light on the labyrinth that so often traps 2e kids and their parents.

How to Help Them

Because of the emphasis on disabilities and special education, our 2e children are drowning in a culture that defines them as broken rather than as bright. The only way to truly save our 2e population will involve a radical paradigm shift in both the psychiatry and psychology fields. The first step in this shift is for parents and professionals to examine their assumptions and beliefs about what it means to be disabled and how giftedness can embrace both exceptionalities.

The study of dual exceptionalities holds the keys to understanding gifted and disabled children. It offers a whole child perspective that supports the gifts while acknowledging the need to identify and minimize the weaknesses. Our message to readers is very similar to that of Thomas Armstrong, expressed in his book *Neurodiversity*:

> [A]mid the damage and dysfunction appearing in the brains of people with mental health labels, there are bright, shining spots of promise and possibility. Rather than viewing people with . . . ADHD or autism as having "broken brains" there is strong evidence for extraordinary gifts in those individuals who might to many people seem least likely to possess them.[4]

In Part Three, "How to Help Them," we explain what can be done both at school and at home to help 2e kids. Chapter Nine offers a variety of ways parents can help their 2e children, from getting an accurate diagnosis and ensuring a nutritious diet to finding specialists in occupational therapy, sensory processing, and counseling. Chapter Ten details the many ways schools can support 2e kids, including the way diagnostic tests are administered, daily instruction, identifying areas of special interest, and social and emotional learning. The information provided in this chapter is useful for educators as well as for parents, who will learn what they need to advocate for at their child's school.

The three of us believe that bringing these groups (giftedness, autism, and related conditions) together is crucial for the well-being of 2e children and our world as a whole. It is our great hope that *Bright Not Broken* helps parents, teachers, and other interested adults ensure that these tremendously gifted children are plucked out of the "problem kid" abyss in which they're often trapped, are properly nurtured, and grow up to make their own contributions to society. As gifted expert Ann Robinson explains, "Future breakthroughs and discovery in science, medicine, and technology will be impossible if we fail to identify and serve today's brightest young minds. The time to act is now."[5] We champion the idea that our children and untold others are bright not broken, and we encourage readers to understand that giftedness has many expressions.

Bright Not Broken

Part I

Who They Are

1

Twice Exceptional

A Nontraditional View of Giftedness

What makes a child gifted and talented may not always be good grades in school, but a different way of looking at the world and learning.

Chuck Grassley, senator

Our future is in jeopardy, and our gifted children are among our best hopes for solving the myriad problems humanity faces. These children are some of our most vital human and national resources. They hold keys to keeping America globally viable, culturally rich, and economically competitive.

When you think of a "gifted" child, the image you conjured in your mind may be quite different from the way you imagine your child. Gifted children are commonly pictured as academically successful, well behaved in class, a bit nerdy or bookish, well organized and easy to teach, natural learners who will succeed regardless of the level of instruction. They are also expected to develop intellectually and emotionally at the same rate; they are thus perceived to be more mature than their peers of average ability. Perhaps the most damaging myth about gifted children is that they are able to achieve in any learning environment and that their high IQs insulate them from academic failure. In short, because they are bright, they are expected to achieve.

We believe that any definition of giftedness must move beyond the idea of academic achievement and excellence to embrace the broad spectrum of unique abilities and talents inherent in gifted children. According to the National Association for Gifted Children (NAGC), many "children demonstrate high performance or have the potential to do so" in one or more areas of expression.[1] This broad definition of giftedness includes *potential* as well as achievement and goes beyond such traditional academic content areas as mathematics or language to embody expressions of intellectual, creative, and leadership abilities.

Despite their unquestionable value to America's future, gifted children, especially the twice exceptional, are among the most neglected groups of students in our nation's education system. Without their unique perspectives and abilities, we as a nation, and perhaps as a species, are at risk for failure. However, as a group, these children are failing miserably because our education and mental health systems are failing them.

Who Are These Children?

In a nutshell, they are children like many of yours and ours. They are this generation's answer to the achievements of Albert Einstein, John Couch Adams, Thomas Edison, Sir Isaac Newton, Vincent Van Gogh, Emily Dickinson, Temple Grandin, Jane Austen, Wolfgang Amadeus Mozart, Mary Englebreit, Alexander Graham Bell, and Bill Gates, among others. They are our future inventors, engineers, philosophers, scientists, authors, musicians, teachers, therapists, and artists. They are our best and brightest hope for answers to the problems plaguing contemporary society and the world as a whole—problems such as world hunger, global water shortages, the energy crisis, environmental changes and their causes, the economy, impending pandemics, and war, just to name a few. They are our gifted children, though to their parents they may not appear gifted.

Like many of our children, the individuals we've named here were clearly twice exceptional. As Temple explains in her book *Thinking in Pictures,* many of our most creative, divergent, and visual thinkers exhibited overt symptoms of what today would be labeled a developmental disability even before their giftedness was recognized. For instance, Albert Einstein did not learn to speak until age three and did not seek out friendships with peers. He struggled with spelling and foreign languages and was not seen as exceptional in school. Yet intensity in his area of passion allowed him to concentrate for hours and even days on a problem. Gregor Mendel, the founder of modern genetics, could not pass the teaching exam to qualify to teach high school, but his experiments eventually led to our contemporary understanding of genetics, which today is standard in most high school biology curricula. Temple herself was an adult before she recognized the extent of her differences from others. As a youngster she did not speak until age four and was extremely hyperactive. Nevertheless, her mother saw glimmers of her visual-spatial brilliance and encouraged her in artistic pursuits, such as drawing, which later became foundational in her development of livestock handling systems used around the world.

How Can My Child Be Gifted?

Within the gifted world and the world of disabilities is a subset of children whose giftedness remains unrecognized or undeveloped because it co-occurs with one or more developmental or learning disorders. Linda Kreger Silverman, psychologist and leading expert in the field of gifted studies, estimates that up to one-sixth of the identified gifted population has a hidden learning disability;[2] the *2e Twice-Exceptional Newsletter* states that this figure may be as high as 20 percent.[3]

Twice-exceptional (2e) children diagnosed with ADHD, Asperger's syndrome, autism spectrum disorders, and related conditions (such as specific learning disabilities, social communication impairments, mood disorders, sensory processing difficulties, and motor skills impairments) are enigmas to parents, medical professionals, and educators—and to the gifted community. Within this 2e group are three categories:

- Children whose giftedness masks the disability
- Children whose disability masks the giftedness
- Children in whom the giftedness and the disability mask one another[4]

Unfortunately, in all but the first category, the children's gifts are unrealized and undeveloped because of the complex interplay among giftedness, disability, and our education and mental health systems. For a majority of these children, the giftedness is lost to the disability: either because the disability balances out the giftedness or because the disability conceals it. As a result, many 2e children remain unidentified in school even though they are likely to be identified as having a learning or behavioral disability. The most common is ADHD, a diagnosis that seldom appears alone.

Many children diagnosed with Attention-Deficit/Hyperactivity Disorder (ADHD), Pervasive Developmental Disorder-Not Otherwise Specified (PDD-NOS), Asperger's syndrome (AS), high-functioning autism (HFA), and related conditions often have exceptional abilities or are exceptionally gifted with an IQ up to 140 or above. When it comes to being able to identify these children as twice exceptional, though, the IQ often masks the severity of the disability, and the disability impairs the IQ.

To account for the confusing variations of development and behaviors within the gifted population in general and among 2e children in particular, a team of gifted experts known as the

Columbus Group created a new definition of giftedness: "Giftedness is asynchronous development in which advanced cognitive abilities and heightened intensity combine to create inner experiences and awareness that are qualitatively different from the norm. This asynchrony increases with higher intellectual capacity."[5] The Columbus Group also states that to reach their full potential, these children require significant adaptations and accommodations on the part of parents, teachers, and counselors.

One defining characteristic of giftedness merits considerable attention when discussing the 2e child: uneven development or "asynchronous development,"[6] otherwise known as asynchrony. This characteristic is well documented in children with HFA/AS,[7] and it is noted to be a trait in ADHD.[8] Children who are gifted often develop faster intellectually than they do physically. Consequently, there are inconsistencies in their performance, their insights, and their abilities to relate to the world around them.

Asynchrony encompasses many aspects of development and accounts for many of the paradoxes seen in gifted children. Silverman identifies several characteristics of asynchrony including "advanced cognitive abilities, heightened intensity and complexity, uneven development, unusual awareness, feeling out-of-sync with societal norms, and vulnerability"[9] and believes that asynchrony increases as IQ increases. Thus when a child has both severe deficits in learning and a high IQ, the unevenness in skills and abilities is exaggerated, making it much more difficult to accurately identify the giftedness as well as the disability or to measure the outer limits of each.[10] As the following list shows, 2e children are an interesting mix of strengths and challenges.[11] Because of this mix, the child's giftedness is often unrecognized, as may his need for educational supports and even medical intervention. Thus many 2e children remain unidentified and never receive the assistance necessary for them to develop their gifts fully.

2e Characteristics

Strengths	Challenges
Is creative, innovative	Has poor social skills
Is a "big picture" thinker	Doesn't "fit in"
Has advanced problem-solving abilities	Is stubborn
Is insightful	Is emotionally intense
Has in-depth interests	Is anxious
Is curious and inquisitive	Is perfectionist
Is highly verbal	Is highly sensitive
Is committed	Has uneven skills and abilities
Is passionate and highly knowledgeable in areas of special interest	Has difficulty paying attention (except in areas of interests)
Has unusual sense of humor	Is disorganized; has poor study skills

Sadly, these children usually are seen by the adults around them as more broken than bright. As moms, we recall the many parent-teacher conferences that focused only on our children's disabilities and behaviors: Rebecca's daughter Erin's dyslexia, her inability to memorize or recall information, and her emotional oversensitivity; Diane's son Sam's and Rebecca's son Graham's energetic, impulsive, noncompliant, and aggressive behaviors, their tardiness and absences, their inattention, and their disorganization.

In all these meetings, giftedness was not a central topic of discussion even though both Sam and Graham had been identified as having gifted IQs: Sam as highly gifted at age four and Graham as gifted at age eight. Similarly, Erin's sharp observational skills, along with her abilities to reason logically and think divergently, were quite evident to her teachers despite her disabilities, and her IQ also fell within the gifted range. Diane's other sons, Jeff and Ben, were also identified as gifted, but it was always the problems with inattention, hyperactivity, and disorganization that were the focus in school conferences.

Because our children did not fit the stereotypical idea of academic All-Americans, their behaviors and challenges eclipsed their strengths in the eyes of educators. Year after year, we listened as frustrated teachers and administrators told us that our children could achieve if they wanted to, that they were simply being lazy, stubborn, and even defiant. In other words, our children's persistent difficulties and their inability to succeed academically did not align with the stereotype of a gifted student.

In the presence of dual exceptionalities, parents and teachers understandably become confused by the interplay between giftedness and disability. The traditional idea of what it means to be gifted flies in the face of what parents often experience, especially when ADHD, HFA/AS, and learning disabilities are thrown into the mix. Even though parents recognize their children's exceptional intelligence, understandably their focus is on the disabilities and problem behaviors, which seem so contrary to the idea of giftedness prevalent in our culture. The following posts illustrate how confusing and frustrating these contradictory symptoms and behaviors can be.

> I'm trying to see if I should definitely bring this up to my [child's] doctor or maybe I am just thinking too much about the possibility that he may be an Aspie with ADHD. My son is exceptionally smart. My main concern is his lack of ability to read social cues. He doesn't appear to be comfortable talking to peers especially face to face. He seems to loose [*sic*] his words or he doesn't know what he wants to say to others until he thinks about it beforehand. His conversations are very short and he seems to loose [*sic*] his audience. Another concern is his reluctance to drive or get involved with

> activities at school or in the community. He is not very coordinated. . . .
>
> He was dx [diagnosed] with ADHD combo type 3 years ago and identified as gifted since kindergarten. On one IQ test (CoGAT), he hit the test ceiling at 140. It seems he has gotten by his elementary school years without too much complaint except he underachieves and looses [*sic*] most of his assignments. These are some other observations since he was young:
>
> - Hypersensitive to light, sound, touch...
> - Uncoordinated—at 10 yrs of age, it seemed difficult for him to wipe up spilt water.
> - Has difficulty maintaining friendships.
> - Seems like he is on a different page when he is with friends.
> - Can get into specific morning rituals where he needs to do things in order and gets very angry if he cannot follow the order.[12]

> My child is in second grade. His behavior is becoming a real issue.
>
> Positives:
>
> Very smart, reads, gets along with his sisters (mostly), plays games, helps around the house (sometimes), enjoys school (often), plays piano, engages in conversations, likes Boy Scouts.
>
> Negatives:
>
> Sleep problems, gets very upset when something is changed or missing or broken, will not do some school work (such as creative writing), yells and throws tantrums when upset, very picky about food (eats primarily peanut butter and jelly but must be of correct

brand and type), refuses participation in karate, soccer, and other group sports.

He has been diagnosed as Asperger's and Gifted by a Neurologist, Psychologist, Developmental Pediatrician and social worker. ADHD and ODD were brought up as possibilities.[13]

My child is 12 years old. He was first diagnosed with ADHD. Later on he developed OCD, and most recently ODD. He has a high IQ and is extremely gifted in math and science. He has seriouse [*sic*] peer problems, and doesn't seem to fit in any setting. He's extremely inquisitive, and always has a book in his hands.

He is currently taking three different medications (one of them a stimulant), which help him "control" himself for a while, at least while he's in school.

I have battled the school system for years to get him appropriate education, but they just keep targetting [*sic*] him as a problem child. I feel that as he gets older, more issues appear, and I believe he has a bright future. . . .

Is there anything else I can do for him?

Has he been misdiagnosed?[14]

Twice Exceptional: Challenging the Intelligence Stereotype

Fortunately, in the past two decades, contemporary theories in learning and aptitude paint a varied and diverse portrait of giftedness: one that includes many intelligences, abilities, and expressions, as well as disabilities and limitations. The idea of multiple intelligences, developed by Howard Gardner in his seminal work *Multiple Intelligences: New Horizons*, allows for intelligences beyond the verbal or computational intelligences typically valued in academics. According to Gardner, there are eight areas where intelligence can be demonstrated:[15]

Linguistic intelligence: the capacity to use words orally or in written form. Writers, poets, and public speakers enjoy these abilities.

Logical-mathematical intelligence: the capacity to use numbers and logic. Accountants, computer analysts and programmers, and scientists have these capacities.

Spatial intelligence: the ability to perceive the visual-spatial world accurately; to visualize; and to perceive the relationship among lines, space, form, and color. Graphic designers, artists, architects, interior designers, mechanical engineers, and tool-and-die specialists have this type of intelligence.

Bodily-kinesthetic intelligence: the ability to use one's body to express ideas; the ability to use one's hands to build or create; and coordination, balance, and dexterity. Dancers, athletes, and gymnasts enjoy these abilities.

Musical intelligence: the ability to perceive, create, or perform music and to understand how tone, pitch, and rhythm interact. Musicians, music producers, orchestral conductors, and singers have these abilities.

Interpersonal intelligence: the ability to understand the motives, moods, and emotions of others; the ability to read verbal and nonverbal cues. Politicians, business leaders, military leaders, and teachers exhibit this intelligence.

Intrapersonal intelligence: the ability to understand one's motives, emotions, needs, strengths, and weaknesses and to act on this knowledge. Individuals who are spiritually intuitive exhibit this intelligence.

Naturalistic intelligence: the ability to identify and classify the elements in our environment. Botanists, biologists, and entomologists exhibit this type of capacity.

Although every person demonstrates intelligence in each of these areas, and all the intelligences function together to create the individual, the degree to which each person expresses strength in particular intelligences is an excellent indicator of where his gifts and talents may lie.[16] In Gardner's theory, giftedness extends beyond IQ and is proven by more than academic achievement in one or two subject areas (though these may indeed be evidence of a particular intelligence or aptitude). Instead, giftedness is evidenced by focus, commitment, and passion in one or more of the intelligences.

Temple describes three types of specialized thinkers within the 2e population with autism. *I am a photorealistic visual thinker. The HBO movie* Temple Grandin *shows exactly how I think. All my thoughts are in photorealistic pictures like using an Internet search engine set for photos. Children with my type of thinking are usually good at art.*

A second type of thinking is the pattern thinker. These children are the mathematical, music, and computer programmer minds. They think in more abstract patterns. These kids are often poor readers. They may be three grades ahead in math, but need special education in reading. It is important to let them advance in math. If you force them to do "baby" math, they will get frustrated and turn into behavior problems, or they will shut down.

The third type of thinker is the word mind. These people think mainly in words, and they are not visual thinkers.

The strengths of all types of minds need to be developed. These different types of thinking are most likely to start showing up when kids are seven to nine years old. Kids can also be mixtures of thinking types.

These patterns Temple describes fall in line with the main learning styles found in children and widely recognized by learning specialists. Two main learning styles are what Silverman describes as auditory-sequential and visual-spatial. The following list shows the characteristics of each style.[17]

Learning Styles

Auditory-Sequential	Visual-Spatial
Thinks primarily in words	Thinks primarily in pictures
Has auditory strengths	Has visual strengths
Is a step-by-step learner	Learns concepts all at once
Is an analytical thinker	Sees the big picture; may miss details
Follows oral directions well	Must visualize words to spell them
Is well organized	Creates unique methods of organization
Can show steps of work easily	Arrives at correct solutions intuitively
Follows oral directions	Learns best by seeing relationships
Develops fairly evenly	Learns concepts permanently; is turned off by drill and repetition
Is academically talented	Is creatively, mechanically, or technologically gifted

Regardless of the kind or kinds of intelligence that are dominant, one common trait exhibited by most gifted individuals is intensity.[18] Intensity is a hallmark of the gifted, driving the individual's emotional, intellectual, and even physical responses. Gifted individuals feel deeply, question relentlessly, and often seem to be restless and on the move. They are also perfectionistic, a double-edged attribute that can either compel an individual to greatness or generate paralysis that leads to failure.[19] Along with intensity and perfectionism, gifted individuals also are highly sensitive to the emotions of others and to the environment, responding to stimuli that most people do not even recognize. As Silverman says, "The gifted are 'too' everything: too sensitive, too intense, too driven, too honest, too idealistic, too moral, too perfectionistic, too much for other people."[20]

These intensities and sensitivities have been best explained in the context of the work of Kazimierz Dabrowski, a Polish psychiatrist whose theory of personality development has been applied to the gifted population. In their important work *Living with Intensity*, researchers Susan Daniels and Michael Piechowski show how Dabrowski's concept of "overexcitabilities" can explain the heightened sensitivities of gifted individuals. Just as children are born with innate sensitivities to the world, children with higher intelligences are often more sensitive to their internal and external realities and respond with more intensity than would children with average intelligences.[21] Specifically, there are five areas or overexcitabilities (OEs) that Dabrowski identified:[22]

1. **Intellectual OE**. Children with this OE are extremely inquisitive and curious, are capable of intense concentration, and generally have highly active minds. These children tend to seek answers and truth, enjoy theory, and are often highly moral.
2. **Psychomotor OE**. Children with this OE have increased excitability in the neuromuscular system. They are highly active, energetic, and talkative, and they love to move.
3. **Sensual OE**. This OE makes children extremely sensitive to pleasurable and uncomfortable sensations from touch, sight, smells, tastes, and sounds.
4. **Emotional OE**. This OE is characterized by intense feelings, increased emotional sensitivity and identification with the feelings of others, and strong emotional attachments.
5. **Imaginational OE**. This OE is marked by a tendency for creating vivid imaginary worlds, thinking visually, using metaphorical language, and having a rich dream life.

Although these OEs provide an excellent framework for understanding the intensity and sensitivity of gifted individuals, they can also lead to confusion when looking at the 2e child. Each OE can lead to behaviors identical to those found in children with ADHD, Asperger's or autism, and related conditions.

Further, when an OE is expressed to a greater degree, the potential for confusion grows. As Daniels and Piechowski explain, "More often than not, aspects of intensity are mistaken for indicators of potential pathology rather than signs of a strong developmental potential."[23] For instance, a child with psychomotor OE will tend to be more active and talkative than his peers, but when this OE is even more prominent, this same child may become a disruption in the classroom, prompting an evaluation for ADHD. This confusion between traits of giftedness and traits of disability often leads to misdiagnosis, missed diagnosis, and even missed giftedness in 2e children.

The Whole Child Approach

Once we understand the many factors that underlie a child's giftedness and his unique intensities, we can more deeply appreciate and support the whole child. As parents, we have a responsibility to embrace our children's giftedness and discover ways to nurture their strengths and abilities. At the same time, we must advocate for them in their areas of weakness.

When it comes to successful life outcomes, taking a whole child approach is what works best for 2e children. Our overriding goal as parents should be to cultivate the wonderful and original talents in our children. Everything else—supports, interventions, therapies, education—should be undertaken with this goal in mind. Only then, when the focus is on the abilities and not the challenges, will it be easier for us to see how to help our 2e children navigate in a world that desperately needs their gifts but unfortunately defines them by their weaknesses.

2

Recognizing 2e

A Confusing Mix of Abilities and Challenges

The question is not what you look at,
but what you see.

Henry David Thoreau

The term *twice exceptional (2e)* embraces two very complex and apparently contradictory exceptionalities. On the one hand, there is giftedness with its myriad intelligences, expressions, and strengths. On the other hand, there is the world of disabilities with its confounding mix of behaviors, abilities, and difficulties. When these two exceptionalities combine within an individual, the result is a puzzling blend of strengths and weaknesses. Our challenge as parents and educators is to tease out the abilities from the disabilities, even when the behaviors that accompany each are inherently similar.

Two of the most common disabilities associated with giftedness in 2e children are ADHD and high-functioning autism or Asperger's syndrome (HFA/AS). As we delved deeper into the nature of giftedness, we began to see that the similarities among the gifted, the gifted with ADHD, and the gifted with HFA/AS paralleled many points of comparison we developed between ADHD and autism in our first book, primarily with regard to behavioral, communication, and social characteristics. Unfortunately, we also discovered that because a diagnosis of ADHD pathologizes the disruptive behaviors commonly associated with giftedness, in many cases this label causes parents and educators to focus too much on the behavioral challenges rather than recognize the gifts or the possible autistic deficits that may be driving the "ADHD" behavior.

Derek, a third grader, seems always to be in trouble even though he's a shy, withdrawn child. His parents don't understand why a child who could read books for fourth and fifth graders while still in kindergarten can't manage to succeed in elementary school. Across the board, his grades are unsatisfactory. The teacher accuses him of never listening, describing him as a daydreamer who's lost in his own world. His inattention is so extreme, at times it interferes with her teaching: *Derek, put away your book. Derek, look at me. Derek, pay attention. Derek, you're not trying.* As for friends, Derek believes his classmates are his friends even though they never invite him to play. However, Derek doesn't seem to care. After school and on the weekends, when other children are busy with sports or other activities, Derek prefers to play on the computer or to read. His parents worry about his isolation and his failure in school, but his teacher insists that Derek has the ability to succeed. The psychologist diagnosed him with ADHD, inattentive type, and the pediatrician prescribed stimulant medication. However, Derek began to socially withdraw even more and developed tics. His parents quit giving Derek the medicine but are lost as to what to do next to help their son.

Lauren, a highly bright, restless fifth grader never finishes anything, including her running conversation with classmates. Although she sets out with great enthusiasm, her teachers complain that she seldom finishes an assignment or project, and loses the ones she does manage to complete. Although Lauren prefers to work alone, when a project requires that others join in, Lauren's frequent interruptions and bossiness lead to conflict. Her teachers complain that her stubbornness makes it difficult for them to redirect her when necessary, and her outbursts and talking in class interfere with their teaching. At home, Lauren's unpredictable rages over simple schedule changes create tension; her apparent unwillingness to complete homework assignments just compounds the turmoil. Having tried behavioral programs to control their "out of control" daughter, Lauren's parents feel like failures and don't know where to turn next.

As these examples show, too often our children's giftedness remains hidden, trapped behind an invisible wall of disability that often leads to a lifetime of disappointment and despair. They disappoint their parents, who know they are smart despite their not appearing gifted. They disappoint their teachers, who expect better behavior and focus in the classroom. Ultimately, though, they are a disappointment to themselves because although they are smart, often smarter than everyone around them, they can't behave, they can't make friends, and they can't seem to get anyone to see that they have value and purpose.

What Is Driving My Child's Behaviors—Giftedness, ADHD, or HFA/AS?

Although there are numerous similarities among giftedness, ADHD, and HFA/AS, the most easily recognizable ones to parents and professionals are, of course, the behaviors. As you can see from Table 2.1, there are several characteristics that are nearly identical among these three groups: hyperactivity, impulsivity, inattention, behavior, and social communication difficulties. Each field has its own explanation for the presence of these traits, but the overwhelming similarities in these characteristics are a source of confusion for parents, clinicians, and educators, especially when looking at inattention, behavior, and social communication.

Table 2.1 Common Characteristics Leading to Confusion

	Giftedness	ADHD	Autism
Hyperactivity	Has a high degree of energy and apparently limitless verbal and physical enthusiasm and energy; talks constantly	Has high energy and enthusiasm; talks incessantly	Is hyperactive; overactivity is common
Impulsivity	Misbehaves and acts out; blurts out answers; interrupts others; is impatient	Acts without thought of consequence; interrupts others; makes careless mistakes; does sloppy work; disrupts others	Works impulsively; often makes careless mistakes; work is sloppy
Inattention	Daydreams; focuses for long periods on subjects of interest; perseverates on interest	Is easily distractible; daydreams; may appear not to be listening when spoken to directly; hyperfocuses if motivated; is unable to shift attention	Daydreams; may not appear to be listening; prefers hobbies or narrow interests; hyperfocuses on interest; is unable to shift attention

Behavior	Tends to question authority; is stubborn and determined; is bossy; has tantrums	Challenges authority; is stubborn, bossy, defiant; has frequent tantrums	Has frequent tantrums; has strong preference for routines
Social Communication Difficulties	Has difficulty finding and keeping peer relationships; gets feelings hurt easily; is frequently bullied	Has difficulty making and keeping friends; has difficulty reading social cues; gets feelings hurt easily; is frequently bullied; has difficulty taking turns	Has difficulty making and maintaining peer relationships; has difficulty understanding nonverbal communication (reading social cues); has difficulty taking turns

Sources: Adapted from *Diagnostic and Statistical Manual of Mental Disorders* (4th ed., text rev.), by American Psychiatric Association, 2000, Arlington, VA: Author; *Delivered from Distraction*, by E. M. Hallowell and J. J. Ratey, 2006, New York: Ballantine Books; *The Autistic Spectrum*, by L. Wing, 2001, Berkeley, CA: Ulysses Press; *Autism and Asperger Syndrome*, by U. Frith, 1994, Cambridge, England: Cambridge University Press.

These characteristics are too frequently the basis for misdiagnosis, which robs our children of timely and appropriate interventions.

Hyperactivity and Impulsivity

Hyperactivity and impulsivity are commonly associated with all three groups. Hyperactivity is defined as excessive levels of activity in various settings. In giftedness, hyperactive behavior is believed to arise from the excessive energy of psychomotor overexcitability, causing a child to sleep less, talk more, and move even when unnecessary. This behavior is frequently confused with ADHD, in which hyperactivity is described as a core symptom, and with HFA/AS, in which hyperactivity is also recognized as a feature of the disorder.

Impulsivity in the gifted is seen as arising from passionate intensity about an area of interest. This intensity can lead to interrupting others, making careless mistakes, and producing sloppy work, as well as starting but not completing projects once curiosity is satisfied.[1] In ADHD, impulsivity is viewed as the inability to inhibit impulses and desires, a trait that results in careless mistakes, blurting out answers, and not completing tasks. Likewise, in HFA/AS, impulsivity also is recognized as poor impulse control that results in sloppy work, careless mistakes, and frequent interruptions.

Inattention

A hallmark characteristic of giftedness, ADHD, and HFA/AS, inattention is viewed as stemming from two primary causes: hyperfocus or distraction. Inattention that results from hyperfocus is described in all three fields as arising from an obsession with specific areas of interest. Ellen Winner, author of *Gifted Children: Myths and Realities*, says that when engaged with their special interest, gifted children "exhibit an intense and obsessive interest, an ability to focus sharply," and she describes them as being in the "flow" or in "optimal states in which they focus intently and lose all sense of the outside world."[2]

A child with ADHD will also hyperfocus, or attend only to tasks that are of high interest to him while "totally ignoring or losing track of everything else."[3] Along these same lines, Uta Frith, author of *Autism: Explaining the Enigma,* describes autistic hyperfocus as a focus on things that many people would find unremarkable, which "seem to hold inexplicable fascination" for individuals with autism. This interest leads to a focus so strong that "they cannot be interrupted in their intense preoccupations."[4] For example, Temple describes her absolute absorption with sand:

> I remember studying the sand intently as if I was a scientist looking at a specimen under a microscope. I remember minutely observing how the sand flowed.... My mind was actively engaged in these activities. I was fixated on them and ignored everything else.[5]

As you can see, there are striking similarities in the way each field describes inattention in relation to hyperfocus.

Similarities also are evident when each field accounts for the second cause of inattention, distraction. Distraction is tied to boredom in all three fields. In gifted literature, distraction is frequently linked with boredom, especially when gifted children are "often two to four grade levels above their actual grade placement."[6] Also, a gifted child with several interests may appear distracted as he bounces from one to the other. Russell Barkley, a pioneer in the field of ADHD, asserts that inattention and the inability to stay with a task arise when the child is assigned boring, lengthy, or repetitive work that lacks "intrinsic appeal" to the person.[7] Similarly, in HFA/AS, inattention and boredom are most frequently tied to giftedness in this population.

Behavior

Another characteristic that leads to confusion among giftedness, ADHD, and HFA/AS is behavior. (Unfortunately, behavior is what frequently leads 2e children to receive an Emotional Behavior Disability [EBD] label in school.) All three fields recognize oppositional behaviors (such as tantrums, stubbornness, and challenges to authority) in their populations, but disagree about the origins of these behaviors. For instance, the field of giftedness says that oppositional behaviors arise in gifted children for several reasons, notably a strong commitment to ideals and beliefs, the deeply rooted feeling that no one truly "gets them," and power struggles with authority.[8] These behaviors are seen as a natural expression of giftedness that must be tempered by teaching children appropriate strategies for handling disagreement and confrontation.

In the field of ADHD, oppositional behavior is viewed from a more negative perspective. Children with ADHD are often characterized as stubborn, self-willed, and defiant.[9] Oppositional behaviors are seen more as a choice to behave badly and are approached through behavior modification programs such as 123 Magic and the Total Transformation Program aimed at teaching parents consistent discipline techniques. In contrast to ADHD, in the field of HFA/AS, such behaviors as tantrums, power struggles, and refusal to comply with rules are viewed as stemming from neurological deficits.

Social Communication Difficulties

Another trait shared among all three categories is social communication difficulties, especially in relating to peer groups. However, each group approaches these difficulties differently: the giftedness field explains that the social problems arise because of IQ, asynchrony, and perfectionism; the field of ADHD attributes them to impulsivity; and the autism field recognizes social deficits as a central core impairment in its population.

Experts in giftedness recognize that giftedness itself can lead to a child's not having an equal peer group with which to socialize. Barbara Klein states that "very smart children may have socialization problems and feel awkward because of their intellectual superiority in comparison to their peer group."[10] Silverman says that gifted children are "likely to be out-of-sync with their agemates and with age-related cultural norms."[11] Their perfectionism leads to their being ostracized from peers because they are perceived as "control freaks" who are highly critical, hard to please, and very demanding.[12] In short, these three traits of giftedness make the gifted child feel alone because he does not fit in intellectually or emotionally with his peers.

Children with ADHD also have trouble with social relationships, but the reasons for these difficulties are described very differently in ADHD literature. Experts attribute most of these difficulties to impulsivity or the inability to delay gratification. For instance, Barkley claims that because they "fail to consider future consequences, they often don't see that their selfishness and self-centeredness in the moment result in their losing friends in the long run."[13] Hallowell and Ratey note that social difficulties often arise because the child with ADHD has difficulty taking turns in games and conversations or may be unable to slow his mind down long enough to recognize social cues.[14]

In autism, social problems are believed to arise from what is known as "mind-blindness," or an inability to understand the way other people think—that others have motives, experiences, beliefs, and personalities, which shape the social interaction. Mind-blindness also impairs a child's ability to read social cues, such as facial expressions, tone of voice, and body language, which is one of the most recognized symptoms of an autism spectrum disorder.[15] It is important to understand that a gifted child with HFA/AS often develops social skills through compensatory learning, but this learning comes at great cognitive costs: "The individual who does well with compensatory education is the individual who has large cognitive resources."[16] In other words, a child with autism who can compensate for his social deficits by "faking it" is most likely a child with tremendous intellectual ability. In fact, it is in AS and in what is considered the "high functioning" group of children with autism that giftedness is most often missed or mistaken for ADHD.

Clearly, the gifted, ADHD, and HFA/AS populations share more than behavioral characteristics. On the surface, the explanations for these characteristics are strikingly similar as well. Inattention occurs when a child becomes bored; hyperfocus, when the child is extremely interested. Impulsivity results from passionate intensity about a subject and the child's inability to restrain his responses. Hyperactivity arises when a child's activity level exceeds the demands of the environment or task. Finally, these children commonly experience social difficulties that arise from their inability to relate to their peers, either intellectually or socially. However superficially common these similarities may appear, we must not lose sight of the fact that because of them, the 2e child is too often mislabeled or misunderstood.

How These Characteristics Lead to Disabilities

As parents, we are the first to recognize our children's unique gifts and talents. We see how quickly they master skills, how intensely curious and driven they are, and how voraciously they learn. Yet we are also the first to see the intensity of their behaviors, especially when they are frustrated or angry; the difficulty they have following directions; the problems with schoolwork that seem so incongruous with their intelligence; the trouble they have with making and maintaining friendships. When our perceptions are echoed in the comments of our children's teachers, our concern about our children naturally increases: "If he would just try harder"; "If he would just live up to his potential"; "If he would just focus more"; "If he would pay attention"; "If he would not take everything so seriously"; "If he would just learn to get along with his classmates."

A parent's first instinct is to try to understand the causes of her child's behavior. Often, when confronted with inattentive, hyperactive, and impulsive behaviors, parents and teachers immediately think of ADHD, as this is a highly popularized disorder in our culture. So the pediatrician is naturally where many parents begin. Others begin with the school counselor, requesting that the school assess the child for ADHD and learning disabilities. Rarely, however, do parents turn to professionals specifically trained in giftedness, because ability is seldom associated with disability in our minds.

How the Professionals See These Characteristics (Professional Blindness)

Frequently, the course of a child's future is determined by the parents' initial choice of professional. In most cases, the direction for any treatments and interventions will emerge from the child's initial assessment and from the professional perspective of the clinician who conducts the evaluation. Unfortunately, too often professionals view symptoms only within the context of their professional training. Silverman sees this as a major impediment to developing the whole child because professionals from various fields seldom consider the ways that giftedness interacts with disability: "The ADHD specialist sees AD/HD, the Asperger specialist sees Asperger Syndrome, and the school psychologist may see no disabilities at all because the child scores in the average range on IQ and achievement tests."[17] In short, even though "giftedness is an inherent part of the child's total nervous system and must be considered at every turn,"[18] most professionals are so narrowly focused on the disability that the gift is overlooked.

A perfect example of this professional blindness occurred when Diane's son Sam was first evaluated at age four. The psychologist, an ADHD expert, acknowledged that Sam scored in the highly gifted range for IQ, calling him a very gifted and intellectually talented child. However, in the summary, the focus was primarily on Sam's potential for attention deficits and oppositional behaviors: "The examiner sees a combination of early Attention-Deficit/Hyperactivity Disorder and Oppositional Defiant Disorder of Childhood. Young children with the Attention-Deficit/Hyperactivity Disorder are very likely to develop specific levels of oppositional behavior."

Although Sam finally received an Asperger's diagnosis, subsequent approaches by medical and educational professionals focused on his disabilities rather than on his gifted potential.

Diane's example illustrates the way that professional training can lead parents and professionals down one of two corridors: gifted or disabled. Unfortunately, because of the professional blindness that arises from our current diagnostic system, when it comes to mental disabilities, although the gifts are recognized, seldom are children identified and treated as twice exceptional.

As you may imagine, the 2e child presents a tremendous challenge to health care providers who must label his troubling behaviors. Unfortunately, because these behaviors most often include hyperactivity, impulsivity, and inattention, a large number of 2e children receive a diagnosis of ADHD. In fact, the American Academy of Pediatrics advises doctors to screen for ADHD when a child ages six to twelve years presents with these symptoms,[19] thereby nearly guaranteeing that the 2e child will receive this diagnosis even though the behaviors may be better explained by giftedness or HFA/AS.

So, What Is ADHD?

Recognized by the National Institute of Mental Health as the most commonly diagnosed disorder of childhood, ADHD is characterized by problems with paying attention or staying focused, difficulty controlling and regulating behavior (impulsivity), and hyperactivity. The *Diagnostic and Statistical Manual of Mental Disorders, Fourth Edition, Text Revision* (DSM-IV-TR) identifies three core symptoms of ADHD: inattention, impulsivity, and hyperactivity, and describes three subtypes: predominantly hyperactive-impulsive; predominantly inattentive; and combined hyperactive-inattentive. (See the box "Diagnostic Criteria for Attention-Deficit/Hyperactivity Disorder" for more detail.)

Diagnostic Criteria for Attention-Deficit/Hyperactivity Disorder

(A) Either (1) or (2):

(1) six (or more) of the following symptoms of *inattention* have persisted for at least 6 months to a degree that is maladaptive and inconsistent with developmental level:

Inattention

(a) often fails to give close attention to details or makes careless mistakes in schoolwork, work, or other activities

(b) often has difficulty sustaining attention in tasks or play activities

(c) often does not seem to listen when spoken to directly

(d) often does not follow through on instructions and fails to finish schoolwork, chores, or duties in the workplace (not due to oppositional behavior or failure to understand instructions)

(e) often has difficulty organizing tasks and activities

(f) often avoids, dislikes, or is reluctant to engage in tasks that require sustained mental effort (such as schoolwork or homework)

(g) often loses things necessary for tasks or activities (e.g., toys, school assignments, pencils, books, or tools)

(h) is often easily distracted by extraneous stimuli

(i) is often forgetful in daily activities

(2) six (or more) of the following symptoms of *hyperactivity-impulsivity* have persisted for at least 6 months to a degree that is maladaptive and inconsistent with developmental level:

Hyperactivity

(a) often fidgets with hands or feet or squirms in seat

(b) often leaves seat in classroom or in other situations in which remaining seated is expected

(c) often runs about or climbs excessively in situations in which it is inappropriate (in adolescents or adults, may be limited to subjective feelings of restlessness)

(d) often has difficulty playing or engaging in leisure activities quietly

(e) is often "on the go" or often acts as if "driven by a motor"

(f) often talks excessively

Impulsivity

(g) often blurts out answers before questions have been completed

(h) often has difficulty awaiting turn

(i) often interrupts or intrudes on others (e.g., butts into conversations or games)

(B) Some hyperactive-impulsive or inattentive symptoms that caused impairment were present before age 7 years.

(C) Some impairment from the symptoms is present in two or more settings (e.g., at school [or work] and at home).

(D) There must be clear evidence of clinically significant impairment in social, academic, or occupational functioning.

(E) The symptoms do not occur exclusively during the course of a Pervasive Developmental Disorder, Schizophrenia, or other Psychotic Disorder and are not better accounted for by another mental disorder (e.g., Mood Disorder, Anxiety Disorder, Dissociative Disorder, or Personality Disorder).

Source: From *Diagnostic and Statistical Manual of Mental Disorders* (4th ed., text rev., pp. 92–93), by American Psychiatric Association, 2000, Arlington, VA: Author.

Physicians and clinicians elicit the comments of parents, teachers, and others who work with the child to determine how many and what types of symptoms the child has. If the child has enough of the symptoms to qualify for one of the subtypes, ADHD is diagnosed even though the clinician has not directly observed these behaviors in the child.

What's in a Label? Two Views of ADHD

Although experts within the field of ADHD have several explanations for the difficulties associated with ADHD—underachievement, disorganization, difficulties with time management, social difficulties, low frustration level, and inconsistent performance, there are primarily two schools of thought with regard to the nature of the disability itself. Each of these views has a serious impact on the way in which we as a culture perceive individuals diagnosed with ADHD and the way the individual views himself. Unfortunately, as is too often true in matters of human nature, the voices of negativity are much louder than the voices of those who see the unique potential of children who receive the ADHD label.

The more recent and more positive school of thought adopts the whole child approach common in the gifted field. Professionals who subscribe to this view see the gifts as well as the challenges associated with an ADHD diagnosis. They recognize the high levels of creativity, original thought, energy, focus, and intensity that individuals diagnosed with ADHD often exhibit, and urge patients to concentrate on developing these positive attributes as a means of succeeding. For example, psychologist Laura Honos-Webb sensitively celebrates the positive attributes of ADHD even as she recognizes the disabilities. Her descriptions of these attributes parallel many of Dabrowski's overexcitabilities, most notably psychomotor, emotional, sensual, and imaginational although she does not equate them with giftedness. Even as she recognizes that the "tension between the promise and pitfalls of ADD is evident,"[20] she focuses on strengths as a means of minimizing the very real struggles that individuals with this label face daily.

Likewise, Hallowell and Ratey take a more balanced approach to recognizing gifts and difficulties in ADHD. Although they clearly identify the major difficulties that individuals with the disorder face, Hallowell and Ratey state that the ADHD diagnosis "provides a spectacular opportunity to … change a life of frustration into a life of mastery by developing talents and strengths, not just shoring up weaknesses."[21] They then give numerous suggestions for "mastering the power and avoiding the pitfalls of ADD," presenting several methods for minimizing or working around some of the deficits in time management, organization, and attention.

Although we certainly agree that it is important to see the strengths in these children, we also assert that the ADHD label obscures both the giftedness and the struggles of those who battle academic, relational, and economic failure, along with depression and anxiety. With the ADHD diagnosis, developing the child's strengths too often becomes subsumed by minimizing the disability—especially when, as a matter of course, characteristics of giftedness are viewed as intrinsic to the disability. As Thomas Armstrong explains in his book *Neurodiversity*, the ADHD label is a "tragic decoy" because "the child is reduced to an 'ADD child' where the potential to see the best in him or her is severely eroded (since ADD/ADHD puts all the emphasis on the deficits, not the strengths)."[22] This concern is echoed in the field of dual exceptionalities, which recognizes that many characteristics of giftedness are commonly misdiagnosed as ADHD.

The second school of thought on the disorder takes a wholly deficits-based approach. Unfortunately, most of the research that is foundational to our scientific and cultural understanding of ADHD originates from this deficits-based perspective and ignores much of the giftedness inherent in this population. Barkley, considered by many to be one of leading experts in contemporary views of ADHD, believes that "ADHD is no gift." He takes the approach that giftedness and talents are distinct from ADHD and asserts that "there is no evidence in any research on any of hundreds of measures ... that shows that ADHD predisposes to anything positive in human life."[23]

Advocates of this school of thought typically see ADHD as a medical disorder to be treated. This view of ADHD characterizes the child as lacking in areas essential to achievement, notably the ability to inhibit their behavior and responses, which results in an inability to follow rules and directions and inconsistency in their ability to do work.[24] In short, according to Barkley, the child's difficulty does not arise from "a lack of skill but from a lack of self-control." ADHD "is not due to a failure of knowledge or reasoning"; rather, "it is a problem with doing what the child knows."[25] This explanation assumes that the child knows how to behave and to pay attention; he just does not control the impulsivity enough to apply this knowledge.

Another expert, Thomas Brown, also subscribes to the disease model even as he recognizes that many children with ADHD have high intelligence and are emotionally sensitive. In fact, like professionals in the 2e field, Brown believes that in cases where the child has a high IQ, the gifts mask the severity of the ADHD syndrome.[26] Like Honos-Webb, Brown attributes such characteristics as emotional sensitivity, overactivity, and passionate single-mindedness to ADHD rather than recognizing them as traits of giftedness. Yet, like Barkley, he takes primarily a deficits-based approach to describing the child with ADHD, explaining that a lack of inhibition underlies some of the child's difficulties in regulating behavior, especially in the hyperactive-impulsive subtype; however, he adds to this the idea that there are several other deficits in the functions of attention, monitoring, and regulation that combine with lack of inhibition to create the ADHD syndrome.[27] Thus, although Brown sees the strengths of these children, he relies on a deficits-based model and sees characteristics of overexcitabilities as evidence for ADHD.

Unfortunately, in even the most positive school of thought, where the strengths of children diagnosed as ADHD may be recognized, their giftedness usually is not. Instead, the ADHD label carries with it a host of associations, most of which are fundamentally negative.

The Limitations of Merging Giftedness with Disabilities

As you can see, the behaviors and symptoms associated with giftedness, ADHD, and HFA/AS are so similar that confusion is certain to arise. Fortunately, experts in the field of giftedness already recognize this potential and have worked diligently to bring the likelihood of misdiagnosis to the forefront of gifted scholarship. Instead of focusing almost exclusively on a child's weaknesses, experts in dual exceptionalities, such Baum, Webb, Silverman, and others in the field of giftedness, promote a whole child approach to fostering the 2e child's potential.

Understandably, experts in the field of giftedness see that the best way to help 2e students develop their full potential is to cultivate awareness of giftedness in the fields of ADHD and autism. Correctly, the field of giftedness operates from a strengths-based model that urges parents, educators, and psychologists to view the gifts as equal to the disability in importance and to consider it first and foremost when developing treatment plans. However, the predominance of the disabilities view of ADHD at the professional level limits parents and care providers from taking the whole child approach. This deficits-based approach to ADHD keeps parents and educators from recognizing challenging, disruptive behaviors as possible signs of giftedness or symptoms of autism. As a result, the ADHD label does more harm than good to 2e children by increasing the likelihood that neither giftedness nor disability will be accurately identified and wholly supported.

3

2e, ADHD, and Labels

Misunderstanding Behaviors and Missing Deficits

The will to label will always prevail over what's being labeled, usually at the expense of either truth or understanding.

Boyd Rice

Labels influence our perception, especially when they are used to identify a person's ability or disability. As Temple explains, *teachers and parents often have higher expectations for a child who is labeled gifted than for a child who has some other label.* Similarly, when a child is labeled as stubborn or angry, our perception of his character is far less negative than if he is labeled as having Oppositional Defiant Disorder (ODD) or Conduct Disorder (CD).

In the same way, a child labeled as having Asperger's syndrome or an autism spectrum disorder is viewed as much more severely impaired than if he is labeled as having ADHD. Typically, when we think of autism, we picture the idiot-savant from *Rainman*, whereas when we think of ADHD, we see "little Johnny hyper." We equate autism with obvious differences in appearance, speech, and ability, whereas we associate ADHD with disruptive, disorganized, and inattentive behaviors. In short, ADHD is seen as the better label to have because it is more palatable and less severe. However, as you will see, it is also the more damaging for these important reasons:

- The symptom set called ADHD does not stand alone as a disorder. Hyperactivity, impulsivity, and inattention are symptoms of numerous other disorders and conditions. Affixing the ADHD label to these behaviors leads to additional labels in an attempt to present a complete diagnostic picture of a child.
- An ADHD diagnosis emphasizes the disruptive behavioral symptoms of these impairments, leading parents and professionals to view and treat the child as behaviorally or emotionally disturbed.
- The ADHD label stands in the way of recognizing the hidden impairments affecting the 2e child.

ADHD: The Confusion Begins

Too frequently, inattention, impulsivity, anxiety, depression, social difficulties, and differences in intellect lead our children to withdraw and lead us as parents to seek labels for these troubling symptoms. Bright, gifted children often struggle with extreme emotional oversensitivity, processing difficulties, and delays, weaknesses, or deficits in social development, causing parents to seek help from mental health professionals.[1] Unfortunately, too many psychologists see disabilities rather than gifts. As 2e expert James Webb explains, "Most psychologists don't think giftedness is an important area of study. The belief exists that gifted kids will make it on their own. But a gifted mind doesn't always find its own way,"[2] as these e-mails clearly illustrate.

> I'm a 49 year old man recently diagnosed with Asperger's Syndrome, but diagnosed earlier with ADHD, Bipolar Disorder, and dyslexia. Although academically bright and college educated, I've never held a job or had a

> relationship. . . . The reason I am writing is because I want a chance to participate in society. I believe I have much to offer others I'm just so alone ... (Lee)
>
> My 14 year old son was recently diagnosed with Asperger's Syndrome after being labeled as ADHD/ ODD with mixed depression and anxiety. He's extremely bright with an IQ of 125. But I am concerned for his safety. Lately he seems to realize how isolated and different he is from other people his age. Are there any social groups I can get him to join? He's already expressed his feelings that no one would miss him if he died ... (SRC)

Although each of these individuals is clearly identified as twice exceptional, their giftedness languished in relation to their disabilities, a situation that is very common. Whenever and wherever we engage in conversation with others about ADHD, the autism spectrum, and giftedness, invariably we hear the all-too-familiar and heart-wrenching story of yet another child whose giftedness remained uncultivated because parents were consumed with finding answers for the child's multiple disabilities, the most common being ADHD. Instead of allowing parents an integrated perspective on a child's strengths and weaknesses, an ADHD diagnosis often leads to additional labels in an attempt to explain each symptom as it emerges. Unfortunately, multiple labels create a splintered view of the child. When a troublesome behavior appears, parents are prone to wonder which label best explains it. Thus their focus is on the parts, and the most difficult ones at that. In the end, the gifts are overlooked and the disabilities magnified.

Differential Diagnosis and ADHD

Before we begin discussing labels in general and ADHD in particular, it is important to pause and give a bit of background on how the DSM-IV-TR, the manual used to diagnose mental disorders, is arranged to sort symptoms into labels. The DSM is organized by broad categories. Each category is distinct from all others and contains one or more diagnostic labels. This arrangement can be compared to makes and models of automobiles. Ford is the make, and under it are the Taurus, Fusion, and Focus models. Chevrolet is the make, and the Malibu, the Impala, and the Cobalt are models. Likewise, under Attention-Deficit and Disruptive Behavior Disorders (the make), ADHD, ODD, and CD (the models) are categorized; under Pervasive Developmental Disorders are PDD-NOS, Asperger's Disorder (the DSM term for what is more commonly referred to as Asperger's syndrome), and Autistic Disorder. Similarly, the category of Mood Disorders includes Depressive Disorder and Bipolar Disorder; Anxiety Disorders such as OCD are categorized separately. The placement of these disorders in different categories is intended to promote what is known as "differential diagnosis" or the diagnosis of one disorder independent from the other. (For more about the diagnostic system, see Chapter Five.)

To diagnose ADHD, physicians and clinicians commonly use checklists of symptoms to elicit the comments of parents, teachers, and others who work with the child, to determine how many and what types of symptoms the child has. If the child has enough of the symptoms to qualify for one of the subtypes, ADHD is diagnosed even though the clinician has not directly observed these behaviors in the child.

However, the DSM-IV-TR also includes a very specific statement that ADHD is *not* to be diagnosed when another disorder better explains the presence of ADHD symptoms. In fact, DSM-IV-TR states that ADHD *can only be diagnosed* when

> The symptoms do not occur exclusively during the course of a Pervasive Developmental Disorder, Schizophrenia, or other Psychotic Disorder and are not better accounted for by another mental disorder

(e.g., Mood Disorder, Anxiety Disorder, Dissociative Disorder, or a Personality Disorder).[3]

In other words, an ADHD diagnosis is not to be given if Asperger's Disorder; an autism spectrum disorder; a Mood Disorder, such as Bipolar Disorder or Depressive Disorder; or an Anxiety Disorder, such as Obsessive-Compulsive Disorder, can be diagnosed. Yet, as you will see, this guideline is rarely followed.

ADHD: The Main Ingredient in the Alphabet Soup

In America today, as many as one in ten school-age children is diagnosed with ADHD, making this the most commonly diagnosed disorder of childhood.[4] Often this diagnosis is accompanied by a prescription for Ritalin, Adderall, Concerta, Focalin, or any one of the newest ADHD medications on the market. ADHD is defined as a behavioral disorder with symptoms that change over the course of a lifetime, prompting new evaluations, new labels, and new treatments. The diagnoses of "secondary" conditions, though, often lead to multiple labels and to a cocktail of psychiatric medications that can include antidepressants, mood stabilizers, and antipsychotics, along with the ADHD stimulant medication. These medications often come with side effects that exacerbate a child's social or sensory problems or create new ones, such as tics, permanent tremors, cardiac events (heart attacks), and manic, explosive, or introverted behaviors.

When a child is diagnosed with more than one disorder, each additional diagnosis is known as a *comorbid condition* or *comorbidity*, meaning that besides the primary disorder, in this case the diagnosis of ADHD, one or more additional conditions are also present in the child. Clearly, the use of multiple labels creates confusion, stress, and frustration for parents because each label changes their perception of their child and his abilities and leads them to believe that their child suffers from multiple mental disorders. As we've noted, the child's giftedness often becomes lost in an alphabet soup of labels, as these parents' comments show:

> My son is six, and very smart. He has been diagnosed with ADHD, Bi-Polar, Social Anxiety Disorder, ODD, and dyslexia. He also hates loud noises. . . . I was wondering if any one else had a kid with so many diagnoses.[5]
>
> My 10 year old daughter (IQ 128) was diagnosed with significant ADHD first and then, later, with Aspergers also. . . . She also has OCD and some symptoms of anxiety. Her doctor wants to add a mood medication to see if it will help calm her. She's already taking her ADHD medicine, an antidepressant, and a low dose of Zyprexa.
>
> My oldest [16 year old son] started with an ADHD diagnosis, and they wanted to give him the ODD label but I refused. He then received a bipolar diagnosis, and an anxiety disorder diagnosis. Now he's on multiple meds and a walking zombie.
>
> My scary smart 10 yr old daughter has ADHD, Aspergers, and an Anxiety/Depression issue which we are currently working with a Cognitive Behavioral Therapist to help her out with. The ADHD overshadowed ALOT [*sic*] of her symptoms when she was younger and it was very difficult to get the doctors to test her for the Autism Spectrum disorders. I had to fight like mad and be a down right pain in the butt to get them to listen to me.
>
> What a vortex. My son was diagnosed at the age of 4 with ADHD. At age 6 he was diagnosed with Aspergers by a developmental paediatrician who specializes in autism diagnoses. Getting to that point was a long journey. My son is having a lot of difficulty with school

> (non compliant, oppositional, aggressive, running away, etc.).... He also has a lot of anxiety.... So we have sought out more help and support.... We are seeing a pediatric psychiatrist who told us he doesn't think my son has Aspergers. He thinks he's gifted.... But, he does not think a person can have Aspergers AND be gifted.... This has been a real blow. I want to know the truth. Of course, I thought I did.[6]

As you can see, the particular mix of labels varies from child to child. No two children are alike, so the ways in which deficits are expressed vary across the population. One child may externalize his frustration and have a tantrum at an abrupt change in schedule; another will internalize the same feeling and become silent and withdrawn. (For example, when we [Diane and Rebecca] discuss our children, we refer to them as our hypers and hypos, in terms of their responses. As youngsters, our children Ben, Sam, and Graham were the in-your-face hypers; Jeff and Erin were our internal meltdown hypos. As they have aged, though, the hypers' external meltdowns have become more internalized.) Yet these variations lead professionals to apply different labels to explain the children's responses.

The child's stage of development at the time of assessment will influence the diagnosis, so the mix of labels also depends on the age of the child, as shown in Table 3.1.

As you can see, the child's symptoms change over time. In preschool, the first symptoms that typically lead to the ADHD diagnosis are hyperactivity and impulsivity. Thus the child is labeled as ADHD, predominantly hyperactive-impulsive type. This was the case with Diane's sons Sam and Ben. Later in childhood, however, the child may begin experiencing problems in school and appear to have trouble staying focused, though the hyperactive behaviors seem to have slowed.

As ADHD expert Mark Wolraich explains, even as the hyperactivity diminishes, "academic problems and problems with peers

Table 3.1 Developmental Course of ADHD and Common Diagnoses

Preschool	Childhood	Adolescence and Adulthood
Hyperactivity	Hyperactivity	Hyperactivity
Impulsivity	Impulsivity	Impulsivity
Inattention (sometimes)	Inattention:	Inattention:
	Problems paying attention/daydreaming	Problems paying attention/daydreaming
	Problems maintaining attention	Problems maintaining attention
Disobedience/ defiance	Disobedience/defiance	Executive function impairments
Problems controlling and expressing emotions	Problems controlling and expressing emotions	Problems controlling and expressing emotions
Social/relational difficulties with peers and adults	Social/relational difficulties with peers and adults	Social/relational difficulties
	Executive function impairments	Inability to predict future outcomes/consequences
	Disorganization	Disorganization
	Anxiety	Anxiety
	Depression	Depression

	Poor school performance	Poor school or work performance
		Anger/aggression
		Poor planning abilities
		Increased chance of substance abuse
Common Diagnoses	**Common Diagnoses**	**Common Diagnoses**
ADHD-hyperactive type	ADHD-combined type	ADHD-inattentive type
ODD	ODD (possible Conduct Disorder)	Conduct Disorder
Bipolar Disorder	Bipolar Disorder	Bipolar Disorder
Asperger's Disorder	Asperger's Disorder	Asperger's Disorder
	Depressive Disorder	Depressive Disorder
	Learning disabilities	Learning disabilities
	Anxiety Disorder	Anxiety Disorder

Sources: Adapted from *Neuropsychological Assessment and Intervention for Childhood and Adolescent Disorders*, by C. Riccio, J. Sullivan, and M. Cohen, 2010, Hoboken, NJ: Wiley; *Diagnostic and Statistical Manual of Mental Disorders* (4th ed., text rev.), by American Psychiatric Association, 2000, Arlington, VA: Author; *The ADHD-Autism Connection: A Step Toward More Accurate Diagnosis and Effective Treatment*, by D. M. Kennedy and R. S. Banks, 2002, Colorado Springs, CO: WaterBrook Press.

become more pronounced."[7] This time, the child's label is more likely to be ADHD combined hyperactive-impulsive and inattentive subtype. Or, as in the cases of our sons Jeff and Graham, hyperactive behaviors were not a problem in early childhood, but in early adolescence the inattention became problematic, as did anxiety, depression, and social problems. This clinical picture is common for children diagnosed with the inattentive subtype in adolescence, and they are described as "exhibiting less disruptive behavior but higher degrees of social impairment, unhappiness, and anxiety or depression, compared with children with the combined type."[8] Regardless of the ADHD type with which a child is labeled, the recommended first line of treatment is stimulant medication, along with possible behavioral therapy or counseling.[9]

ADHD and Additional Labels

When a child is given a diagnosis of ADHD, there is an excellent probability that at least one additional label will be added. In fact, up to 100 percent of ADHD patients will have another disorder,[10] and 55 percent will have a third one.[11] For example, Diane's son Sam was diagnosed with ADHD, ODD, Asperger's, anxiety, sleep disturbances, and specific learning disabilities. Rebecca's son, Graham, was labeled with ADHD, depression, anxiety, sleep disturbances, and specific learning disabilities; along with these, her daughter carried the additional label of OCD.

Although every child is different, there are several disorders and conditions routinely diagnosed with ADHD:

- Oppositional Defiant Disorder and Conduct Disorder
- Bipolar Disorder
- Obsessive-Compulsive Disorder
- Anxiety and depression
- Asperger's Disorder
- Learning disabilities (including central auditory and visual processing disorders)

- Language disorders
- Sleep disturbances
- Sensory processing and motor skills disorders

As Figure 3.1 shows, ADHD is highly comorbid with many of these disorders. Recent trends in ADHD research show an increase in studies on and diagnoses of anxiety. The most frequently recognized Anxiety Disorders are Generalized Anxiety Disorder (GAD) and Obsessive-Compulsive Disorder (OCD); the most

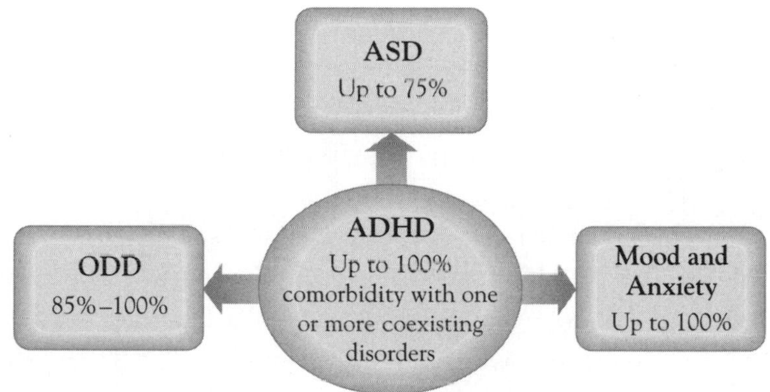

Figure 3.1 ADHD's Excessive Comorbidity

Sources: Adapted from "Discriminating Between Children with ADHD and Classmates Using Peer Variables," by S. Mrug, B. Hoza, A. C. Gerdes, S. Hinshaw, L. E. Arnold, L. Hechtman, and W. E. Pelham, 2008, *Journal of Attention Disorders*, *12*, pp. 372–380; "Comorbid Depression and ADHD in Children and Adolescents," by G. L. Brunsvold, G. Oepen, E. J. Federman, and R. Akins, 2008, *Psychiatric Times*, *25*(10), www.psychiatrictimes.com/adhd/content/article/10168/1286863; *A New Concept in Mental Health: What Is ESSENCE?* by C. Gillberg, 2010, www.docstoc.com/docs/69854703/Child-mental-health-problems-in-preschool-epilepsy; "Autistic Traits in a Population-Based ADHD Twin Sample," by A. M. Reiersen, J. N. Constantino, H. E. Volk, and R. D. Todd, 2007, *Journal of Child Psychology and Psychiatry*, *48*, 464–472; "Shared Heritability of Attention Deficit/Hyperactivity Disorder and Autism Spectrum Disorder," by N. N. Rommelese, B. Franke, H. M. Geurts, C. A. Hartman, and J. K. Buitelaar, 2010, *European Child and Adolescent Psychiatry*, *19*, 281–295.

common Mood Disorders are Depressive Disorder and Bipolar Disorder. As you can see, the prevalence of these disorders is very high, with anxiety disorders and mood disorders being diagnosed in up to 100 percent of patients.

Twice-exceptional children are diagnosed with depression for several reasons, including concern about performance. They frequently judge themselves as incompetent because they never know if they will forget something or say the wrong thing,[12] and repeated school failure leads to depression. Likewise, their social difficulties often lead them to perceive themselves as incompetent and foster negative self-esteem, especially in adolescents. We (Diane and Rebecca) have heard our children express despair over their inability to maintain peer relationships, and we have heard from parents that their children have considered suicide as a possible option for relief from social isolation.

Another common mood disorder, Bipolar Disorder, is frequently confused with ADHD. Experts recognize that up to 100 percent of children who receive a diagnosis of Bipolar Disorder also have symptoms commonly associated with comorbid ADHD and disruptive behavior disorders.[13] Some symptoms that look similar in Bipolar Disorder, ADHD, and ODD and CD include high levels of energy, impulsivity, inattention, problems controlling emotions, rages and tantrums, and sleeplessness.[14]

Controlling Their Symptoms or Compromising Their Gifts?

The symptoms of explosive behaviors, hyperactivity, and impulsivity are leading clinicians increasingly to diagnose Bipolar Disorder and ODD in preschool children.[15] This is a dangerous practice, considering that mood stabilizers and powerful atypical antipsychotic agents (Risperdal, Zyprexa, Seroquel) used to treat schizophrenia "are generally considered one of the first lines of treatment for childhood Bipolar Disorder."[16] The issue of prescribing these medications for our children is a huge source of controversy and a pressing public policy issue, especially in light of the possible long-term effects of these drugs.

Even though these medications are marketed to pediatricians and psychiatrists for use in children accompanied by claims that they are safer than the older antipsychotics, tremendous controversy exists about their safety and use in *adults*, let alone in children. In an attempt to see if the newer antipsychotics are indeed safer and more effective for adults than the older ones, the NIMH funded the Clinical Antipsychotic Trials of Interventions Effectiveness (CATIE) study in 2005. CATIE compared an older antipsychotic, Trilafon, which has the fewest side effects of the older medications, to the newer antipsychotics Risperdal, Zyprexa, Seroquel, and Geodon.[17] The study, which was the largest, longest, and most comprehensive independent trial ever conducted to study these medications, found that the newer medications have no substantial advantage over the older medication. Likewise, a clinical trial known only as Study 15 unexpectedly showed that Seroquel is no more effective than Haldol, which has been available since the 1960s.[18] In other words, these powerful, more expensive medications are no safer or more effective than the older antipsychotics in adults. Yet they are routinely prescribed to one in five children who visit a psychiatrist.[19]

Temple has witnessed the increased use of psychoactive medications, especially risperidone, in children with autism and stands strongly against this trend.

I am absolutely appalled at the huge quantities of medication given to kids like candy. Recently a mom told me that the doctor wanted to put her smart, fully verbal eighteen-year-old on Risperdal because he had difficulty concentrating. This is a heavy-duty drug that has many serious side effects, such as obesity and tardive dyskinesia (tremor disorder). Likewise, at a recent talk for an autism meeting, a psychiatrist came up to me afterwards and praised me for bashing the indiscriminant use of powerful medicines in young children to treat irritability, aggression, temper tantrums, and moodiness. She said it "makes them fat and stupid." Risperdal may be approved by the FDA for five-year-olds, but that doesn't make it right. Most of the studies that were used for this approval were too short to show long-term safety.

As a matter of fact, with the exception of a very limited number of studies on stimulants and anticonvulsants used as mood stabilizers, most medications used to treat our children's various comorbidities have not been tested for use in children under eighteen years of age and certainly not in children ages six and under. According to the *Handbook of Preschool Mental Health*, although stimulant treatment is a recommended treatment option for this age group, "there is still a great deal we do not know, such as whom to treat with medications and what doses are most effective."[20] Yet members of the current DSM committee on Mood Disorders; influential researchers in ADHD, ODD, and CD; and such organizations as the American Academy of Child and Adolescent Psychiatry recommend off-label use of not only stimulants but also atypical antipsychotics and antidepressants in preschoolers.[21]

The phrase *off-label use* refers to the practice of prescribing medications for conditions or age groups other than those approved by the FDA. This practice is legal, and estimates are that off-label prescriptions represent as much as 75 percent of pediatric medication use.[22] Historically, off-label use has been a frequent practice with regard to physical illness in pediatric medicine, as most clinical trials are conducted in adult populations where medications have been proven safe and effective.

With regard to psychiatry, however, off-label use is not supported by research and is in fact strongly cautioned against because of the potential danger. Nevertheless, in a recent radio interview, ADHD expert Joseph Biederman stated that over 20 percent of all Risperdal prescribed is used to treat children.[23] In 2008, an estimated 2.5 million children were taking atypical antipsychotics,[24] with over half being given for Attention-Deficit/Hyperactivity Disorder.[25]

Off-label use also means that no one has tested how the drug will affect children—no research has been conducted to determine how the drug is metabolized, its immediate and long-term side effects (which can include death), or its overall effectiveness in treating the disorder. Even more alarming is the practice of "combination pharmacotherapy" in which more than one psychiatric medication is used to treat a child.

Unfortunately, this practice is prevalent not only in the treatment of children diagnosed with Bipolar Disorder but also for children diagnosed with autism, ADHD, and any number of comorbid conditions, leading to the use of stimulant medications, antidepressants, antipsychotics, and anticonvulsants in varying combinations. A Columbia University study found that in children prescribed antipsychotics, about a third had behavior disorders, a third had developmental problems, and a third had mood disorders; further, "more than 40% were taking at least one other psychiatric medication."[26]

Even more disconcerting is the possibility that these medications may be harmful to children's, and especially preschoolers', developing brains. Studies in neuroscience suggest that brain changes arising from "external environmental influences" more profoundly affect the brains of children under the age of five years because of *neuroplasticity*, the brain's ability to rewire itself by forming new neural pathways in response to events or injury.[27] Young children's brains are more responsive than the brains of adults; thus the potential for harmful and possibly irreversible changes in brain development is heightened when psychoactive drugs are used in preschoolers.[28] Likewise, because "many of the neurotransmitter systems … targeted by psychoactive medications undergo rapid change in the preschool period,"[29] neuroplasticity increases the chance of negative outcomes.

If the safety of a medication has not been established in children, especially very young children, then prescribing two or more medications to a child of any age flies in the face of

"First, do no harm." Yet physicians, influenced by professional treatment guidelines and aggressive marketing by pharmaceutical companies, are increasingly prescribing two or more of these agents. This is the growing trend in the treatment of childhood psychiatric disorders, especially when the child carries multiple diagnoses or when his behavior is difficult to control.

Clearly, when physicians are uncertain as to which symptom belongs to which disorder and as to how one or more medications may affect a child, they should be extremely cautious and conservative in their approach to treatment. As parents and authors, we readily admit that when used judiciously, medication can be a useful adjunct to other therapies in older populations, but even then, it should be prescribed *only* as a last resort. Temple herself has benefited from careful use of medication to treat symptoms of anxiety in early adulthood; through her twenties, she became increasingly nervous and had constant panic attacks, so in her early thirties she started taking a low dose of an antidepressant. Temple believes there is a place for medications when they are used sparingly to help a child achieve his potential, not to turn the child into a compliant zombie.

ADHD and Disruptive Behavior Disorders: A Dangerous Category for 2e Children

Within the Disruptive Behavior Disorders category there is a hierarchical structure among the disorders: ADHD predisposes a child to ODD; ODD predisposes a child to CD; CD predisposes a child to antisocial behavior. Recent studies in ADHD suggest that as many as 85 to 100 percent of children diagnosed with ADHD will also carry an ODD diagnosis;[30] ODD is two to three times more common than CD.[31] Research has also shown that up to 30 percent of children with ODD will be diagnosed with CD, and the risk is three times greater for children who were initially diagnosed at a very young (for example, preschool) age.[32] A recent article in *American Family Physician* states that as many as 40 percent of these children will develop Antisocial Personality Disorder.[33]

DSM-IV-TR describes ODD as "a recurrent pattern of negativistic, defiant, disobedient, and hostile behavior toward authority figures" that includes arguing, tantruming, being angry or resentful, being touchy, being annoying, and refusing to take blame. It is usually apparent before the age of eight years and is seldom diagnosed past early adolescence.[34] The American Academy of Child and Adolescent Psychiatry and the American Academy of Family Physicians suggest that treatment for ODD would optimally begin in preschool and would include family therapy, cognitive behavioral therapy, and psychopharmacological treatment with stimulants, anticonvulsants (mood stabilizers), and antipsychotics (for aggression).[35]

Although we recognize that poor parenting practices and deliberately defiant children do exist in our culture, most oppositional behaviors in 2e children—stubbornness, impatience, low frustration levels, and tantrums—are caused by underlying deficits in emotional regulation and in social cognition (mind-blindness) or by characteristics of giftedness. For a large portion of the 2e population, oppositionality is not simply a learned behavior. The diagnosis of ODD is a very real danger to 2e children because it opens the door to their being seriously misunderstood, misjudged, and medicated.

Unfortunately, the notion that ODD is a learned behavior arising from poor parenting echoes a long-held assumption that parents somehow "cause" their children's disorders. Early literature on ODD echoes Bruno Bettleheim's description of the "refrigerator mother," who was detached and unresponsive to her child's needs and thus caused autism.[36] DSM-IV-TR states outright that ODD is more frequent in families "in which harsh, inconsistent, or neglectful child-rearing practices are common."[37] Likewise, indulgent, passive child-rearing practices in which the parents and child relate as peers or when parents cannot recognize the child's unique needs are also recognized as contributing factors to ODD.

This label does more character damage to 2e children and their families than perhaps any other label in the DSM. Because of the assumptions surrounding this label, a diagnosis of ODD nearly ensures that professionals and others will make negative moral and character judgments about the child, as well as the parents. When the impulsivity and inattention of ADHD are added to the unwilling, stubborn tendencies described as ODD, the stage is set for the child to be seen as willfully disobedient, disruptive, defiant, explosive, unyielding, selfish, self-centered, and morally deficient.

Even the best professionals in the 2e field unwittingly echo these judgments. As a well-respected book on giftedness reports, gifted children with ADHD and ODD have difficulty with empathy and may "choose to be kind or caring, but only because it is a means of exerting control."[38] Sadly, this perspective on a child's behavior can lead professionals to a conclusion of psychopathology, especially in cases where "argumentativeness, defiance, anger, aggression, teasing, stealing, and lying are particular problems."[39] These labels and judgments follow children throughout their lives, branding them as disruptive, devious, and lacking in moral character.

Regrettably, rather than recognizing that these troubling behaviors often accompany giftedness and HFA/AS in many 2e children, teachers and health care professionals are conditioned by experts within the field of ADHD to view these behaviors as signs of character defects that may lead to psychopathology. In fact, Barkley estimates that one in five children with the ODD diagnosis will eventually become a psychopath.[40] However, we must wonder how many of this group are actually 2e children with HFA/AS who have been misdiagnosed with ADHD or ODD and whose behaviors are seriously misperceived as a result of this labeling. Consider Temple's meltdowns throughout the course of her childhood. How much more harshly would her behaviors have been judged had she been diagnosed with severe ADHD and ODD instead of autism?

Moving Beyond Labels to Understanding

An ADHD diagnosis often leads parents down an exhausting, hazardous path of chasing labels and using medications to treat their child's behaviors, moods, and social problems. As the following e-mails demonstrate, once parents set out on this course, it is difficult to change direction, especially when alternative explanations to the child's problems are not readily available.

> After prior ODD, ADHD, and depression diagnoses, my son, who is very bright, was labeled emotionally disturbed (ED).... It took evaluations from three different neuro-psychologists, consultations with two other psychologists, and a few tests by the school psychologist to finally see the Asperger's in him because his symptoms are so subtle...
>
> As a parent whose eight-year-old child was diagnosed with alphabet soup ADHD, Tourette's Disorder, OCD, ODD, Bipolar Disorder, anxiety, Dyslexia, seizures, developmental delay, and finally PDD-NOS, which led me to autism, I believe the autism community is on to something.... It made the most sense out of them all. It explains all of his behaviors at different times of his life.

This second e-mail testifies to how firmly embedded the ADHD paradigm is in the medical community. Notice also how difficult it was for these parents to obtain a diagnosis of Asperger's for their children. In both of these cases, it took years to obtain an autism spectrum diagnosis, years that could have been spent obtaining more effective treatment to minimize their children's weaknesses and finding ways to nurture their natural talents and gifts.

We call attention to the problem of labels hoping to encourage parents and professionals to look outside the narrow categories to discover a more integrated understanding of the children they seek to help. Parents turn to the experts for the answers and for explanations of their child's difficulties. In turn, the child receives a label, most often ADHD. Unfortunately, ADHD is an incomplete explanation for the child's symptoms and difficulties, so most children wind up with at least three labels, and parents remain discouraged and frustrated. In short, the diagnosis of ADHD often prohibits parents from understanding the unique nature and giftedness of the 2e child and derails them in their quest to identify his deficits and intervene with supports.

A prevailing belief we hear from parents is that something must be terribly wrong with their child because he has so many labels and has trouble getting the help that he needs in school. Instead of questioning what is wrong with your child, we encourage you to consider that something may be fundamentally wrong with the diagnostic and education systems that are failing your child, a subject we examine more fully in Part Two.

Because we understand the pain of viewing your children as broken rather than bright, we want to share two other perspectives, which offer a more balanced view of your child's strengths and better explanations for his deficits. As you will see in the next chapter, the field of autism has a solid, comprehensive understanding and explanation of the deficits underlying the disruptive behaviors that lead to the alphabet soup of labels. Together, the fields of dual exceptionalities and autism bring a clear, more compassionate view of the whole 2e child with his unique set of strengths and weaknesses.

4

Autism and 2e

A Better Understanding of Deficits and Behaviors

Effective strategies can only be employed if the true nature of a condition is known.

The National Autistic Society Web site

As we discussed in Chapter Three, an ADHD diagnosis interferes with identifying giftedness and deficits. It forces parents into the uncomfortable role of advocating for a child whose behavior perplexes and sometimes frightens them—a child who, by all appearances, chooses to behave badly. Sadly, in the absence of a true understanding of their impairments, 2e children often end up identifying themselves by their difficult behaviors and others' opinions, not by their unique abilities, as the following recollection of a 2e thirteen-year-old shows.

> I thought I was stupid, because I was always getting bad grades, doing dumb stuff, or freaking out in a panic attack. I wasn't stupid, though. . . . I'd never been stupid. I could read "big kid books" when I was still in the 1st grade, stuff for 5th and 6th graders. I'd taken an IQ test and scored as high as could be measured. For some reason, though, I, and others, still found myself a fool.

> "Wake up!" "Put down that book!" "Look at me when I'm talking to you!" "Are you listening to me?" "PAY ATTENTION!" These were the fences that divided me from my peers, the lines that defined the territory of my conversations with my teachers. I shrank further into myself, an impressive feat of shame.[1]

As long as professionals focus on disruptive behaviors and call these ADHD, they will continue to miss the true underlying impairments, and they will continue to pile on additional diagnoses, frustrating parents and losing the child in the mix. We have heard this frustration from countless parents, as the following letters to us illustrate:

> It absolutely mystifies me why the "experts" can't put it together when it comes to these diagnoses.... I have an eighteen year old son who was originally diagnosed ADHD/ODD/NVLD with depression. He finally was diagnosed as having Asperger's Syndrome.
>
> My five year old has a dual diagnosis of ADHD and Asperger's ... we began noticing social issues, speech issues, and anxieties but once I started reading about Asperger's it all started making sense.... I'm going to be honest here and say, "I don't get this." Why would a child have a dual diagnosis of ADHD/autistic spectrum? It seems to me the ADHD would be ruled out once the autistic spectrum diagnosis is given.

Notice how difficult it was for these parents to obtain a diagnosis of Asperger's for their children. In both of these cases, the time spent moving through multiple labels to the autism diagnosis[2] could have been spent obtaining more effective treatments to minimize their children's weaknesses and finding ways to nurture their children's natural talents and gifts. These e-mails also illustrate the emphasis on differences that the categorical diagnostic system encourages among professionals. Even in the face of undeniable similarities in behaviors, populations, and comorbidly diagnosed conditions, the buzzword in professional literature continues to be "overlap," implying that two or more separate entities are present.

However, this idea of overlap results in confusion and frustration for parents of 2e children who have discovered that autism spectrum disorders comprehensively account for the symptoms diagnosed as ADHD and for many of the characteristics of giftedness, especially overexcitabilities, that are so often indistinguishable from ADHD. Yet because of the categorical system, children are given an ADHD diagnosis even when a diagnosis of autism might lead to more appropriate therapies, interventions, and supports for the 2e child.

The following responses to us during an international autism conference show how parents are frustrated that an autism diagnosis is so difficult to obtain.

> So glad ADHD was mentioned. My son is a young adult now but I have always felt that there is more to it than ADHD. He needs to have a correct diagnosis to get the correct help, which has not been very forthcoming. We have all kinds of titles for his condition, but to me it all comes under autism at different levels.
>
> My 10 yr old daughter has been given the diagnosis of ADHD but I am certain it was ASD. She fits the ASD profiles I've read but I'm still trying to get my head around the fact that her Developmental Paediatrician says no it's not. He explains all her other behaviors as being what they call comorbid conditions. But I think he might be wrong. So how many doctors are we going to have to go through to convince me that it's ADHD and not ASD?

Clearly, these parents are frustrated by the incomplete profile of the ADHD label, even as they question the logic of adding comorbid conditions to round out a diagnostic picture that is already complete in autism. They actively sought the answers found in the field of autism, but two significant barriers stood in the way of their children receiving an autism diagnosis:

1. The categorical system requires clinicians to diagnose ADHD with comorbid conditions when a child does not meet the required number of symptoms for HFA/AS or when the symptoms are not obviously impairing.
2. The restricted definition and description of autism prohibits children with higher IQs and less obvious impairments from receiving the diagnosis.

In short, the system frequently keeps parents, educators, and health care providers from a better understanding of 2e children.

What Are Autism Spectrum Disorders?

The Centers for Disease Control define autism spectrum disorders as a set of developmental disabilities causing "significant social, communication, and behavioral challenges" depending on the degree of severity of the disorder, the child's developmental stage, and the child's IQ.[3] Autism spectrum disorders account for a range of disorders, including autism, AS, and PDD-NOS, although currently the criteria for each disorder is listed separately in DSM-IV-TR; the following box shows the criteria for AS. (In DSM-5, whose publication is projected for 2013, it is proposed that all forms of autism be diagnosed under one label, Autism Spectrum Disorder. See Chapter Seven for more about this.)

Diagnostic Criteria for Asperger's Disorder

The essential features of Asperger's Disorder are severe and sustained impairment in social interaction and the development of restricted, repetitive patterns of behavior, interest, and activity. The disturbance must clinically show significant impairment in social, occupational, and other important areas of functioning. In contrast to Autistic Disorder, there are no clinically significant delays in language. In addition there are no clinically significant delays in cognitive development or in the development of age-appropriate self-help skills, adaptive behavior, and curiosity about the environment in childhood.

A. Qualitative impairment in social interaction, as manifested by at least two of the following:
   (1) marked impairment in the use of multiple nonverbal behaviors such as eye-to-eye gaze, facial expression, body postures, and gestures to regulate social interaction
   (2) failure to develop peer relationships appropriate to developmental level
   (3) a lack of spontaneous seeking to share enjoyment, interests, or achievements with other people (e.g., by a lack of showing, bringing, or pointing out objects of interest to other people)
   (4) lack of social or emotional reciprocity

B. Restricted repetitive and stereotyped patterns of behavior, interests, and activities, as manifested by at least one of the following:
   (1) encompassing preoccupation with one or more stereotyped and restricted patterns of interest that is abnormal either in intensity or focus
   (2) apparently inflexible adherence to specific, non-functional routines or rituals

(3) stereotyped and repetitive motor mannerisms (e.g., hand or finger flapping or twisting, or complex whole-body movements)

(4) persistent preoccupation with parts of objects

C. The disturbance causes clinically significant impairment in social, occupational, or other important areas of functioning.

D. There is no clinically significant general delay in language (e.g., single words used by age 2 years, communicative phrases used by age 3 years)

E. There is no clinically significant delay in cognitive development or in the development of age-appropriate self-help skills, adaptive behavior (other than in social interaction), and curiosity about the environment in childhood.

F. Criteria are not met for another specific Pervasive Developmental Disorder or Schizophrenia.

Source: From *Diagnostic and Statistical Manual of Mental Disorders* (4th ed., text rev., pp. 83–84), by American Psychiatric Association, 2000, Arlington, VA: Author.

It is important to note that in the prose description of Asperger's Disorder, the DSM states that "Symptoms of overactivity and inattention are frequent in Asperger's Disorder, and indeed many individuals with this condition receive a diagnosis of Attention Deficit/Hyperactivity Disorder prior to the diagnosis of Asperger's Disorder,"[4] suggesting an awareness of the possibility of diagnostic confusion between these labels.

ADHD and HFA/AS: Identical Characteristics but Different Perspectives

After nearly thirty years, researchers have been unable to differentiate ADHD from HFA/AS in any meaningful way that precludes misdiagnosis. In fact, research continues to show that these disorders are indistinguishable in their symptoms, deficits, and related conditions. They differ only in degrees of severity, and their presentation depends on the child's stage of development.

Autistic impairments in the 2e population can be debilitating because they are frequently hidden by the child's ability to compensate. As Wing and Gould explain, a triad of underlying impairments in social interaction, communication, and imagination (or executive function) form the basis of any autism spectrum disorder.[5] (*Executive function* refers to self-control, planning, reasoning, and abstract thought.) The interaction among these three impairments, combined with IQ, accounts for the seemingly endless variety of children's behavior and abilities within the autism spectrum. In other words, the extent to which a child is impaired in any one of these areas determines the diagnosis he receives, ranging from classic autism to HFA/AS.

In addition to this triad of impairments, though, researchers recognize several "ADHD-like" behavioral symptoms "including hyperactivity, short attention span, impulsivity, aggressiveness . . . and temper tantrums."[6]

It is important to understand that researchers in ADHD view these common impairments and symptoms quite differently from researchers in autism. As you can see from Table 4.1, the core symptoms of ADHD are considered the associated features of autism spectrum disorders, and the associated features of ADHD are the core deficits in autism spectrum disorders.

Is it any wonder, then, that although children suffer from identical social, communication, and executive function impairments, as well as identical attention and oppositional behaviors, they can be diagnosed with ADHD, HFA/AS, or even both disorders? As early as the 1940s, Asperger himself observed that these children suffer from significant attentional deficits; and as recently as 2010, researchers recognized that "attentional dysfunction is one of the most consistent findings in individuals with ASD."[7] Yet because

Table 4.1 Core Symptoms and Associated Features of ADHD

Core Symptoms of ADHD (Associated Features of ASD)	Associated Features of ADHD (Core Deficits of ASD)
Hyperactivity	Social difficulties
Impulsivity	Communication problems
Inattention	Imagination–executive function impairments

Sources: Information from *Diagnostic and Statistical Manual of Mental Disorders* (4th ed., text rev.), by American Psychiatric Association, 2000, Arlington, VA: Author; L. Wing, interview with the authors, February 17, 2011.

of our diagnostic system, these deficits are most often diagnosed as ADHD with comorbid conditions.

Shared Core Impairments in ADHD and HFA/AS (and Gifted)

As we have watched the fields of both ADHD and autism evolve, one striking trend has emerged: the field of ADHD continues to "discover" and study impairments that have already been established as part of the autism spectrum, namely social impairments, communication deficits, and executive function challenges. However, as you will see, the ADHD explanations for these impairments pale in contrast to the understanding offered by autism.

Impairments in Social Abilities

Within the last decade, the field of ADHD has been giving more attention to the social difficulties within its population. Yet social impairments are the central core deficit in ASD, as evidenced by the DSM-IV-TR description of the disorder.

ADHD's descriptions of the social deficits and the impact these have on functioning are identical to those that have long been found in the field of autism. However, ADHD's explanations for these deficits fall short of the comprehensive understanding found in autism. For instance, in autism it has been recognized that impairments in the realms of communication and imagination–executive function seriously impact the child's social functioning. In ADHD, though, impairments in these areas, if recognized, are diagnosed comorbidly, and the child is all too frequently blamed for the social difficulties arising from these impairments.

The following e-mail illustrates the devastating effect that unaddressed and misunderstood social issues can have when ADHD is diagnosed instead of ASD. This high school student wrote to an ADHD chat room called Outside the Box! to see if anyone could tell him where to get help:

> Hi, my name is Jared. I am fifteen and I was diagnosed with ADHD in second grade.... This year I find myself out of the circle of friends I once thought I was in.... My main issue with other kids is "small talk" (short conversations that don't really have any intellectual values, yet are useful for building strong, long-lasting relationships). I am either completely involved in the conversation or I really don't care. I often interrupt people and dominate conversation.... I take 50mg of Adderall XR every morning including weekends... I have been getting more and more depressed about my situation every day. My question is: Where can I practice/learn/develop social skills or strategies to better my social situation in my school?[8]

Jared clearly blames himself for losing the friends he believed he once had. Yet his perception of his social shortcomings—the inability to make small talk, interrupting others, and monopolizing conversation—suggests that these were not close friendships at all. Sadly, even as he is aware of his poor social understanding, he believes that he is simply missing a set of social skills. But Jared's problems with social communication go deeper than a learned skill set, as experts in autism recognize. In fact, Jared's difficulties arise because of an impairment in his *ability* to learn social skills.

Social Difficulties and Theory of Mind For years the field of autism has used the term *theory of mind* to refer to a child's ability to understand and take the perspective of others in social situations. Experts in autism recognize that children on the spectrum lack theory of mind—that they suffer from a sort of social blindness that makes them unaware of another's motives, needs, interests, feelings, or drives.

These children suffer social isolation because they dominate conversations with monologues on special interests, impulsively interrupt conversations, trample over the feelings of others, and misread or miss common social cues that support reciprocity. Most of these cues are related to nonverbal aspects of social communication, including facial expression and body language, which serve to reinforce the speaker.[9] Consequently, when a child has impaired theory of mind, he will not pick up on social cues. Sadly, such deficits in theory of mind can also lead to social victimization because social blindness often makes them perfect victims for all types of bullying.

Interestingly, although ADHD's description of the social difficulties are identical to those found in autism, the explanation of the *reasons* for these deficits is strikingly different. A 2008 study of peer rejection in ADHD includes the following description:

> [T]he child is actively rejected and disliked by peers, has little insight into these problems, and does not have any mutual friends ... [though] the child may claim many friends, they are just acquaintances and other children avoid this child.[10]

These sorts of social difficulties go beyond merely the missing of social cues and point instead to deeper impairment in theory of mind. Most children with ADHD are unaware of their "negative social status" and of their negative social behaviors.[11]

Unfortunately, the way the field of ADHD attempts to explain these social problems all too often assumes that the child's performance is to blame. In fact, Barkley states that "ADHD is a disorder of performance not of skill." It is "not a disorder of knowing what to do, but of doing what one knows."[12] A *performance deficit* is described as a "won't do" problem in which "the child is failing to exhibit the desired behavior in the appropriate situation despite the presence of the skill in the child's behavioral repertoire."[13] Clearly, viewing a child's social difficulties as a "won't do" problem sets the stage for the child to be seen as willful and to be blamed for his failures in social interactions.

When it comes to social difficulties, a frequently repeated refrain in ADHD literature is that the child does not "put on the brakes," meaning that he does not slow down his mind enough to pay attention to social cues. As Sam Goldstein, longtime ADHD researcher, explains, "Children with ADHD are cueless. They tend to miss important cues in their environment. . . . They know what to do but often don't do what they know because they miss the cues."[14] Likewise, Thomas Brown states that

> Persons with ADHD also report problems in monitoring the context in which they are interacting. They fail to notice when other people are puzzled, or hurt or annoyed by what they have just said or done and thus fail to modify their behavior.[15]

These explanations rest on the assumption that the child with ADHD has the capacity to develop social understanding, has developed it, but is not applying it. However, as the following comments by a thirteen-year-old girl diagnosed with ADHD show, this assumption is often inaccurate: "I didn't really know how to be a good friend. I didn't realize if I was hurting or annoying anyone else. . . . The other kids would try to avoid me."[16]

In short, although both fields recognize and describe the same social deficits, autism's long-standing assumption of an impaired theory of mind offers a more thorough explanation of why our children struggle socially than does the assumption that they simply do not slow down enough to pay attention or to apply social knowledge they have.

Theory of Mind and Oppositional Behaviors Impairments in theory of mind are often expressed through explosive, oppositional, and emotionally detached behaviors that are frequently misjudged by parents and professionals as simply "bad behavior." We cannot stress enough the differences in understanding that the field of autism offers with regard to oppositional behaviors. Unlike the judgment-laden, psychosocial explanations found in ADHD literature, the explanations found in autism are grounded in the knowledge that the child is neurologically impaired and that the behaviors stem from these impairments. Disabilities consultant and advocate Roger N. Meyer cautions that

> [Parents] should exercise extreme caution when a clinician slaps the Oppositional Defiant Disorder (ODD) label on their children. It is a very inappropriate diagnosis. ODD is a catchall, old-time, psycho dynamically oriented explanation for "inappropriate" behavior and is unsuitable for persons on the autistic spectrum.[17]

As we noted in Chapter Three, the progression from ODD to CD to antisocial behavior is assumed in the field of ADHD. This progression poses a very real danger to a child with ASD who is misdiagnosed with ADHD/ODD because the child with ASD often appears callous and emotionally detached. Often this child is described as lacking empathy and is mistakenly assumed to have "a full understanding of what is going on in his own and other people's minds,"[18] leading teachers, professionals, and parents to believe that like the antisocial psychopath, the child is being manipulative to achieve his own ends. This assumption is incorrect, however; as we've discussed, a child with autism has an impaired theory of mind, the executive function that allows a child to *mentalize*, or attribute mental states to another person.[19]

When explaining theory of mind, Uta Frith distinguishes between sympathy and empathy to explain the apparent callousness in children with autism. *Instinctive sympathy*, according to Frith, is an autonomic response to fear and sadness that "is *not* dependent on the ability to mentalize."[20] Contrary to the popular belief that children with HFA/AS are unable to relate to another's emotions, many HFA/AS children feel sympathy for others; it is their inability to express it appropriately that leads people to judge them as callous and unemotional, characteristics strongly associated with conduct-disordered, antisocial behavior.

Empathy, in contrast, requires the ability to mentalize or understand *why* the other person is sad in order to respond. From this understanding, the child can create an appropriate, socially acceptable response even in the absence of shared emotion.[21] It is important to understand that the truly conduct-disordered child is able to mentalize, and may in fact be quite accomplished at this. However, it is theorized that such a child may lack instinctive sympathy, "leading him to be adept at feigning empathy but impaired in the ability to understand the guiding moral principles that would prevent him from hurting another person."[22]

In short, there is a distinct difference between a child with ASD and a psychopath. However, the only way this difference can be recognized is if the child's behavior is understood not as ODD but as autism. Although we are certainly aware that there are truly conduct-disordered children in our world, we cannot stress enough how tragic it is that a child with HFA/AS, who already suffers from social communication impairments, is labeled and judged as a bad child who acts intentionally to harm others.

Impairments in Communication

Remember our sons Sam and Graham? They both received diagnoses of different subtypes of ADHD, but they also exhibited symptoms of social communication impairments and disruptive behaviors. Sam, who was diagnosed with ODD, has problems understanding a person's tone of voice, which makes it difficult for him to gauge whether someone is angry or joking. He also interprets language literally, meaning that when he is told "to take a hike," he may ask, "to where?" Graham, too, has some trouble interpreting facial expressions and body language, though he comes across as an effective communicator. However, he has severe problems with interpreting meaning—that is, he can recall verbatim what someone says, but is unable to interpret the message so that he can act on it. This discrepancy in abilities leads to frequent misunderstandings and seriously impacts Graham's relationships: he is judged as being oppositional and defiant because he does not follow through.

Both Sam and Graham illustrate communication problems that are recognized as aspects of autism spectrum disorders but that are often missed or are diagnosed separately in ADHD. Both of our sons illustrate common difficulties in two major aspects of communication: semantics and pragmatics, which lead to problems in *all* social situations and relationships. Unfortunately, these difficulties in communication are seen as secondary issues in ADHD, whereas autism recognizes them as core impairments.

Semantics refers to the relationship between thought and language. It is the understanding of the meaning and interpretations of language and symbols. Pragmatics is the practical use of language to convey meaning to others. It refers to how a child uses language to relate to those around him. Table 4.2 illustrates the elements of these aspects of language.

As you can see, a child with impairments in these areas will have trouble with all aspects of communication: telling a story that has a point, maintaining the flow of conversation (taking turns or staying on topic), and constructing or understanding messages. Sam and Graham illustrate how different children have different difficulties—one child is able to interpret facial expressions but unable to understand figurative language, for example; another can make eye contact but is unable to initiate conversation when help is needed. Whatever the manifestation, communication impairments

Table 4.2 Semantic and Pragmatic Uses of Language

Semantics: The Abstract Meaning of Language Thought ⇒ Language	Pragmatics: The Social Use of Language Language ⇒ Expression
Recognizing the need to initiate conversation	The ability to ask for help or information
Organizing thoughts and message	Clear content in speech and writing
Conveying message	Use of body language, eye contact, body space, reciprocity
Understanding the relationship between tone and meaning	Use of vocal qualities—intonation, modulation
Understanding figurative, indirect language	Interpreting idioms or figures of speech

Source: "Semantic and Pragmatic Difficulties and Semantic Pragmatic Language Disorder," by C. Bowen, 2001, www.speech-language-therapy.com/spld.htm.

often result in sudden, explosive behaviors because of a child's frustration at his inability to communicate effectively with others, to understand their expectations, and to get his needs met.

It's clear that a large number of children diagnosed with ADHD have communication difficulties, but in the ADHD paradigm, disruptive behaviors are viewed as the primary problem; communication problems are seen as secondary. These communication problems may go undetected because the focus is on a child's behavior—behavior described "as difficult or inflexible and explosive," according to a 2006 ADHD study[23] or as self-centered (DSM-IV-TR).

Experts in ADHD contend that communication problems result from a child's inability to focus his mind and control his behavior. Children with ADHD have trouble verbalizing and listening because "their brains are racing ahead to the next thought."[24] This explanation is fraught with negative connotations: it suggests that a child's approach to communicating with others is fundamentally out of control because the child is out of control. Brown describes children with ADHD as "too impulsive in what they say."[25] Likewise, Barkley views verbal impulsivity and the inability to control behavior in the presence of strong emotion as central to ADHD.[26]

In contrast, autism views these same oppositional behaviors as tied to communication, indeed even as part of the communication process. As Brenda Smith Myles, a respected speech-language pathologist, explains, behavior *is* communication. Rita Jordan and Glenys Jones recognize that "difficult or challenging behaviour is … a common reaction of pupils with these [autism spectrum] disorders" because they are "faced with limited abilities to communicate their frustrations."[27] Likewise, Sally Jackson believes that "whether it is an inability to process the verbal and non-verbal information given or an inability … to verbalize their own needs or frustrations, both play an important part in the resulting challenging behavior displayed" by children with ASD.[28] Similarly, Robert Koegel and Lynn Kern-Koegel, founders of the Koegel Autism Center, see a direct correlation between communication, language difficulties, and disruptive behaviors, and they believe that language therapies can lessen these inappropriate behaviors as a child becomes more able to communicate.[29] In other words, rather than treating disruptive behaviors independently, researchers in autism believe that communication therapies will improve the behavior as well as the communication.

Executive Function Impairments

The term *executive function* refers to the processes that regulate cognitive and emotional control. Executive functions allow us to

- Keep several tasks going at once and switch smoothly between them
- Keep items in working memory
- Set goals and plan how to reach them
- Break with routine and make a transition in the face of sudden change

- Monitor thoughts, feelings, and performance
- Regulate attention
- Organize thoughts and language into messages
- Control emotional and physical responses

As you can see, executive function plays a significant role in a child's ability to interact socially with the world around him as well as to develop his individual gifts and talents.

In the field of ADHD, numerous authorities, including Barkley, Brown, Goldstein, and Biederman, have associated executive function impairments—such as problems with working memory, regulating attention, planning and organizing, and regulating emotion and motivation—with the hyperactive-impulsive subtype. Both Brown and Barkley have hypothesized and revised their individual executive function models in their attempts to define ADHD.[30] For example, in his presentation *Advances in the Understanding and Management of ADHD*, Barkley says, "ADHD is a disorder of inhibition and self-regulation, which arises from the executive system," and states that "there are no other disorders I'm aware of that produce these problems chronically, unremittingly, dating from childhood."[31] Yet well-respected authorities in autism, including Wing, Gould, Frith, Volkmar, and Klin, have long recognized that executive function impairments are highly associated with autism spectrum disorders;[32] specifically, impairments in the areas that control working memory, planning and organization, shifting attention, self-monitoring, and inhibiting responses underlie most autistic behaviors, such as difficulties in communication, learning, setting goals and directing behaviors, controlling attention, regulating emotional responses, and dealing with changes in routine. In fact, Wing and Gould believe that impairment in executive function may be the most disabling result of having an autism spectrum condition because of its negative impact on life outcome.[33]

Numerous researchers have examined the efficacy of using executive function deficits as a means of differentially diagnosing

ADHD and autism spectrum disorders. Over a decade ago, when we researched executive function in ADHD and autism, we uncovered numerous similarities between the two. Since the publication of our first book, research studies in both fields continue to confirm that the executive function deficits targeted in these disorders are nearly identical. This calls into question the idea that executive function can be used to differentially diagnose ADHD from ASD. In fact, recent studies in both fields comparing executive function between ADHD and ASD populations show that "the cognitive profiles are consistent" between these groups[34] and that executive function "assessment is not useful for differential diagnosis between ADHD and ASD."[35] In other words, recent research shows that using executive function to distinguish between the diagnoses of ADHD and ASD is ineffective.

Autism's Explanation for Oppositional Behaviors

So-called oppositional behavior in ASD has its roots in several deficits and impairments. It is up to the parent, educator, therapist, and clinician to look beyond the behavior to its source, and to see what the child is attempting to communicate. In ASD, there are several sources of oppositional behavior, including sensory processing problems related to smells, textures, lighting, temperature, sounds, and crowds.

As we discussed earlier, an underlying communication impairment can often lead to apparently defiant behavior because the child "refuses" to follow directions or rules. Or, if he acts on the message inappropriately because he misunderstood it, then he is seen as reactive, impulsive, and intentional. However, in the presence of a semantic or pragmatic language processing difficulty, it is highly likely that the child *heard* what was said, but was *unable to process the "why"* of the message.

Likewise, other oppositional behaviors evident in ASD children arise from internalizing disorders, such as anxiety and mood disorders, which result in externalized reactions such as explosive behavior. Anxiety is highly persistent and common in ASD, and leads to frequent meltdowns in response to social demands and situations. Children with ASD "live in a world that is more unpredictable and uncertain than it is for others ... and repetitive and ritualized behaviors, slowness, aggression, and irritability are likely to worsen" when the child becomes anxious.[36] These behaviors are frequently the child's response to anxiety, but all too often he is accused of deliberately annoying others, attempting to control, or being manipulative or coercive. However, for a child with ASD, attributing intention to such behaviors is a gross injustice and serious misjudgment.

Explosive and inflexible behaviors are commonly associated with ODD, a disorder that is almost always diagnosed comorbidly with ADHD. Interestingly, the fields of ADHD and autism both attribute this explosiveness to impaired emotional regulation and impulsivity. But whereas Barkley has only just recently theorized that children diagnosed with ADHD may have deficiencies in emotional regulation, autism researchers have recognized *for years* that children with ASD have "difficulties in emotional regulation including frequent temper outbursts, a tendency to cry, rapid mood changes, a tendency to be easily frustrated ... and clinically significant issues with perfectionism."[37]

Autism: A Blend of Gifts and Deficits

As we have shown, the field of autism holds many more answers and offers a deeper understanding of 2e children's deficits, challenges, and gifts than do the labels ADHD and ODD. Autism recognizes the ways in which social, communication, and behavioral symptoms change over the course of a child's development, and therefore allows parents to avoid the pitfalls of an alphabet soup of labels. Likewise, although the condition is still strongly associated with the most severely impaired populations, the field of autism does recognize that degrees of impairment and IQ significantly impact the presentation of the disorder, even to the point of misdiagnosis.

Also, although the autism field acknowledges that many in its population are uniquely and extremely gifted with high IQs and wonderfully creative abilities, as well as learning disabilities, the answers for developing these talents is found in the field of giftedness. In fact, the area of dual exceptionalities offers the best of both worlds for parents because it enables them to see the whole child—one with gifts, not just deficits. In short, the best approach for a 2e child may emerge from the union of these two fields.

The Whole Child Approach: Bringing Together Giftedness and HFA/AS

For decades it has been recognized that high IQ and special abilities are significant traits in the HFA/AS population. This unique aspect of autism predisposes children to "a particular originality of thought and experience, which may well lead to exceptional achievements in later life."[38] In fact, because intelligence in both autism and in giftedness occurs along a continuum, "it is not surprising that the two populations are matched at several points."[39] The late Bernard Rimland, a highly respected autism expert, found it nearly impossible to distinguish between autism and genius at young ages.[40] After much research into the overlapping behaviors in giftedness and HFA/AS, Isabelle Rapin, a neurologist and autism expert, "questions where autism ends and oddness begins."[41]

Obviously, besides IQ, children with HFA/AS share a significant number of strengths with children who are gifted, such as excellent memory skills, focused interests, extensive knowledge, and a strong vocabulary.[42] Another important similarity is in development: both populations show uneven development—a confusing mix of skills and deficits—and they are often out-of-sync with their peers. Important similarities in behaviors and personalities also exist between these two populations, further adding to the confusion as parents seek to see the whole child.

Understanding Both Parts of Twice Exceptional

The 2e concept requires that each exceptionality be clearly identified and understood so that interventions can be designed to target the precise needs of the individual child. In light of this goal, it becomes increasingly urgent that the fields of autism and giftedness come together, especially as the 2e concept continues to evolve. Many experts see ADHD as the primary disability in dual exceptionalities. However, as we have shown, ADHD is a questionable diagnosis, fraught with misconceptions about the nature of the disability itself, whereas autism offers more scientifically sound explanations for those impairments and behaviors described as ADHD. Yet because more traditional stereotypes of autism are prevalent in our culture, the idea that autism can be associated with giftedness is one that is only beginning to garner much-needed attention in both fields.

As we begin to tease out the complexity of dual exceptionalities, tough questions arise as to what exactly an ADHD diagnosis adds to an understanding of the 2e child. The ADHD diagnosis thwarts attempts to accurately assess such conditions as specific learning disabilities, autism spectrum disorders, anxiety, and giftedness, which result in the difficult behaviors, learning problems, or impaired social development common in dual exceptionalities. In other words, the diagnosis of ADHD confuses rather than clarifies because all of its symptoms can be accounted for by other aspects of dual exceptionality, which are more scientifically and reliably assessed and defined.

As we have noted, accurate identification is foundational to 2e children's obtaining a strengths-based education that ensures a successful outcome. However, as you will see in Part Two, the current diagnostic system all but prohibits proper identification of hidden social, communication, and imagination–executive function impairments in children with high IQ, and 2e students remain unidentified and underserved by our educational system.

Part II

Why They're Stuck

5

A Layman's Guide to the DSM

The Flawed System That Traps Our Children

Unthinking respect for authority is the greatest enemy of truth.

Albert Einstein

As parents, the two of us (Diane and Rebecca) sought answers as to why our children were so trapped by the alphabet soup of labels; our search led to a research project beyond the scope of what we imagined. Somewhere in your journey with your own child, like us you have no doubt encountered the DSM and its awesome power to dictate the diagnoses, the medications, the therapies, and the educational services your child receives.

This mother's e-mail to us illustrates the frustration we ourselves experienced as we returned for repeated evaluations to explain our children's difficulties:

> I have a child who was diagnosed with ADHD at a very young age of 4. In trying to figure out what was really going on, I read everything I could possibly find. . . . I found so many of the symptoms of the [*sic*] Autism Spectrum Disorder I could apply to my child with ADHD. After an evaluation by a well-known psychiatrist, it was determined that although he [my son]

> may exhibit some of the symptomology, it was not intensive enough to consider the diagnosis of ASD. . . . I just had another evaluation done and the diagnosis is now described as PDD-NOS. We need more definitive guidelines so that our children can get the appropriate help they need.

It is unfortunate that parents have to go to such lengths to find answers to advocate effectively for their children, especially when they trust that the diagnostic system will give them those answers. Parents are in a highly vulnerable position, balancing extraordinary concern for their children with the necessity of placing their trust in the DSM and the professionals who use it.

All too often, the system fails us and fails our children, leading us to blame the professionals when, in all honesty, they are simply following the rules of their profession. In fact, in a recent article titled "Psychiatrists Call for Overhaul of Unwieldy DSM," several psychiatrists voiced their own frustration with the current system, saying, "The DSM is too wordy"; "It is a nightmare in terms of gathering and analyzing data . . . many of the terms elicit misunderstandings about the patient's condition"; "We need a substantial modification of the diagnostic system."[1] If the current diagnostic system is not serving its practitioners or their patients, we must ask where the failure occurs and why.

Much literature in the fields of dual exceptionalities, ADHD, and autism addresses the consequences of the system's breakdown—the alphabet soup and the medication cocktails—but stops short of questioning the system itself. These well-intentioned works attempt to help parents sort out the multiple labels their children receive and encourage parents to look beyond the labels to the whole child. However, these works share a basic acceptance of the DSM system of diagnosis as reliable and valid—a view that leads experts to shuffle and reshuffle similar symptoms in order to explain the differences among the labels.

As we examined current and past research in ADHD, autism, and dual exceptionalities, we seemed to be the only ones asking questions no other book has addressed: Why does the DSM system lead to an alphabet soup of labels? Could it be that our diagnostic system is fundamentally flawed when it comes to meeting the needs of practicing clinicians and parents? Who, really, does this system serve?

One night as we attempted to answer these questions, we stumbled upon information from a group of researchers who were examining the larger context of the system. These professionals were questioning the fundamental design of the DSM and the accuracy of the ways disorders are defined, and acknowledging the need for new approaches to diagnosing these disorders. To our surprise, this group turned out to be the very professionals responsible for creating and revising the current DSM. The experts included high-ranking members of the American Psychiatric Association (APA), the organization that authors and publishes the DSM. Among them were Robert Spitzer and Allen Frances, past and present chairs of the DSM task force; Michael First, editor of DSM-IV and DSM-IV-TR; David Kupfer, chair of the DSM-5 task force; and others with vested interests in the existing system and the diagnoses it includes.

The grim reality is that the DSM system breeds tremendous disagreement, both among members and leaders of the APA and among parents and the professionals in the trenches who work with our children. Although we humbly acknowledge that it is not our responsibility as mothers to unravel the intricacies and nuances of the DSM, we also recognize that in order to understand the complexity of the forces that come to bear upon our children's futures, we need to examine how the system evolved, the numerous controversies within the professional community, and what the future holds if people continue to be complacent about these issues.

Although our perspective on the DSM is a provocative one, we feel compelled to share our view of this very complicated topic. It is quite enlightening to look at the creation of the DSM system and see the very real controversies that have a serious impact on our children's diagnoses, controversies that began in 1980 and are still hotly debated today.

DSM-II to DSM-III: The Changing Paradigm from Practice to Research

Historically, in the period including the publication of DSM-II, the power rested with practicing psychiatrists in a sort of "bottom-up" system in which the descriptions of psychiatric syndromes as broad constellations of symptoms and treatment were based on the data collected from rank-and-file clinicians.

The publication of DSM-III in 1980 represented a fundamental change: the system flipped to a "top-down" approach, shifting power away from practitioners to academicians and researchers. This change established the primacy of research, because one goal of the new paradigm, as explained in DSM-IV-TR, was to establish "operational" diagnostic criteria, which were regarded as more "reliable than the traditional ones based on clinical descriptions."[2] As a result of this shift, the broad syndromes were broken down into specific disorders based on narrowly defined clusters of symptoms. These disorders were then diagnosed comorbidly and treated according to guidelines established by the research.

DSM-III marks the transformation of psychiatric diagnosis into the methodology we recognize today: one that works with narrowly defined, symptom-based disorders grouped together into categories that imply relatedness. Significantly, along with the paradigm shift in this DSM, authorship shifted from practicing psychiatrists to academic researchers, headed by Columbia University's Robert Spitzer, a consultant on DSM-II.[3]

Under Spitzer's leadership, experts defined and grouped diagnoses by their clusters of symptoms, giving them the appearance of being discrete, independent disorders. This is when ADD was first introduced as a disorder of attention instead of as Hyperkinetic Disorder of Childhood, which had focused on hyperactivity as the main impairment. The authors of DSM-III added lengthy descriptions of each disorder, checklists of symptoms or criteria required to make a diagnosis, as well a minimum number of symptoms that the patient must have in order to qualify for a diagnosis.[4] Since its publication, as public policy professor Rick Mayes and sociologist Allan Horowitz explain in their article "DMS-III and the Revolution in the Classification of Mental Illness," researchers "took for granted that the proposed criteria for the DSM-III provided the optimal method for classifying mental disorders."[5]

In addition to checklists of criteria and extended descriptions of disorders, the authors of DSM-III developed several other products, such as structured interview protocols and screening tools to guide practitioners in gathering information from their patients. In short, DSM-III not only provided the detailed descriptions and categorical groupings of disorders but also helped assemble fairly homogenous groups for clinical trials. This in turn created new research and funding opportunities, leading to the present-day symbiotic relationship among researchers, the National Institute of Mental Health (NIMH), pharmaceutical companies, and clinicians.

The New and Improved DSMs: DSM-III-R and DSM-IV

By the time DSM-III-R (the revision of DSM-III) was published, several important changes had been made: categories were added, reorganized, and deleted to reflect the research that began with the scramble to support the new paradigm of DSM-III. DSM-III-R also added twenty-seven *new* disorders in just seven years. What had been known as ADD in DSM-III was revised to include hyperactivity and became ADHD. It was with this revision that pharmacological research into various categories exploded as the DSM led to more highly refined, homogenous groups for clinical trials.

Two significant changes in DSM-IV that had an impact on 2e children were the addition of Asperger's Disorder and the addition of the clinical significance criterion, which states that "the disturbance causes clinically significant distress or impairment in social, occupational, or other important areas of functioning."[6] This revision made the criteria for diagnosis more restrictive. With DSM-IV-TR, more disorders were added, pushing the number up to well over 350. This is the version still in use today, though a new edition, DSM-5, is projected to be published in 2013.

Screening Tools

As the descriptions for each disorder became more specifically defined with each revision of the DSM, so did tools developed to diagnose the disorders. The aim was to promote differential diagnosis—that is, a diagnosis of only one disorder that preempts others. Because the DSM established a specific set of criteria and a specific number of items required to make a diagnosis, screening tools were developed that are tied to each specific disorder and that screen for that disorder only. In this way, the screening tools are used to validate the existence of a disorder, to determine who qualifies for a diagnosis, and to help refine research populations. Unfortunately, because most researchers specialize in specific areas, they seldom communicate their findings to experts in other fields. As a result, the right hand does not necessarily know what the left hand is doing, so to speak.

The Cultural Impact of the DSM Paradigm

Few documents rival the stature and power of the DSM to dictate public policy. As Mayes and Horowitz explain, the shift in the DSM paradigm did not arise because of increased scientific knowledge or an ability to recognize these disorders by their biological causes.

Instead, they attribute the change in the diagnostic system to four specific factors in our culture:[7]

1. Politics and conflicts within the psychiatric field
2. The government becoming more involved with research and policymaking in mental health
3. Insurance companies demanding that psychiatrists validate their diagnoses and treatments as medically effective
4. Pharmaceutical companies needing markets for their products

The paradigm shift not only opened the door to more involvement and influence from government and industry but also established an urgent need for a standardized approach to diagnosing mental disorders.

It is no understatement to say that DSM is one of the most powerful systems of classification in use around the world. Besides the United States, twenty-two other countries use the DSM to diagnose mental disorders. However, DSM's influence transcends the boundaries of research into mental health; it has an impact on several critical segments of our culture and our world. Insurance companies require a DSM diagnosis to reimburse doctors and therapists, so mental health professionals must use the manual. Social service and governmental agencies use it to help decide who qualifies for services and disability compensation. Prisons use it to diagnose and place inmates in proper settings; court systems use it to determine whether a defendant is competent to stand trial. Finally, universities use the DSM in multiple disciplines ranging from medicine to social work; education systems use it to label our children and to help decide whether they qualify for services.

With so much riding on a system, it is important for the public to understand that there is still widespread disagreement about the system's reliability, validity, and even usefulness. Debates about the DSM still rage at the highest levels of the APA as well as among treatment professionals and academicians and reveal the limitations and fallacies of the categorical system.

The Criteria for a Sound Categorical System

With the paradigm shift from a practitioner-based approach to a research-based approach, the DSM-III claimed to serve two masters: the clinician and the researcher. One major goal of DSM-III was to provide "a medical nomenclature for clinicians and researchers,"[8] one that practitioners could use in their offices for diagnosing patients. In fact, the APA maintains that its "highest priority has been to provide a helpful guide to clinical practice."[9] However, this claim rings hollow in light of the continued debates about the reliability, validity, and usefulness of the DSM system at the clinical level. In the trenches, where these issues immediately affect diagnosis and treatment, arguments about the accuracy and dependability of the DSM continue among professionals.

Within the context of scientific disciplines, the definitions of reliability, validity, and utility differ from the way that these terms are defined in everyday use. In the sciences, *reliability* means that the same results can be reproduced in different clinical settings. For our discussion, the term *validity* refers to how effectively the current system describes and categorizes distinct diagnostic entities that have clear boundaries from each other and from normal behavior. We focus on what is known as *construct validity*, meaning that the disease or disorder has clear boundaries from other diseases or disorders. The definition of the term *utility* is most akin to everyday use. It refers to how useful a description of a disease or disorder is in communicating essential information about the malady, its treatment, and predicted outcomes.

Reliability

When the DSM-III categorical system was conceptualized, Spitzer's main argument for the paradigm shift was that the existing system for describing and classifying mental disorders was unreliable and therefore invalid, especially with regard to the medical model of mental illness.

Reliability, or the ability for practitioners to consistently produce the same diagnosis from patient to patient using the same information, is the *absolute* standard for evaluating a classification system's effectiveness.[10] By framing their argument for DSM-III around this concept, Spitzer and his associate Joseph L. Fleiss made a strong case that the unreliability of DSM-II threatened the very field of psychiatry.[11] In their article, "A Re-analysis of the Reliability of Psychiatric Diagnosis," they strongly argued for the importance of reliability, saying that "The reliability of psychiatric diagnosis as it has been practiced since at least the late 1950s is not good," and going so far as to declare that "assuredly an unreliable system must be invalid."[12] They proposed the categorical system as a way to solve the problems with reliability and validity in DSM-II.

To improve reliability, Spitzer and his associates attempted to standardize the diagnostic process by providing a "foolproof little recipe" for each disorder, which included lengthy prose descriptions, checklists of symptoms, and cutoff points for making a diagnosis.[13] In fact, Spitzer sold DSM-III on the basis of claims about specialized field studies that proved "the reliability of the radically new diagnostic system,"[14] implying that because it was reliable, the new system was scientifically sound. However, there is sufficient evidence to suggest that Spitzer's claims were exaggerated and perhaps unjustified.[15]

Although the Introduction of the DSM states that the manual is designed to meet the needs of both researchers and clinicians, clearly the most powerful purpose the DSM serves is to generate reliable, standardized criteria and homogenous populations to support research into the causes and treatments of mental disorders. According to former DSM-IV and DSM-IV-TR chairman Allen Frances, DSM-IV editor Michael First, DSM-IV science editor Ruth Ross, and associate Avram Mack, "During the past 25 years, the DSM and psychopharmacology have 'grown up' together and have had a strong influence upon one another," with the main areas of influence being "the development of explicit and reliable diagnostic criteria" for research.[16] This research, in turn, generated scientific data that were used to validate the categories and disorders, which were included in subsequent revisions of the manual.

However, this approach creates a sort of false reliability because of its circular nature. As Frances and colleagues explain, with regard to carefully controlled psychopharmacological studies, "it is almost always possible with any given ... diagnosis to achieve satisfactory to excellent reliability using the DSM system."[17] Apparently, within the context of research, the problem of reliability appears to have been satisfactorily resolved.

The more pressing issue for parents is how or even if reliability in research translates into diagnostic reliability at the clinical level. Recent comments by Spitzer and Frances in an interview with Alix Spiegel for *The New Yorker* reveal that this issue remains a very real challenge for practitioners. As Frances explains, "To my way of thinking, the reliability of the *DSM*, although improved, has been oversold." Likewise, Spitzer frankly commented on the reliability of the DSM, saying that *any* claim that this problem has been solved "is just not true.... If you're in a situation with a general clinician it's certainly not very good. There's still a real problem"[18]—a problem that, ironically, as Spitzer argued nearly forty years ago, undermines the validity of the diagnostic system and threatens the very field of psychiatry, as we noted earlier.[19] Still today, this problem with reliability continues to challenge the efficacy of the DSM. As Frances explains, without reliability, "The system is completely random and the diagnoses mean almost nothing—maybe worse than nothing, because they're falsely labeling. You're better off not having a diagnostic system."[20]

Validity

In the DSM system, to say a syndrome or disorder is valid, or has construct validity, means that it has clear, natural boundaries that distinguish it as a discrete entity separate from other disorders.[21] In fact, the DSM was based on the assumption that the classification system would lead researchers to uncover isolated disease entities and to identify their etiology, or underlying biological causes.

Clearly, this has not happened. As a matter of fact, the researchers responsible for creating the research agenda for DSM-5 admit that the DSM has "failed to identify a single neurobiological marker or gene that is useful in making a diagnosis of a major psychiatric disorder or for predicting response to psychopharmacologic treatment."[22] Likewise, in their pivotal article on validity and classification systems, psychiatric experts Robert Kendell and Assen Jablensky state that

> Despite historical and recent assumptions to the contrary, there is little evidence that most currently recognized mental disorders are separated by natural boundaries. Researchers are increasingly assuming that variation in symptoms is continuous and are therefore questioning the validity of contemporary classifications.[23]

When Spitzer and his associates developed DSM-III, the available science in the field of psychiatry was still pretty limited, so "individuals who were considered experts in their fields"[24] made the decisions about which disorders and categories would be included or excluded. Spitzer described this process as a highly subjective one in which decisions "for most of the categories" were based on "the best thinking of people who seemed to have expertise in the area."[25]

In reference to questions about decisions with regard to the number of symptoms required to receive a diagnosis, "It was just consensus," Spitzer replied. Even after conducting field trials and asking experts for their opinions on the number of symptoms needed, Spitzer said "we came up with the arbitrary number ... because we don't understand the neurobiology."[26]

This final statement is quite significant in light of the topic of comorbidities and the validity of DSM. The categorical system rests on the presumption that these disorders are decidedly distinct. Nevertheless, a disclaimer in DSM-IV states "there is no assumption that each category of mental disorder is a completely discrete entity with absolute boundaries dividing it from other mental disorders or from no mental disorder."[27] In other words, the authors of the DSM themselves acknowledge that the system does not conform to the criterion for validity established by DSM-III.

As former DSM-IV committee members Frances and First, along with colleagues Ross and Mack, state, "Most of the disorders in the DSM lack clear boundaries with near neighbors and could as well have been defined with alternative items or thresholds," so there is no basis for assuming that DSM "follows nature with any degree of precision."[28] As a result, multiple diagnoses are commonly given to account for a patient's full range of symptoms. In fact, a recent study estimates that 56 percent of psychiatric patients in the United States are diagnosed with two or more disorders.[29]

The problem with comorbidities suggests that the current diagnostic categories do not accurately reflect the true disease entities that affect our children. As Mario Maj, a DSM-5 work group member in Mood Disorders states, "Artificially splitting a complex clinical condition into several pieces may ... represent a new source of diagnostic unreliability."[30] Although in some cases the presence of multiple conditions may point to the existence of distinct disorders with different origins, some researchers insist that in the majority of cases, comorbidity suggests the existence of "a common, shared pathology,"[31] as may be the case with such conditions as autism spectrum disorders, ADHD, OCD, and tic disorders.[32]

Another issue that continues to plague clinicians and parents is differential diagnosis; that is, how do clinicians differentiate between disorders that have similar presenting symptoms? For instance, with respect to HFA/AS and ADHD, the symptom sets are nearly identical and, depending on developmental stages, can be indistinguishable, leading one to question whether these are distinct entities or expressions of a larger syndrome.[33] Likewise, how can clinicians reliably diagnose and treat conditions that appear identical but are defined differently, especially when the explanations for the symptoms differ from disorder to disorder? Clearly, professionals are likely to diagnose the disorder with which they are the most familiar.

In short, the current DSM categorical system lacks diagnostic validity because it has failed to lead to proof that each disorder is a distinct entity, as evidenced by the serious issue of comorbidity, one of the most troubling by-products of the DSM system for parents and professionals seeking to understand the 2e child. Comorbidity likely occurs because boundaries for the disorders have been established where they do not exist in nature; as a result, "the probability that several diagnoses have to be made in an individual case will obviously increase."[34]

Utility

One final consideration to be addressed when examining the DSM system is the concept of utility, which refers to "how useful a definition is in conveying information about a disorder."[35] However, utility, or usefulness, is variable depending on the context. Obviously, the two contexts in which the utility of diagnostic concepts are most relevant are in research and clinical practice.

For researchers of most disorders, the current categorical system possesses high utility. The literature for most DSM-defined disorders transmits high-quality, voluminous information about suspected causes, defining characteristics, recommended treatments, and anticipated outcomes.[36] For researchers using the DSM system, the manual fulfills its stated purpose and is quite useful. As we discussed earlier, it has been instrumental in helping assemble relatively homogenous groups based on specific diagnostic criteria for clinical trials into all areas, especially diagnostic imaging and psychopharmacology. These data in turn bolster the apparent reliability and utility of the DSM for research purposes, and even at the clinical level when "breakthroughs" are marketed to professionals and parents.

A vastly different view of DSM's usefulness emerges at the clinical level, though. Managed health care requires primary and emergent care physicians to provide quick diagnoses and inexpensive treatments in response to patients' complaints. Considering that practitioners in psychiatry, general practice, pediatrics, and now psychology are using the DSM as a diagnostic tool, the concept of usefulness becomes increasingly important.

Despite its claims about the importance of clinical utility, the DSM appears to be failing in meeting its stated goal of usefulness for diagnosticians. Clinical and medical psychologist Michael G. Connor states that at the clinical level, "there does not appear to be any clearly useful relationship between the DSM diagnosis, treatment, and outcome of treatment."[37] As Wing explains, "The categories have not proved helpful in prescribing type of education, behavior management, medication or other treatment."[38]

In fact, there appears to be a substantial number of practitioners who rely on their general impressions of disorders rather than on the checklists of symptoms and lengthy descriptions in the DSM to make diagnostic decisions.[39] Clinicians, "if they use the manuals at all, use them in a loose, informal manner and are comfortable ignoring diagnostic criteria," or they use them for reference about uncommon disorders or for coding.[40]

Perhaps Frances's observation best illustrates the disparity between experts and practitioners with regard to usefulness in clinical settings:

> It is inherently difficult for experts, with their highly selected research and clinical experiences, to appreciate fully just how poorly their research findings may generalize to everyday practice—especially as it is conducted

> by harried primary care clinicians in an environment heavily influenced by drug company marketing.[41]

In short, even though the DSM may be useful at the research level, it falls seriously short of utility where the sole meets the asphalt, so to speak—in the practitioner's office.

Whom Does the DSM Serve?

Parents of uniquely gifted children who are identified more by their labels than by their exceptional abilities must understand how DSM has permeated every aspect of our culture and too often directs them down the path of misdiagnosis, comorbidities, and medications.

As we have shown, even though the DSM aims to support both research and clinical practice, this system has more rigorously promoted the interests of research over the needs of the clinician. The DSM and such fields as neurobiology, genetics, and especially psychopharmacology have shared a symbiotic relationship since the time of DSM-III-R. The DSM system has helped researchers assemble groups for clinical trials to study brain imaging, genetics, and medications. Admittedly, important discoveries have been made in these areas, particularly in advancing our understanding of how the brain functions, which genes may predispose us to certain disorders, and what medications may be the safest for targeting certain symptoms (though the question of exactly what these medications are treating remains elusive).

That being said, the DSM appears to have fallen short of proving its claim to support clinical practice. In over thirty years, the DSM system has not been proven reliable in helping clinicians consistently diagnose patients. Even with lengthy descriptions, checklists of criteria, structured diagnostic interviews, and multiaxial domains, in most cases the DSM system requires practitioners to diagnose several comorbid disorders to round out the clinical portrait. Clearly, this is not the clinician's fault. Rather, the DSM is behind the practice of giving a child multiple labels and prescribing multiple medications as doctors attempt to treat each symptom. Unfortunately, when treatments fail to minimize the disability, or a child has a negative reaction to a medication, or another label is warranted, parents understandably blame the clinician, even though these professionals are doing their best to operate within the constraints of a flawed diagnostic system.

Instead of criticizing the clinicians, whose hands are tied by the DSM and managed health care, we need to pull back, seriously examine the system at large, and ask some tough questions, beginning with "How did the DSM system, which is a wholly theoretical construct, attain such stature?"

This abstract, arbitrary system has permeated our thinking and our culture to a degree most parents do not recognize. It has given us a shared language that we use to describe ourselves and others: *I'm so ADD today ... He's acting really bipolar ... He's so Aspie ... She's so OCD about her room.* Each time we use one of these labels, it becomes more real in our minds and in our culture.

The DSM system has been "reified" or made to appear as a concrete, natural law in our culture. Although researchers have cautioned against our thinking about the disorders as real diseases, the very act of labeling symptoms as disorders and including them in the DSM gives them scientific validity in our minds. Their "validity" is reinforced for us when the labels are used to market medications that were developed as treatment for the disorder. Likewise, because a medication is purported to alleviate the symptoms associated with a disorder, its existence confirms our belief that the disorder is a discrete entity and is therefore "real" when in fact only the symptoms are authentic.

After over thirty years of living with managed health care, the DSM, and psychopharmacological treatments, a generation of parents has been conditioned to expect and to believe that an appointment and a prescription will "fix" their children. We all must remember, though, that because we are human beings, psychiatric problems have not only a biological component but also social and psychological ones, which cannot be identified and addressed in a fifteen- or thirty-minute office visit or treated with medications. Nevertheless, with the disease model firmly entrenched in our consciousness since the late 1900s, we blindly accept a medical model of psychiatry that splits the symptoms of mental disorders from their social and psychological components and divides larger syndromes into many separate disorders.

Given this cultural context, it is understandable for us to believe that the biology of mental disorders has been discovered and that the DSM system is the key to finding the best answers to help us advocate for our children. However, as the editors of *A Research Agenda for DSM-V* point out, "research exclusively focused on refining the DSM-defined syndromes may never be successful in uncovering their underlying etiologies,"[42] especially as the limitations of the DSM and its corresponding treatments become increasingly troublesome for practitioners in the trenches and the children they seek to serve.

Yet at the highest levels of psychiatry, government, and managed care, leaders throw up their hands and declare the DSM system too huge to be changed. As a matter of fact, experts involved in the DSM-5 revision due out in 2013 offer seven disadvantages to changing diagnostic criteria:[43]

1. If there are changes, thousands of clinicians must learn them.
2. Any changes in criteria will require that medical forms, standardized treatment procedures, and any other health-related documents be changed.
3. Changes in criteria "impair the cumulative capacity of research," thereby interfering with the goal of "creating a rigorous database of the major psychiatric disorders."

4. Changes in criteria create problems for longitudinal research projects that are based on existing criteria because the researcher is then faced with the dilemma of choosing to stay with the former system and appear behind the times or change to the new system and disrupt the flow of the research.
5. Changes in diagnostic criteria require "a new generation of structured psychiatric interviews to evaluate the new criteria."
6. Changes will generate questions about the new and old criteria.
7. Changes can discredit the diagnostic system and potentially cause the DSM to become "a subject of ridicule."

Clearly, the rationale against change is rooted in the goal of preserving the system itself, regardless of how the system continues to affect the lives of countless patients. Consider carefully the reasons the experts offered. Are we to believe that because "clinicians are accustomed to thinking in terms of diagnostic categories, and most existing knowledge … was obtained, and is organized, in relation to these categories,"[44] these are grounds to persist in working within an admittedly flawed paradigm that continues to be criticized at all levels of psychiatry? Not only does this paradigm generate questionably reliable and useful research for clinicians, but it also hinders those clinicians from achieving the goal that compelled many of them to practice in the first place: to help patients understand themselves and reach their full potential in society.

Likewise, as the reasons suggest, to change the system would create far too much work in all the related industries, including insurance, education, research, clinical practice, and general medicine, and at all levels from clerical to administrative to governmental. As parents, are we to blindly accept that the system is just too big to change? In the interest of convenience, should we continue to fail our children by committing their mental health and treatment to an admittedly artificial and flawed system?

Current research perpetuates the flawed system by refining research populations for clinical trials and validating artificially defined categories and disorders. As one astute neuropsychiatrist commenting on BrainTalk, an online medical forum, stated, "It isn't a question of whether we have to rearrange these categories in an appropriate way, but whether the whole system of categories that we have depended upon works."[45] Although the call to change the DSM system has been voiced at the highest levels of psychiatry, it continues to be ignored "because of the powerful inertia of the interests and traditions that supports the current form of the classification system," as psychologist and professor Jeffrey Poland explains in his commentary on the DSM.[46] Nevertheless, the existing paradigm must be changed for the good of our children and our society, regardless of the amount of work it requires or the number of industries it affects. As Dr. Martin Luther King Jr. said, "The time is always right to do what's right."[47]

Given the ongoing problems with reliability, validity, and utility, as well as the tremendous amount of resources devoted to perpetuating the DSM system, we must conclude that this diagnostic system is fundamentally flawed. Although the DSM system continues to be debated within the field, these debates can no longer remain confined to the annals of psychiatry and be treated as a mere exercise in academic argument or political mudslinging.

Parents deserve to know the controversies surrounding the DSM because it so powerfully contributes to our seeing our children as broken instead of bright, and it determines the services our children do or do not receive. Likewise, the debates about the reliability and validity of the DSM must be brought to the public's attention because the system affects our whole society. As Abraham Lincoln said, "I am a firm believer in the people. If given the truth, they can be depended upon to meet any national crisis. The great point is to bring them the real facts."[48]

Clinicians in the trenches struggle every day to help our children, and as parents we understandably accept that they are the authorities. However, as you have seen, DSM is of questionable use in helping parents and practitioners understand the unique profile of disabilities in 2e children. As victims of this system, our 2e children remain trapped in misdiagnosis and misunderstanding, and are too often prescribed dangerous, untested medications that threaten their mental and physical well-being and, ultimately, the future welfare of our society.

6

Fact or Fallacy

Questioning the Validity of the ADHD Diagnosis

Fallacies do not cease to be fallacies because they become fashions.

G. K. *Chesterton*

Before we begin, we must acknowledge that we are not scholars or experts in the DSM, ADHD, or ASD. Two of us (Diane and Rebecca) are simply mothers who did as Barkley directs in his book, *Taking Charge of ADHD: The Complete and Authoritative Guide for Parents*: "Read! Listen! Seek! Question! Find out as much as you can about your child's disorder ... question everything. Be prepared to abandon every theory or hypothesis that does not stand up to critical scrutiny."[1] We read, listened, sought, and questioned. What we have discovered and report on here and in the following chapter are controversies about ADHD and ASD. Sometimes it takes a view from the outside to see what is really going on in a field.

Unfortunately, 2e children often get caught between categories, in part because of the DSM system's failure to take into account the impact that higher intellect has on the presentation of the disorders it describes. Instead of emphasizing the clinical importance of considering intellectual giftedness when making a diagnosis, the DSM system splinters the disability away from giftedness. As a result, children whose IQ masks the disability often appear less significantly impaired and more functional than their average counterparts with the same disorder because of their ability to compensate. This often results in misdiagnosis or missed diagnosis in the 2e population.

However, as you will see, a more fundamental problem within the design of the DSM system may also explain why our 2e children get trapped between categories. Most criticism of the diagnosis of ADHD centers around the symptoms and the screening tools as being too vague, too general, too subjective, and therefore too inclusive. In contrast, the central concern for parents of children with HFA/AS is that the criteria are perhaps too exclusionary.

IQ and the DSM Categories: Behavior Versus Development

As we explained in Chapter Five, the current DSM system groups disorders together under different categories. When these categories were established, the relationship among the disorders within each category was assumed because the behavioral symptoms appeared so obviously similar. As a result, ADHD and Disruptive Behavior Disorders are in one category, and Pervasive Developmental Disorders, which include Autistic Disorder and Asperger's Disorder, make up another.

It is important to understand that at the time these categories were created, the field of what is now called ADHD and the field of autism were in their infancy, so to speak. ADHD had evolved from what was known in the 1960s as Hyperkinetic Reaction of Childhood, a term used to describe children with behavioral and conduct disturbances tied to hyperactivity, impulsivity, and inattention. Associated features of ADHD included academic underachievement, deficits in social skills, language impairments, learning disabilities, sleep problems, and mood lability.

The field of autism was emerging at this time as well. With DSM-III, autism also became a separate diagnostic category after being seen as part of Schizophrenic Reaction, childhood type, through DSM-II. Initially coined Early Infantile Autism in DSM-III, the category changed to Autistic Disorder by DSM-III-R. Although researchers recognized social impairments, language impairments, and repetitive patterns of behavior and routines in their populations, as well as oppositional behaviors, the disorder was associated primarily with intellectual disability until Wing's work established Asperger's Disorder as a form of autism.

The similarities between ADHD and autism, coupled with the presence of high intellect, continue to generate a tremendous amount of diagnostic confusion in the 2e population. As we begin examining possible reasons for this confusion, we'll start with ADHD, the more commonly diagnosed disorder of the two. In the next chapter, we'll continue with the autism paradigm and examine how some of the proposed changes in DSM-5 may affect our 2e children.

ADHD: The Emperor Wears No Clothes!

From the outset of this discussion, we want to state *strongly* that hyperactivity, impulsivity, and inattention are very real and debilitating symptoms that frequently interfere with a child's ability to function in social and academic environments. Our concern centers not on the symptoms but on labeling these symptoms as a separate disorder called ADHD.

For most parents of 2e children, getting an ADHD diagnosis for their child is a great relief. At first, knowing that there is a name for their child's hyperactive, inattentive, impulsive, and oppositional behaviors along with his apparent functional difficulties (such as not finishing projects or being disorganized) provides a strange comfort because parents now know where to turn for answers, and they know they're not alone. National parent support groups, Web sites, and informational pamphlets, forums, and blogs remind parents that ADHD is the most commonly diagnosed childhood behavioral-psychiatric disorder, so parents quickly assume that help for their child will be readily available.

Yet this relief quickly gives way to desperation as parents realize that they are still at a loss as to how best to help their smart but struggling child. Many parents discover that the volumes of information about ADHD provide little understanding of their child's actual social, behavioral, and emotional difficulties and how to treat these. No matter where they turn to help their child, parents are often thwarted by incomplete answers, redundant literature, dangerous medications, and ineffective therapies. Nevertheless, armed with an ADHD diagnosis, parents continue to seek the magic bullet that will free their child even as years pass, additional diagnoses are added, and their child grows into adulthood still struggling to function, as Lee's e-mail showed in Chapter Three.

Given this all too common experience, we need to ask some hard questions about the ADHD label. Why, after more than thirty years of being included in the DSM and researched for just as long, does the ADHD diagnosis continue to be mired in controversy about whether it is a real disorder? Why does an ADHD diagnosis keep parents and children stuck in a seemingly endless search for answers and treatment? Does the ADHD diagnosis do more harm than good?

Cultural Assumptions About the Validity of ADHD

As a culture, we believe in ADHD. It is a disorder that permeates our very consciousness. We have a label, ADHD or ADD. We have a prescribed course of treatment: stimulant medications. We have national support and advocacy organizations, such as CHADD (Children and Adults with Attention Deficit Disorder) and ADDA (Attention Deficit Disorder Association), where we can find listings for doctors, coaches, and local support groups. We have Internet forums that address every issue from diagnosis and treatment to sexuality and relationships. And if a child is officially diagnosed with ADHD, we assume that one of the many ADHD medications on the market will solve his problems. The prevailing assumption among parents and professionals is that ADHD is a valid, common, and treatable disorder.

Marketing efforts on the part of pharmaceutical companies also support the assumption that ADHD is a separate, discrete disorder with symptoms that are easily controlled. In the waiting rooms of pediatricians and family physicians across America, medical "educational" material on ADHD and its treatment abounds, most of it sponsored by pharmaceutical corporations, such as Eli Lilly, Shire Pharmaceutical, Merck, and others. Likewise, full-page ads for treatments for ADHD continue to appear in parenting and general interest magazines, keeping alive the message that stimulant medications are safe, effective answers to a proven diagnostic entity.

For pediatricians and family practice physicians, this assumption is reinforced not only in the media but also at the highest levels of their profession. For instance, the American Academy of Child and Adolescent Psychiatry provides the "Practice Parameter for the Assessment and Treatment of Children and Adolescents with Attention-Deficit/Hyperactivity Disorder," which cites the prevalence of ADHD as ranging from 6.7 to 10 percent, depending on the survey.[2] Similarly, consider the American Academy of Pediatrics (AAP), the premier organization for professional development and treatment information. The AAP "Clinical Practice Guideline" for diagnosing ADHD states that "Attention-deficit/hyperactivity disorder (ADHD) is among the most prevalent chronic health conditions affecting school-aged children,"[3] underscoring the idea that ADHD is a scientifically proven diagnosis.[4]

Needless to say, the marketing of ADHD through professional literature and the attention it receives in the media support the assumption that ADHD has been proven valid by DSM standards (that is, has clear, natural boundaries). Over time, through advertising, news articles, and medical and educational materials, proponents of ADHD have carefully moved the public from an attitude of skepticism about the diagnosis to one of optimism.

Yet even as doctors, teachers, and the media reinforce the idea that ADHD is a disorder of hyperactivity, inattention, and impulsivity, the diagnosis remains controversial, as these headlines attest:

- Three-Quarters of ADHD Diagnoses Wrong[5]
- Gray Area Exists in Diagnosis of ADHD[6]
- The ADHD Quandary[7]
- What to Do About the ADHD Epidemic[8]
- Fix the Diagnosis, Not the Children[9]
- Nearly One Million Children in U.S. Potentially Misdiagnosed with ADHD, Study Finds[10]
- Is ADHD Overdiagnosed?[11]

Likewise, Wikipedia has a multiple-page entry titled "Attention Deficit Hyperactivity Disorders Controversies," citing over 160 references. Countless Web sites and blogs (not all sponsored by such fringe elements as the Church of Scientology) challenge ADHD's existence and the use of medications to treat our children. Likewise, numerous credible, respected professionals within and outside psychiatry also question the validity of ADHD, leaving us to wonder: if ADHD is such a valid, treatable disorder, why are so many different factions disputing its legitimacy?

Issues with Validity

The most obvious place to begin when examining the validity of any disorder is the DSM. You may recall that according to the DSM, for ADHD and any other disorder to be valid, it must meet two criteria:

1. It must be clearly distinct from normal behavior.
2. It must exist as a distinct diagnostic entity apart and separate from others through natural boundaries.

The evolution of ADHD through the various versions of the DSM reveals just how determined researchers have been to prove that this diagnosis meets these DSM requirements.

You may recall that when the change to DSM-III occurred, ADD was included as well. As a construct, ADD, now known as ADHD, was created using the top-down approach wherein researchers identified a cluster of symptoms, named it, and established the criteria to diagnose the disorder. Understandably, after DSM-III, there was a rush to generate as much scientific support as possible for ADHD in order to confirm its place in the new paradigm. This effort continues into the twenty-first century, leading experts, including the American Professional Society of ADHD and Related Disorders (APSARD), to claim that ADHD is one of the most researched psychiatric disorders of childhood.[12]

Changing Models of ADHD

As you can see from Table 6.1, as the clinical constructs of ADHD changed through the various versions of the DSM, so did the models developed by Barkley and other ADHD researchers to explain the ADHD symptom set. Initially, ADD was conceptualized as a disorder of attention regulation. Then, in the 1980s, between DSM-III and DSM-III-R, as the model shifted to focus on impulsivity, disruptive behaviors, and self-regulation, so did the focus of the research. In DSM-IV, the model changed again, identifying three subtypes. Presently, there are several proposed changes to the DSM-5 model and subtypes, which are being debated.

In the face of so many changes to the models and explanations for ADHD, is it any wonder that the validity of the disorder has been debated at the highest levels of the scientific research community and the government agency that governs it, the National Institutes of Health (NIH)? Significantly, eighteen years after DSM-III, in 1998, the NIH held a two-day Consensus Development Conference on ADHD, which included presentations from the most prominent experts in ADHD, including Russell Barkley, Joseph Biederman,

Table 6.1 The Changing Models and Diagnoses of ADHD

DSM and Model of ADHD	Category	Diagnosis Type(s)	Core Symptoms of Subtypes
DSM-II (1966) Model: Hyperkinetic	Hyperkinetic Reaction of Childhood or Adolescence	Hyperkinetic Reaction of Childhood	Hyperactivity
DSM-III (1980) Model: Inattention	—	Attention Deficit Disorder	
		1. ADD with hyperactivity	1. Inattention, hyperactivity, impulsivity
		2. ADD without hyperactivity	2. Inattention, impulsivity (without hyperactivity)
DSM-III-R (1987) Model: Hyperactivity/Impulsivity	Disruptive Behavior Disorders	Attention-Deficit/Hyperactivity Disorder	Inattention, hyperactivity, and impulsivity (all one)

DSM-IV (1994) Model: Hyperactivity/Impulsivity	Attention-Deficit and Disruptive Behavior Disorders	Attention-Deficit/Hyperactivity Disorder	
		1. ADHD: Predominantly Combined Type	1. Hyperactivity-impulsivity, inattention
		2. ADHD: Predominantly Inattentive Type	2. Inattention
		3. ADHD: Predominantly Hyperactive-Impulsive Type	3. Hyperactivity-impulsivity
DSM-IV-TR (2000) Model: Hyperactivity/Impulsivity	Attention-Deficit and Disruptive Behavior Disorders	Attention Deficit Disorder	
		1. ADHD: Predominantly Combined Type	1. Hyperactivity-impulsivity, inattention
		2. ADHD: Predominantly Inattentive Type	2. Inattention
		3. ADHD: Predominantly Hyperactive-Impulsive Type	3. Hyperactivity-impulsivity

Source: Information from "The Nature of ADHD," by R. A. Barkley, 2006, in R. A. Barkley, *Attention-Deficit Hyperactivity Disorder: A Handbook for Diagnosis and Treatment* (pp. 3–55), New York: Guilford Press; *Diagnostic and Statistical Manual of Mental Disorders* (4th ed., text rev.), by American Psychiatric Assocation, 2000, Washingtcn, D.C.

Peter Jensen, and William Pelham. After hearing evidence and deliberations, the NIH panel, headed by David J. Kupfer, an editor of *A Research Agenda for DSM-V*, issued a consensus statement saying, "Basic research is needed to better define ADHD," and emphasizing that "additional efforts to validate the disorder are needed."[13] One particular area that the panel targeted for more research was comorbidities, as "ADHD often does not present as an isolated disorder... which may account for some of the inconsistencies in research findings." The consensus statement concluded by saying that "after years of clinical research and experience with ADHD, our knowledge about the cause or causes of ADHD remains speculative."

Likewise, in an international consensus statement critiquing the science of ADHD, Sami Timimi, psychiatrist and director of postgraduate education for the National Health Service in England, along with thirty-three co-endorsers from around the world, commented on the various models of ADHD saying,

> There is obvious uncertainty about to how define this disorder, with definitions changing over the past 30 years depending on what the current favourite theory about underlying aetiology [cause or causes] is, and with each revision producing a higher number of potential children deemed to have the disorder.[14]

Increasingly, the diagnosis of ADHD is being made in adults as well as children. Although figures vary from source to source, the APSARD Web site states that as of 2009, "Hundreds of millions of people worldwide have ADHD."[15]

Despite ongoing attempts to address the concerns voiced in the 1998 consensus statement, problems with the ADHD diagnosis continue. Apparently, for many clinicians, making a diagnosis of ADHD can be frustrating, so much so that a 2006 survey of more than two hundred specialists found that "One third of child psychiatrists, 41 percent of psychiatrists and 24 percent of pediatricians reported a lack of consensus among doctors on ADHD symptoms and diagnosis."[16] Still, over a decade after the NIH Consensus Statement was issued, visitors to the NIH Consensus Development Program Web page on the diagnosis and treatment of ADHD are advised that the statement "is provided solely for historical purposes" and that "new knowledge has inevitably accumulated in this subject area in the time since the statement was initially prepared."[17] Yet as debates continue about how to revise the ADHD model for DSM-5, it appears that many of the original concerns about the definition, validity, and causes of ADHD still remain unanswered.

Arguments Against the Validity of the ADHD Diagnosis

Even as efforts to define and validate ADHD continue, the voices of those who question its validity—neurologists, pediatricians, psychologists, and psychiatrists, as well as experts from other disciplines—grow stronger. It's important to note that the central issues these professionals raise about ADHD focus on the DSM requirements for validity, rather than on popularized controversies about medicating children. In particular, their arguments against the validity of ADHD express concern with regard to the following issues:

- The science in ADHD fails to meet the standards of traditional scientific inquiry.
- ADHD does not meet DSM requirements for validity.
- ADHD does not meet the requirements for differential diagnosis.

The Science of ADHD Fails to Meet Traditional Standards

A good place to begin examining the position that ADHD is not a valid disorder is with the science. Beginning with the publication of the International Consensus Statement in 2002, ADHD experts and organizations such as the American Medical Association, the surgeon general, the NIH, and others have attempted to present indisputable evidence that ADHD is a "real disorder" backed by "real science," with the cumulative conclusion being that because it is the most commonly diagnosed disorder of childhood, it is a valid diagnosis. However, careful examination of weaknesses in the scientific underpinnings of ADHD reveal that its science fails to meet the rigorous standards required by traditional scientific inquiry, especially in the two key practices of using data to create theoretical models for study and of then testing these theories and attempting to refute them.[18]

Theoretical Models

As a theoretical construct, ADHD is, like the DSM categories, created from the top down. Rather than being defined from the bottom up by using research data to develop diagnostic criteria, ADHD was conceptualized from the top down by a committee of experts who "negotiated and eventually arrived at an appellation [name] and established, through a consensus of opinion, diagnostic criteria."[19] This is one reason why what we know as ADHD today has been renamed and revised with each new version of the DSM.

This top-down approach also explains why the theoretical models, especially executive function models, have been subject to so many changes. Professionals from several fields, including pediatrician Lydia Furman; experts in psychological assessment and neuroscience Steven Thurber, William Sheehan, and Richard J. Roberts; pediatrician William Carey; professors John Visser and Zenib Jehan; psychiatrist and director of postgraduate education for the National Health Service in England, Sami Timimi; and numerous others agree that attempts to show specific brain dysfunctions as the cause of ADHD continue to fail;[20] yet in the continued process of trying to prove these causes, ADHD theorists generally disregard basic scientific convention.

As Thurber, Sheehan, and Roberts explain in their article, "Attention Deficit Hyperactivity Disorder and Scientific Epistemology," ADHD researchers, rather than proposing a hypothesis about ADHD and then seeing if the science validates or refutes it, create their models of ADHD post hoc—that is, by developing a model based on the results of their studies.[21]

Confirmatory Studies

Perhaps the largest body of research of ADHD centers on validating the symptoms and the currently prevailing theoretical model. Once they have developed a model, theorists and researchers in ADHD design research studies to *confirm* the model, rather than studies that may refute it.[22] Thurber et al. contrast this approach to diagnostic validity with the criteria for truth established by the scientific method in which studies are designed to *disprove* the theory. The authors conclude that "ADHD currently does not have status beyond that of the 'hypothetical construct' "; in fact, researchers primarily seek confirmatory data in their search to prove the causes of ADHD, so even the most "current brain-based causal models [such as the executive function model] have failed to provide rigorous supporting data that comes from testing falsifiable hypotheses."[23]

In the presence of such questionable approaches to scientific truth, it is understandable why doubts remain about the validity of the ADHD diagnosis. Rigorous scientific tradition requires that a theory, or hypothesis, be falsifiable, meaning that it can be proven wrong. However, because studies of ADHD generate primarily confirmatory data—that is, only data that support the theory, research in support of validity remains unconvincing to professionals in many scientific fields. International opinion is that theorists in ADHD would do better to keep within scientific tradition and work toward specific, falsifiable, and testable hypotheses.[24] In short, a number of scientists, researchers, and theoreticians criticize

ADHD research as being carefully designed to support rather than challenge the ADHD construct.

ADHD Does Not Meet DSM Requirements for Validity

Besides questioning the science in ADHD, challenges to the validity of ADHD fall into two main areas with respect to the DSM. The first, that ADHD symptoms are not clearly distinguished from normal childhood behaviors, holds true, but only to a point. Hyperactivity, impulsivity, and inattention are normal behaviors for children, especially gifted children; however, as we said earlier, there is a point at which these symptoms also cause tremendous upheaval and suffering for children and families (though, arguably, these symptoms may arise from hidden impairments).

The second challenge to ADHD's validity is that there is no objective, biological marker on which to base a diagnosis. With regard to this point, we must note that for nearly all of the DSM disorders, no such marker has been discovered, which was one of the original goals for the shift to the medical model. Instead, brain-imaging studies that attempt to prove the presence of ADHD only verify the presence of symptoms, and the results of these are very similar to the results of brain-imaging studies of children with autism.[25] Also, numerous tests of executive function in ADHD find that the deficits are nearly identical to those in children with an ASD.[26] Likewise, numerous genetic studies that attempted to isolate the origins of ADHD have found that "There is extensive overlap with findings from other psychiatric disorders," quite notably studies of autism.[27]

A commonly held assumption with regard to the biological basis of ADHD is that if a child's symptoms respond to stimulant medication, the presence of ADHD is proven. Gordon Tait, professor of education at Queensland University of Technology in Australia, has written a compelling examination of the logical fallacies used to argue for ADHD. One fallacy among the many he examines is the *non sequitur*, meaning "does not follow," in relation to the premise that a child's response to stimulant medication "proves" an ADHD diagnosis. As Tait explains, this argument is used frequently: "Ritalin helps with hyperactivity, hyperactivity is a symptom of ADHD, therefore ADHD is a valid disorder."[28] Interestingly, several research studies from the late 1970s and early 1980s from researchers in the field of ADHD have also shown that children without a diagnosis of ADHD respond similarly to stimulant medication.[29] The fact that a symptom or set of symptoms responds to a drug does not prove the existence of ADHD. However, in the absence of a biological marker for ADHD, many pediatricians rely on a child's response to medication as evidence to validate the diagnosis, a practice that may lead them to continue prescribing stimulant medication when it is not warranted.

Still, the American Academy of Pediatrics (AAP) instructs pediatricians to screen children ages six to twelve for ADHD when they present with symptoms of hyperactivity, impulsivity, or inattention. Although pediatricians are also directed to evaluate for comorbid conditions, "most primary care practitioners are not trained to make these assessments."[30] As noted pediatrician Lydia Furman explains, the AAP guidelines instruct pediatricians to "make a diagnosis of ADHD based on DSM-IV criteria," using "ADHD-specific Checklists, these including the Vanderbilt ADHD Parent Rating Scale and the Vanderbilt ADHD Diagnostic Teacher Rating Scale, neither of which was developed or validated using interview, observation or independent diagnosis of the rated children."[31] In another article, Furman also states that the AAP warns that these rating scales "were tested under 'ideal' conditions and 'may function less well in primary care clinicians' offices' and notes that [the] questions on which these rating scales are based are subjective and subject to bias."[32] Other commonly used ADHD rating scales, such as Connors Parents Rating Scale, Connors Teacher Rating Scale, and the Child Behavior Checklist, are also based on subjective items.

Despite these caveats, the AAP directs pediatricians to use the results from these questionable rating scales to make the diagnosis without referral to a mental health professional, and then to prescribe stimulant medication for the condition. In this context, the absence of a biological marker is quite troubling, especially because many pediatricians rely on a child's response to medication as evidence for the diagnosis. Likewise, the fact that the symptoms of ADHD have not been proven to be clearly distinguishable from normal variations in behavior also calls into question its validity as a mental disorder.[33]

ADHD Does Not Meet the Requirements for Differential Diagnosis

The third and final area of dispute is that ADHD has not been shown to be distinct from other disorders. This is the issue that affects children the most. The structure of the DSM and the shared symptom set of ADHD are primary causes of comorbidities, a central problem that truly calls into question the validity of both ADHD and the DSM.

Although the DSM presents ADHD as a separate disorder, numerous experts focus on the symptom set of ADHD as being vague, unspecific, and common to many conditions and disorders. World-renowned pediatrician William Carey says that hyperactivity, impulsivity, and inattention are known effects from lead poisoning, brain injury, and fetal alcohol syndrome.[34] Similarly, Furman argues that the symptom set called ADHD is "not a disease per se but a group of symptoms representing a final common behavioral pathway for a gamut of emotional, psychological, and/or learning problems."[35] Likewise, as we show in Chapter Two, numerous experts in the gifted and 2e field recognize that this group of symptoms is also intrinsic to the gifted population.

In fact, since DSM-III, exclusion criteria have been included because it was acknowledged from the beginning that the symptom set called ADHD was already associated with several other disorders. In other words, the founding DSM committee members apparently recognized that the symptom set of hyperactivity, impulsivity, and inattention was inherent in autism, anxiety, mood, and personality disorders, and could be caused by a myriad of other conditions. Perhaps the assumption was that research would eventually bear out that it is a distinct entity. Three decades later, our children's alphabet soups of labels testify that this distinction remains unproven and that ADHD fails to meet the requirements for differential diagnosis.

This issue of comorbidity is one that strongly calls into question the framing of ADHD as a separate disorder. When a disorder claims as high as 60 to 100 percent comorbidity rates with other psychiatric disorders,[36] as ADHD does, it seems reasonable that professionals should question whether it is a distinct disorder. As clinical psychologist, professor, and founder of the Italian Observatory for Mental Health Claudio Ajmone states, "the more the symptoms of a pathology overlap those of other pathologies, the more it is probable that it does not exist."[37] Or, as neurologist Jeffrey Victoroff describes it, "ADHD is a symptom in search of a disorder in search of a syndrome."[38]

Moving Beyond an ADHD Diagnosis

We must ask how ADHD has become the power that it is. As a disorder, it fails to live up to DSM requirements for validity, especially with respect to scientific empiricism, comorbidity, and differential diagnosis. As a disorder, ADHD relies on highly subjective screening tools that allow a clinician to diagnose it without direct observation of the child and that permit a medical doctor to diagnose it without consulting a mental health practitioner. It is also one of the most marketed disorders in the DSM. Pharmaceutical companies underwrite educational materials, professional conferences, online parent support organizations, and research. As a result, a large percentage of the research grants through the Research, Condition, and Disease Categories (RCDC) of the National Institutes of Health goes to fund ADHD research.[39]

At the heart of all of this confusion is the DSM, a flawed system that continues to allow universal symptoms of hyperactivity, impulsivity, and inattention to be identified as a single disorder, ADHD. Pediatricians, primary care physicians, and clinicians have been trained to recognize and diagnose these symptoms as ADHD without screening for other disorders first—disorders that in the case of 2e children may account for the symptoms while offering better explanations for the social, academic, behavioral, and functional difficulties these children frequently face.

One such set of disorders is found in the Pervasive Developmental Disorders category, most notably autism spectrum disorders, which have been the primary focus of our work for the past ten years. Despite the increased awareness of autism in our culture, as pioneers of the ADHD-autism connection, we observe, with growing frustration and dismay, how children with high IQs or learning disabilities (or both) and those who are at the high-functioning end of the autism spectrum continue to be misdiagnosed and misunderstood. As Temple explains, at conferences she talks to parents all the time with children whose diagnosis switches between Asperger's and ADHD. She expresses great concern that these very smart children who should be computer analysts and engineers are getting stuck in special education classes instead of having their abilities nurtured and developed.

Clearly, the diagnosis of ADHD offers parents and professionals an incomplete understanding of the challenges 2e children face. Although it can be frustrating for parents to have their child's behaviors misunderstood and misdiagnosed, the good news is that once parents recognize that underlying conditions such as giftedness, as well as hidden impairments, can cause hyperactivity, impulsivity, and inattention, they can focus on securing educational interventions and therapies to target their child's individual strengths and weaknesses.

7

Misunderstanding the Spectrum of Autism

An Important "e" in 2e

What we see depends mainly on what we look for.
John Morrow

In the following e-mail—sent to a prominent behavioral pediatrician through a Web site—the mother has pulled together what she has learned from her child's ADHD diagnosis and other possible diagnoses, as well as what she thinks may be a possible explanation for her son's behavior, based on her observations.

Dear Expert,

I'm between a rock and a hard place! My son is almost eight years old and is in a regular second grade class though he is very bright. He was diagnosed as ADHD before kindergarten. It's also been suggested that he has Asperger's, but we're exploring that. (The more I read about it the more I'm positive he does.)

Here's the problem: He has been taking either Adderall or Dexedrine since kindergarten for ADHD. His medicine does improve his attention, but a few hours after taking either of them he gets irritable, sometimes violently. It's a balancing act to get enough of a dosage

> to help with attention but minimize the rages. When I talk to his doctors about it, they more or less say, "Oh well … that's how it works." My son is not the only one with this issue! The interesting things about the other kids I've met with this problem is that they have an autistic spectrum disorder as well as ADHD.
>
> Could it be that the social issues (lack of understanding of other people's feelings) and the control issues associated with Asperger's syndrome are being made worse by the ADHD medicine? Or could we be giving these kids too much medicine trying to curb the inattention and distractibility?
>
> I can't find any definite information on this problem. Who would know about this? Can you help me understand?
>
> Worried[1]

The expert, a behavioral pediatrician, answers that "although there is some overlap in the behavioral symptoms [of ADHD and autism], the core 'disorder' is quite different." She goes on to explain that these disorders are different because autistic spectrum disorders are primarily disorders of relatedness (how a child relates to others), whereas attention disorders are primarily disorders of attention and are associated with hyperactive-impulsive behavior.

Yet as we discussed in Chapter Four, there is a growing recognition in the professional literature that social impairments and difficulties frequently occur in individuals diagnosed with ADHD.[2] By now you know that we respectfully assert that as a diagnosis, ADHD in many cases interferes with the proper identification of children's abilities and challenges and the interventions that could support the best possible life outcomes.

Too often, when a child receives an ADHD diagnosis, the attending social, communication, and executive function challenges remain unidentified. Without accurate identification, proper interventions are unavailable, and life outcomes are likely to be compromised. In fact, a 2005 ADHD study found that in America over $77 billion per year in lost productivity can be attributed to "the problems faced by people with ADHD, associated with every aspect of life, ranging from school difficulties to emotional difficulties to problems in the workplace."[3] Given that the most recent statistic from the Centers for Disease Control and Prevention (CDC) states that one in ten school-age children is diagnosed with ADHD,[4] we must question how many of these children may in fact be gifted with HFA/AS.

Still, too frequently, the early identification and the information parents so vitally need and desire to help their children elude them because of the way the DSM system operates. A concerned father writes to the popular, highly entertaining, and wonderfully informative Web site Starkravingmadmommy.com about the problems he's having with getting his son accurately assessed for HFA/AS:

> Wish I had someone knowledgeable to talk to about this who won't assume he's fine b/c he's really smart.... When we took him in to get him tested we were basically dismissed as ridiculous. B/c he passed some of the tests fine they said we were just being over anxious. Well, great. I knew he didn't have full blown, needing major interventions autism. But there's a big space between non-verbal and neurotypical that I think leaves room for other possibilities.... I just want to know what it is so I can help him. I don't like that a lot of things I read about other kids with Asperger's sounds eerily similar to my son, yet he can't get a diagnosis.... b/c he's really smart for a 3 year old [I feel like] they see that and dismiss him.[5]

If the field of autism provides a more comprehensive understanding of both the gifts *and* the deficits in 2e, why are so many parents, educators, and even health care professionals unaware of the relationship between giftedness and autism? Why are parents left to discover on their own, through research and serendipity, this valuable information about their 2e children's behaviors and needs?

One reason that parents are locked out of the understanding that autism provides is also a result of the flawed DSM system. This system forces labels onto children based on whether they do or don't meet the number of symptoms and the degree of severity to qualify for a diagnosis, indicating *Yes, he has it* or *No, he does not.* With regard to autism, the continued emphasis on the severely impaired population often excludes children with HFA/AS who are intellectually gifted. In fact, the most widely used screening tools for autism, the ADI-R (Autism Diagnostic Interview-Revised) and the ADOS (Autism Diagnostic Observation Schedule) originally emerged as a result of research focused heavily on autism in individuals with intellectual disability (IQs below 70) and are admittedly limited in their ability to identify HFA/AS. The University of Michigan Autism and Communication Disorders Center, the major outlet for the ADOS and ADI-R, states that "Our research suggests that . . . children with milder ASDs (such as Asperger or PDD-NOS) may not consistently score in the Autism Spectrum range."[6]

Because of the diagnostic origins of the disorder, the field's continued emphasis on intellectual disability, and its limited focus on the spectrum of compensatory abilities available to children with high IQ, the diagnosis of an autism spectrum disorder is far more exclusive than the diagnosis of ADHD. The DSM system has for so long imposed a terribly rigid idea of what social communication deficits and repetitive, stereotyped behaviors and routines "look like" that any child whose symptoms are outside these established ideas appears "mildly" versus "significantly" impaired, and even unimpaired. Many 2e children are thus failed by a diagnostic system that prohibits a full understanding of their deficits and of the therapies and educational interventions necessary to support those deficits.

The Spectra of Giftedness and Autism

The relationship between giftedness-genius and autism has intrigued scholars and experts in both fields for decades. Both giftedness and autism have been described as occurring along a spectrum. Longtime experts in the field of autism, including Michael Rutter, University of London professor and part of the original workgroup on DSM-III, and Lorna Wing, recognize that IQs in the autism population range from intellectually disabled to highly gifted to savant.[7] Likewise, the field of giftedness recognizes that IQs in its population span from mildly gifted through genius with various gradations between.[8] Abbey B. Cash, a widely respected education expert and consultant to 2e students with autism, explains that although "the two populations are matched at several points ... the difficulties of the twice-exceptional gifted/autistic population are generally neurologically associated and more severe."[9] Temple especially acknowledges the possibly shared origins of giftedness and autism, saying that "the genetic traits that can cause severe disabilities can also provide the giftedness and genius that produce some of the world's greatest art and scientific discoveries."[10]

Because these populations are so closely aligned, it is often difficult to distinguish between them, especially during the very early years, when interventions and support are so important to developing the whole child. The late Bernard Rimland, director and founder of the Autism Research Institute, recognized as early as 1978 that in young children it is nearly impossible to differentiate autism from genius because all that parents initially see is the giftedness.[11] Likewise, Temple states a very valid concern that "intellectually gifted children are being denied opportunities because they are being labeled as either Asperger's or high functioning autism. Before people knew about Asperger's Syndrome, many such children would have received the very positive label of intellectually gifted."[12] Temple collaborated on this book because of her strong belief in the importance of getting parents, educators, and professionals to recognize and develop the abilities inherent in these 2e children.

Stereotyped Ideas of Autism

Traditionally, most of what we envision when we discuss autism is known as classical autism, or early infantile autism, and is based on the work of Leo Kanner, a Viennese physician who was director of psychiatry at Johns Hopkins Hospital. His monograph "Autistic Disturbances of Affective Contact" described severely socially withdrawn children who were unresponsive to others and who had serious language impairments.[13] Although Kanner recognized a range of cognitive abilities including above-average IQ in his studies, his work in autism has been primarily associated with individuals who have severe social, cognitive, and behavioral impairments, a stereotype prevalent in our society.

At nearly the same time that Kanner published his work (1944), Hans Asperger, a pediatrician practicing in Vienna, published "'Autistic Psychopathy' in Childhood."[14] In this paper, Asperger chronicled his observations of children with social and communication impairments. Unlike Kanner's subjects, Asperger's patients had little if any delay in language acquisition. Several had exceptional vocabularies, though their comprehension of meaning was not nearly as sophisticated as their use of language. They also exhibited strong attachments to areas of interest and often would direct conversations to these areas despite the effect such one-sided conversations had on the listener. One of the most striking and important features that Asperger recognized in his population was their above-average IQs.

It was not until 1981 that Asperger's work became popularized through the work of Lorna Wing, a British psychiatrist who published a paper titled "Asperger's Syndrome: A Clinical Account."[15] In this paper, Wing used the term "Asperger's syndrome" to describe a group of patients whose conditions were very similar to the personalities and abilities described by Asperger. Her work sparked an ongoing debate about degrees of severity and impairment along the autism spectrum. Wing's patients demonstrated some language impairments and social aloofness when very young, but went on to develop normal speech patterns and the need to socialize. Although this group developed beyond the traditional diagnosis of autism, they still demonstrated significant difficulties in social skills and reciprocity, narrow areas of intense interest, and the inability to plan or predict future consequences—all characteristics that closely resembled Asperger's group of children.

Wing's work led to the inclusion of Asperger's Disorder in the DSM-IV in 1994, and to the recognition that there is a wide spectrum of abilities that

> ranges from the most profoundly physically and mentally retarded person, who has social impairment ... among a multitude of other problems ... to the most able, highly intelligent person with social impairment in its subtlest form as his only disability. It overlaps with learning disabilities and shades into eccentric normality.[16]

Wing and her associate Judith Gould established the "triad of impairments" in autism, which they described as including impairments in social interaction, social communication, and social imagination.[17] However, as we discuss at the end of this chapter, one of the most significant changes to the autism diagnosis proposed for DSM-5 is to reduce the triad of social impairments to two domains: social communication and fixated interests and repetitive behaviors. Wing, however, has always maintained that "when these impairments [the triad] are present, the individual pattern of activities is narrow and repetitive."[18] In other words, repetitive behaviors are an expression of the presence of the triad; they are not the impairment.

Misunderstanding Imagination in Autism

Imagination is the most widely misunderstood part of the triad of impairments that defines the autism spectrum. It is commonly believed that individuals with autism lack creative imagination, relying on mimicry or imitation instead. Increasingly, though, the picture of autism includes both ends of the spectrum with regard to imagination—with severely impaired on one end and creative genius at the other. Still, certain core features are recognizable in each of these expressions, namely an overriding preoccupation with details, obsessive interests, and difficulties with understanding another person's perspective.[19]

To understand the paradigm of autism, it is important to understand exactly what Wing and Gould meant by *imagination* or *social imagination*. After several conversations with them about imagination, we now see that the ways in which Wing and Gould employ the term differ significantly from the way the term is usually explained in autism literature, especially here in the United States. These differences are pivotal to the changes being proposed in DSM-5, which we discuss at the end of this chapter.

The common definition of imagination is "the ability to recombine former experiences in the creation of new images directed at a specific goal or aiding in the solution of problems ... a plan or a scheme."[20] Imagination as Wing defines it encompasses this general definition and more specifically refers to *social imagination*, or "the capacity to think about and predict the consequences of one's actions for oneself and for other people."[21] This capacity typically "does not develop until after 3 years of age."[22]

In a recent phone conversation, Wing explained that when she employed the term *imagination*, she was describing what is commonly referred to as *executive function*, impairments in which have been recognized by experts in the fields of ADHD, autism, and giftedness as having a severe impact on functioning and quality of life because they affect the ability to plan, to predict, and to set goals. In fact, Wing, Gould, and Gillberg believe that impairment in imagination (executive function) "is perhaps the most important and disabling of all the consequences of having an autism spectrum condition of any kind,"[23] leading to a lifetime of lost job opportunities, broken relationships, and suffering.

DSM-IV-TR describes imagination quite differently than do Wing and Gould. In the DSM system, impairments in imagination are tied to creative expression and are equated with the presence of restricted, repetitive routines, behaviors, and interests. Rather than playing with toy cars, for instance, a child with Asperger's will repeatedly line them up or group them in predictable ways, leading parents and experts to conclude that the child lacks creativity.

Unfortunately, most autism experts commonly interpret the perceived lack of creativity and restricted physical behaviors as an indicator of how severely a child is impaired and even whether a child has an autism spectrum disorder. Many parents and professionals correlate stereotyped behaviors, such as spinning, rocking, head banging, hand flapping, and other physical tics, with severity of autism.

However, Wing et al. caution against using stereotyped behaviors as indicator of functioning.[24] As they explain, expressions of restricted, repetitive behaviors and routines, especially in HFA/AS children, are often internalized and, therefore, harder to see. Recent research suggests that OCD in children with HFA/AS may be an expression of the autistic tendency for restricted, repetitive routines and behaviors,[25] a possibility recognized earlier by Wing.[26] Thus an HFA/AS child with an impairment in imagination can exhibit a range of restricted behaviors extending beyond simple physical movements into the mental realm of highly repetitive thought patterns associated with OCD[27] and with limited approaches to social functioning.[28]

Impairments in imagination–executive function are often internalized in the HFA/AS population instead of being expressed as the more easily recognized hand flapping, rocking, and other stereotyped movements commonly associated with classic autism. As Digby Tantam states, children with HFA/AS "usually lack the marked stereotypies and unusual sensory preoccupations of more handicapped autistic people and, also unlike them, are generally not overly concerned with mere repetition although change usually upsets them and they often cleave to routine."[29] In short, the restricted, repetitive behaviors and routines required by the DSM look different in the HFA/AS population.

Changing Ideas of Autism: Recognizing a Larger Population

A diagnosis of AS often comes after a child starts school; this is likely because the impairments in social interaction along with the inability to engage in reciprocal conversation are first recognized in this environment.[30] A child's inability to take turns in conversation, to read another person's body language, and to understand the unspoken rules for behavior and play becomes readily obvious in a classroom. Likewise, as Wing explains, during this period the rigidity or insistence on sameness on the part of children with AS also becomes apparent.[31] These children do not adapt well to changes in routines or established patterns, and transitioning from task to task during the course of a day can be extremely challenging.

Another reason why a diagnosis of Asperger's is often made later is that these children are frequently extremely bright, which masks their social difficulties. In fact, Asperger recognized that although all autistic individuals struggle with social and academic learning, "The cleverest among them can overcome their difficulties in the end by dint of sheer intellect."[32] As Uta Frith explains, "Autistic people can, and often do compensate for their handicap to a remarkable degree."[33] Diane Twachtman-Cullen, speech-language pathologist and editor in chief of *Autism Quarterly*, recognizes, however, that their greatest strengths are their greatest weaknesses because their IQ and language abilities make them appear socially functional and thus interfere with an early and accurate diagnosis of an autism spectrum disorder.[34]

Recent statistics from the Interactive Autism Network at Kennedy Kreiger Institute show that 73.7 percent of children ages ten and older diagnosed with an autism spectrum disorder have also been diagnosed with ADHD.[35] This high number may be due to the changing faces of autism over the course of a child's development. Initially, as was the case for Diane's son Sam, the hyperactivity, impulsivity, and extreme tantrums often drive parents to seek an assessment during early childhood. The obvious diagnosis is ADHD. Likewise, during elementary school, the excellent verbal skills of the child with HFA/AS will often mask the social impairment; the symptoms of inattention and impulsivity will lead to an ADHD diagnosis. Once the child's ability to compensate for the social impairments becomes insufficient in the face of the increasing social and academic demands of school, an HFA/AS diagnosis is more likely.

Children with HFA/AS are frequently misunderstood because of their IQs, and are even more misjudged and misdiagnosed because of their behaviors, which are often mistaken for ADHD. As early as 1944, Asperger recognized several key characteristics in the population he studied. Specifically, Asperger described his patients as "showing a lack of initiative, aimlessness ... distractedness ... impulsive and bizarre behaviour." He noted that "Both intensity and extent of attention are disordered" and that "One finds obsessional acts, automatic acts, automatic commands, etc."[36] According to Asperger, these characteristics not only affect every aspect of the children's personality but also "explain their difficulties and deficits as well as their special achievements," an understanding that accounts for so many of the challenges our 2e children face.[37]

Some commonalities that Asperger recognized in his subjects with high IQ include advanced language abilities, specialized areas of interest and gifts, learning disabilities, academic underachievement, inattention, impulsivity, hyperactivity, restricted and repetitive routines and behaviors, obstinacy, defiance, inflexibility and stubbornness, aggression, problems regulating social-emotional responses, problems maintaining peer relationships, and uneven development.

Significantly, Asperger made a statement that mental health professionals trained under the DSM categorical system should be reminded of: "Once one has learnt to pay attention to the characteristic manifestations of autism, one realizes that they are not at all rare in children, especially in their milder forms."[38] In fact, Wing et al. explain that "defining the boundaries between autism and the enormous range of 'typical' development" is quite challenging, "especially in individuals who have very high skills in specific areas."[39]

In other words, once a professional has a true understanding of autism and its associated behaviors, he or she will recognize that these symptoms are not limited only to those with autism, AS, or HFA, but are frequently evident in children who are gifted and who have milder autistic symptoms found in PDD-NOS and HFA and often diagnosed as ADHD. As a matter of fact, the differences in behavior that these children show are so subtle that "most professionals who are consulted, unless they have special experience, fail to recognize that there is anything to be concerned about,"[40] although the very presence of autism negatively impacts the children's social functioning.

Even as the DSM recognizes that many children with Asperger's Disorder often have a prior diagnosis of ADHD, and experts in autism acknowledge the breadth of abilities included in the autism spectrum, there is a prevailing belief that most individuals with autism are represented by Kanner's portrait of classical autism with intellectual disability, or mental retardation. Reports on the autism epidemic often focus on children with mild to severe impairments in IQ and verbal and nonverbal abilities; repetitive, stereotyped movements; and oppositional behaviors. Likewise, many advocacy movements focus on regressive autism, in which children appear to have normal cognitive and language development and then lose it suddenly. This form of autism has played a role in the vaccine controversy.

Although the picture of autism is slowly changing, the idea of autism in America is still usually associated with the most severely impaired. Whether or not there is a connection between vaccine injury and autism is beyond the scope of this book. However, we feel compelled to point out a glaring conflict with attempts to link the rising number of autism cases with vaccine injury. The majority if not all of the cases described as vaccine injury claim that the child had prior language or development delays, or at least had shown some normal development and lost it. However, in the DSM description of Asperger's Disorder, there can be no delay or regression in language and cognitive development. Because the HFA/AS population comprises a large percentage of new autism cases, it is unlikely that the rise in these cases can be attributed to vaccine injury.

Changing Autism Rates

As you can see in Figure 7.1, there is a significant discrepancy between the size of populations and the percentages of individuals diagnosed with autism as compared to HFA/AS.

Autism rates in the United States are currently estimated at about one in one hundred, or 1.1 percent of children.[41] Between 2002 and 2006, as awareness of the disorder increased, there was a 57 percent increase in diagnoses.[42] Nevertheless, much of the emphasis is still on assessment of and interventions for the more severely impaired.

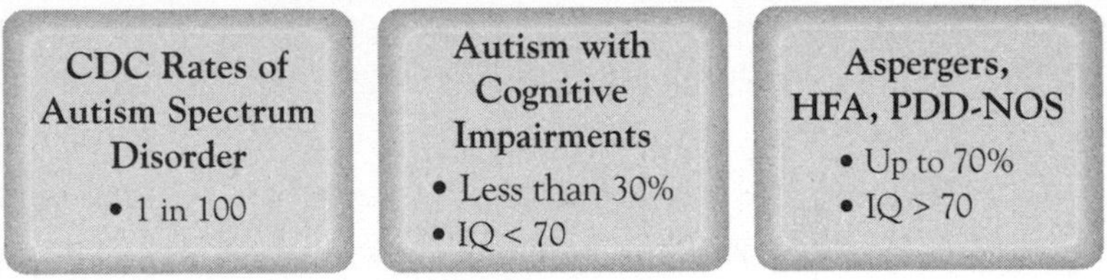

CDC Rates of Autism Spectrum Disorder
- 1 in 100

Autism with Cognitive Impairments
- Less than 30%
- IQ < 70

Aspergers, HFA, PDD-NOS
- Up to 70%
- IQ > 70

Figure 7.1 Autism's Largest Population

Sources: Adapted from "Higher Autism Rates Detected: Now 1 in 100 Kids," by Associated Press, October 5, 2009, Mental Health on msnbc.com, www.msnbc.msn.com/id/33165127/ns/health-mental_health; "The Numbers Guy: How Many Children Have Autism?" by C. Bialik, November 30, 2006, *Wall Street Journal*, http://online.wsj.com/article/SB116481159830835726.html.

Clearly, there is some disagreement within the field of autism about who constitutes the largest population. In fact, a number of statistics from various sources show that the majority of the autism population may actually be high functioning. After Asperger's Disorder was included in DSM-IV (1994), the number of children diagnosed with an autism spectrum disorder and who had an intellectual impairment dropped from 61 percent to only 27 percent, meaning that nearly three-quarters of newly diagnosed cases were in the HFA/AS population.[43] The CDC also recently reported that up to 41 percent of children with autism also have an intellectual disability, which means that well over 50 percent of children with autism have normal to above-normal intelligence.[44] Autism experts Geraldine Dawson and Sally Ozonoff estimate that two-thirds to three-quarters of those affected by autism spectrum disorders "appear to be high-functioning."[45] Likewise, Roy Richard Grinker, in his popular book, *Unstrange Minds: Remapping the World of Autism*, states that 50 to 75 percent of the increase in autism diagnoses are in these milder categories.[46]

It appears that within the population of children with autism, the majority is made up of those with normal to above-average IQs and who are high functioning, which would include those with Asperger's and PDD-NOS. And although some experts, such as Allen Frances, question whether the inclusion of Asperger's Disorder in DSM-IV is responsible for increasing the prevalence of autism,[47] Wing et al. explain that

> [T]he widening of the criteria for autistic conditions has followed from an increase in knowledge of work from Hans Asperger and the belief that his syndrome is part of the autism spectrum. The DSM-IV ... draft followed, not started this trend.[48]

Yet the continued emphasis on the severely impaired in research initiatives, spending, and the media may be due, in part, to the mistaken belief that higher IQ equates with "milder" autism when, in fact, autism is autism. Although IQ may allow a child to compensate for his social communication deficits and thereby minimize the appearance of impairment, impairment still exists and affects functioning as well as quality of life. As Cash explains, 2e children with HFA/AS appear more functional because of their "higher intellect and ability to manipulate and thereby dilute some of their apparent autistic weaknesses and tendencies (e.g., weak social interactions and stereotyped body movements)."[49] Asperger himself believed that the fundamental social, communication, and behavioral deficits of autism were just as severe in his patients, even as he recognized the positive effect that intelligence had upon their ability to function. As explained in *The OASIS Guide to Asperger's Syndrome*, "Asperger Syndrome is a serious, lifelong disability that requires individualized expert intervention and should be treated as such. There is nothing 'mild' about the challenge people with Asperger's face."[50] In short, the ability to function is too frequently perceived as a sign of "mild" autism, when it is more likely evidence of high IQ and verbal ability masking the severity of the autism. Yet IQ cannot take away the loneliness, isolation, and depression that so often results from so-called mild autism.

Increasing the Likelihood of Misdiagnosis and Missed Diagnosis: DSM-5

As this book goes to print, there are several major changes being proposed in DSM-5 that are likely to have a significant impact on the high-functioning population.

The first proposed revision is to rename and restructure the current category of Pervasive Developmental Disorders. The proposed name for this category is *Autism Spectrum Disorder*. The disorders to be classified under this heading include those currently known as Autistic Disorder (autism), Asperger's Disorder, Childhood Disintegrative Disorder, and Pervasive Developmental Disorder-Not Otherwise Specified. Rather than retaining these disorders as separate entities, the proposed revisions will collapse these disorders into a single diagnosis, Autism Spectrum Disorder.

Another important revision is that under the proposed diagnosis, the criteria for Autism Spectrum Disorder will change. Wing's triad of impairments, which you may recall includes social deficits, communication (verbal and nonverbal) impairments, and imagination–executive function impairments, will be reduced to two areas of impairment in DSM-5: *social/communication deficits* and *fixated interests and repetitive behaviors*. A set number of criteria for each domain must be met to qualify for the diagnosis.

Under the domain of social/communication deficits, verbal language development has been removed, and the emphasis is on the use of nonverbal and pragmatic aspects of communication, including eye contact, facial expression, emotional expression (affect), sharing of interests, and adjusting behaviors to suit varied social situations.

The domain of fixated interests and repetitive behaviors includes stereotyped behaviors and speech, insistence on sameness, unusually intense or focused interests, and abnormal sensory responses. However, Lord, whose work has been foundational in changing the DSM-5 criteria, states that although children on the spectrum consistently exhibit social and communication deficits,

> [T]his is not always true for restricted and repetitive behaviors and interests (RRBs), which are much more variable across children. . . . This variability has led some researchers to question the degree to which RRBs are necessarily an inherent part of the diagnosis of ASD.[51]

Another significant revision is that these two areas will be rated according to three severity levels ranging from "Level 1 (Requiring support)" to "Level 3 (Requiring very substantial support)."[52] At this time, although each level includes a description, the DSM Workgroup responsible for these changes has not determined how clinicians are to objectively determine a patient's level of severity.

Potential Impact on High-Functioning Autism Populations

The most immediate effect of these proposed changes will be on individuals currently diagnosed with Asperger's Disorder. Although Wing never intended for Asperger's syndrome to become a separate diagnosis, this label has helped individuals, especially 2e individuals, embrace their autism as the source of their giftedness. For many with the label, eliminating Asperger's is, to some extent, akin to changing their name without permission; it is a major part of how they identify themselves. Furthermore, the diagnosis has led to tremendous advances in the field of autism.

These proposed changes are also likely to increase the possibility that individuals with HFA/AS will be missed altogether, for several reasons. First, as we showed earlier, the ADI-R and ADOS, the "gold standard" in screening tools for autism, have been proven to be of limited use in diagnosing higher-functioning forms of autism, such as Asperger's Disorder and PDD-NOS. Second, these tools will be used with the revised criteria for Autism Spectrum Disorder, criteria that are likely to exclude people in this group rather than identify them. As Yale researcher Fred Volkmar points out, "The focus on a spectrum would seem to imply a broadened diagnostic view but the actual approach proposed may, in some respects, be more stringent than the current one."[53]

Under the proposed changes, individuals must meet criteria for restricted, repetitive patterns of behaviors, interests, or activities as well as for social communication impairments, and these must be shown to impair *everyday functioning*. In the HFA/AS population, there is a strong possibility that young children whose impairments appear mild, as well as older children who use their intellect to compensate for these impairments, will be missed. Further, as we have noted, in this population repetitive behaviors and routines are frequently hidden or internalized, and often appear as OCD. The requirement that these symptoms must obviously "limit and impair everyday functioning" may exclude countless individuals from receiving a diagnosis that provides the answers and services they need for successful life outcomes.

At the same time, by adding levels of severity, these proposed changes may significantly impact the types of services the high-functioning population can receive should they be diagnosed with ASD, leading to the possibility of reduced educational and therapeutic accommodations and an increase in the use of antipsychotics now approved for use in autism.[54]

A final proposed change that is highly likely to impact the high-functioning population is the creation of a new disorder, Social Communication Disorder. This disorder is separate from the proposed Autism Spectrum Disorder, but the possibility of confusion between the two is enormous, especially in HFA/AS individuals, who often do not exhibit obvious restricted, repetitive patterns of behaviors or routines. The workgroup members who framed Social Communication Disorder (SCD) already recognize the potential for confusion between SCD and ASD, as the following statement under the proposed revision illustrates:

> Rule out Autism Spectrum Disorder. Autism Spectrum Disorder by definition encompasses pragmatic communication problems, but also includes restricted, repetitive patterns of behavior, interests or activities as part of the autism spectrum. Therefore, ASD needs to be ruled out for SCD to be diagnosed.[55]

Given that the proposed criteria for an Autism Spectrum Disorder diagnosis will require obvious impairment in the domain of fixated interests and repetitive behaviors, a child whose impairment is hidden will not qualify as having autism. Instead, as we have shown, in all likelihood they will be relegated to an ADHD diagnosis with its attending comorbidities, which may soon include Social Communication Disorder.

Impact on 2e

As you can see, the proposed changes in DSM-5 have the potential to severely impact the identification and education of 2e students with HFA/AS. Wing et al. are very concerned that the autistic impairment in children with high intellect and less obvious autism will be missed under the proposed guidelines. Since DSM-IV-TR, great advances have been made in recognizing the needs of this unique yet vitally important group and in providing the necessary educational interventions to support their deficits in the classroom. Unfortunately, the proposed changes to the PDD category in DSM-5 threaten these advances and the futures of 2e children.

8

2e Students and Education

Too Bright, Too Broken

The worst form of inequality is to try to make unequal things equal.

Aristotle

America's current system of education is under heavy scrutiny, as witnessed by such documentaries as *The Race to Nowhere: The Dark Side of America's Achievement Culture* and *Waiting for "Superman."* As a nation, we recognize that our future depends on how well our students are prepared to face the realities of a global economy, increasing populations, diminishing natural resources, and the ongoing process of negotiating peaceful solutions in the face of diverse and conflicting political, religious, and cultural agendas.

However, we also recognize that our education system largely fails to produce students who are prepared for college and who possess the creativity to face the challenges of the future. How does a nation that champions equal opportunity and guarantees a free and appropriate public education (FAPE) for all its citizens balance its overriding agenda of achieving equality with meeting the unique needs of the individual—especially when it is individual creativity and innovation that will produce the advances in technologies, the natural and life sciences, and the arts that can save this great nation?

Because of No Child Left Behind (NCLB), our education system continues to use test scores and proficiency measures to judge whether schools, administrators, and teachers are effective. Educators across America are subject to data-driven decision making at all levels to guide and assess "learning" and to hold administrators and teachers accountable for attaining student proficiency. The emphasis remains on having *all students*, regardless of ability or disability, meet proficiency standards. For example, a recent report from the Kentucky Department of Education states that school councils and principals should use data to guide decision making that is "focused on *advancing* all students to proficient levels," while "*all* classroom assessments should be aligned with *curriculum standards*" (emphasis ours), which are set by the state.[1] As creativity expert Sir Kenneth Robinson explains, "Education is not a one size fits all. Teaching students to think is pushed aside in the pursuit of proficiency."[2]

When we are considering the quality of an education system, the idea that test scores can accurately predict or reflect academic achievement is a mistaken one, according to Yong Zhao of Michigan State University and cofounder of Challenge Success, an organization that believes that success encompasses more than achievement.[3] Instead of relying on skills and drills, education should focus on developing all types of abilities and talents in our children. As Robinson explains, "Talent is buried deep; an educational system needs to dig deep to discover this"[4] and to foster students' innate creativity. However, as Stephen Krashen, professor at the USC School of Education observes, "The Department of Education clearly thinks that weighing the animal more frequently is more important than feeding it."[5]

Against the backdrop of competing value systems that, on one hand, champion equality as evidenced by accountability measures and mandated standards and, on the other, embrace equity as absolutely necessary to foster individual creativity by meeting individual needs, we have failing schools and failing students, many of whom are our best and brightest, which includes our

2e children. Because NCLB so powerfully pushes states to meet proficiency measures, particularly through inclusion, the emphasis in our education system is on age- and grade-referenced norms for achievement, leading to less concern with students who meet these measures. A recent study from the Center for Evaluation and Education Policy states that "the federal accountability system has resulted in schools and teachers placing greater emphasis on low achieving students than on high achievers."[6] Likewise, according to Elissa Brown, North Carolina's state consultant for gifted education, "The passage of No Child Left Behind underscores the federal emphasis on bringing students 'up' to proficiency and completely ignores those students scoring at and above proficient levels."[7] As a result, 2e students end up in the general education classroom, where many remain unidentified and where their varied learning needs remain unmet.

What Are the Needs of 2e Students?

The complex profiles of 2e learners make identifying these students problematic and nearly ensure that some, if not all, of their educational needs will not be met, especially when it comes to identifying and supporting their needs for gifted programming. The nuances of their unique learning profiles require training and services beyond what is currently available in either special education or gifted education programs across the United States. Although many states have policies that address identification of 2e students and offer support services for them,[8] the dual needs of these learners make accommodation difficult. For these students to receive an appropriate education, accommodations must include enrichment to support their giftedness as well as remediation for their disabilities.

Identifying and Supporting Disabilities

Proper identification for 2e students is often problematic and frequently hinges on parents finding clinicians or evaluators who are highly trained in recognizing and diagnosing developmental disorders and related conditions, such as specific learning disabilities, sensory processing disorders, mood disorders, and others. Ideally, these professionals are also trained in identifying and supporting giftedness, though parents usually have to consult multiple specialists in order for their child's disabilities and giftedness to be properly identified and to develop an appropriate education plan.[9]

As we explained in Chapter Five, because of the DSM, clinicians and pediatricians are conditioned to diagnose behavioral disorders to account for characteristics associated with giftedness, ASD, and developmental disorders and related conditions, leading to interventions and medications that do little to address the underlying difficulties. At the same time, because the DSM informs so much of the professional training in behavior and development that educators receive, teachers frequently interpret student behavior from the perspective of a flawed system that assigns intention and willfulness to difficult behaviors when in reality a developmental or learning disability of some sort may be involved.

In addition, to support the disabilities, teachers of 2e students must be trained and skilled in such instructional strategies as differentiating curriculum, using multimodal approaches to teaching, incorporating visual supports for instruction, and using effective grouping to support the wide range of specific learning disabilities (SLDs), disabilities, and learning styles in the classroom.

Identifying and Supporting Giftedness

Because of their exceptional abilities, 2e students have unique social and learning needs that are often best met in instructional groupings with other gifted children. They may need accelerated curriculum in areas related to their strengths as well as project-based learning opportunities to showcase their talents. They need teachers who are trained to recognize and to support the unique social, emotional, and learning profiles of gifted students. At the same time, though, they need teachers trained to understand their perplexing behaviors, lack of motivation, and social limitations. They also frequently require support that extends well beyond the boundaries of the classroom and even of the school into the larger community.

Most parents, and most Americans, would assume that as a nation we would be heavily invested in developing consistent, high-quality educational programs designed to teach our best and brightest minds and that such educational programming would receive its fair share of attention from the federal government. This is simply not the case. In fact, there is a scarcity of research into gifted and talented students as compared to students with disabilities. At the federal level, notes Brown, "No systematic policies and practices for gifted learners have been formulated and implemented from the research that has been done."[10] Consequently, in the absence of federal guidelines or resources for gifted education, responsibility for funding and regulating gifted programs falls to the states, where "state mandates often lack financial provisions for services for those who learn faster than their age-mates."

Currently, the lack of federal regulation of gifted education has resulted in serious inconsistencies in two major areas that have significant impact on gifted education as well as on 2e students: identification and teacher training. According to the National Association for Gifted Children (NAGC), as of 2008, only thirty-four states required identification of gifted students, only twenty-nine required services be provided, and only six required regular classroom teachers to receive *any* training in gifted education.[11] In most states, even when students have been identified as gifted, curricular and placement changes are not guaranteed. In fact, most students who have been identified as gifted in elementary and middle schools remain in general education classroom settings for most of the day, and thus many do not receive instruction under the conditions most favorable for meeting their unique educational needs.[12]

Clearly, serious deficiencies exist with regard to effectively identifying and appropriately educating students who are gifted. However, when one or more disabilities are added into the mix, recognizing and meeting the unique needs brought about by both ability and disability becomes a challenge even for the most highly trained, well-seasoned professional clinicians and educators.

Federal Law: 504 and IDEA 2004

According to Section 504 of the Rehabilitation Act of 1973, all children, regardless of disability, are guaranteed a FAPE. Although both special education and gifted education are recognized at the federal level, they are not regarded as equally important, in part because of the overarching belief that gifted children do not have as many educational needs as children with disabilities. With the emphasis on proficiency, special education receives the majority of funding and focus under such laws as Section 504 and the Individual with Disabilities Education Act (IDEA) of 2004, whereas funding for gifted education is questionable at best. In 2008, for instance, the federal government allocated only 2.06 cents of each $100.00 in education for gifted education.[13] Similarly, in 2010, the House of Representatives voted to eliminate funding for the Javits Program, which for more than ten years has been a main source of federal funding for gifted and talented education (and which includes a stipulation for identifying 2e students). (This move has been frozen by the current fiscal crisis.)

Because of their dual exceptionalities, 2e students seldom receive a FAPE, which is guaranteed by law to each child. Although their education may be free, whether it is appropriate is questionable. Even Child-find, a federal program developed under IDEA for the early identification of *all* children with disabilities, can fail to identify children whose giftedness cloaks disability. In the classroom, the student likely will meet the requirements for proficiency, and both the giftedness and the disability will remain unrecognized. Or, if the student does not meet the proficiency standard, then it is likely that only the disability will be recognized.

Attempting to Improve Access to Services for Disabilities: 504 Amended

With the amendments to Section 504 of the Americans with Disabilities Act (ADA) in 2008, Congress opened the door for students who have been diagnosed with a disability to obtain an evaluation and services if the disability restricts their ability to learn, think, concentrate, or communicate. At the same time, the amendments to 504 also give parents the right to request an evaluation though no adverse educational impact has been demonstrated. Even if the child earns average or even above-average grades, should parents suspect that their child has an educational disability, they have every right to request in writing that the child be evaluated.

This is extremely significant for the 2e student, as now it is considered a violation of civil rights for a district to refuse to evaluate a child whose disability may not have an apparent educational impact. Regardless of academic performance, if a child is *regarded as* having a disability, then parents have the right and obligation to pursue services for the child.[14]

Attorney Lisa M. LaVardera, a special needs advocate in New York, graciously shares her interpretation of how the amendments now affect Section 504.

Section 504 Under the 2008 ADA Amendments

In 2008, Congress amended the Americans with Disabilities Act, significantly broadening the definition of disability, beginning in January 2009. The ADAA (Americans with Disabilities Act Amendments) resulted in changes to what constitutes "major life activities," as well as a lowering of the standard of "substantially limits" to "materially restricts." These changes affected the definition of disability under Section 504, one of two statutes through which children receive special education services in school (the other being the Individuals with Disabilities Education Act, or IDEA). The changes as they pertain to schoolchildren with disabilities, including bright children who may not have qualified for special education services or accommodations previously, are summarized herein.

1. Originally, the definition of disability was described in Section 504 of the Rehabilitation Act of 1973. Under Section 504, a person was considered to be a person with a disability if he (1) had a physical or mental impairment that substantially limited a major life activity and (2) had a record of such impairment or (3) was regarded as having such an impairment. Once a person met that standard, he could receive a "reasonable accommodation." Over the years, a few landmark employment law cases made it to the Supreme Court; its opinions tightened the requirements by which a person could be considered disabled for purposes of employment and disability law. Congress thought that those Supreme Court decisions contradicted its congressional intent of protecting people with disabilities, so it revised the Americans with Disabilities Act (the ADAA) to clarify and broaden the interpretation of disability. The ADA as revised by Congress has now clarified "substantially limits" with a lower standard of "materially restricts." Although the wording of Section 504 did not change, because of the ADAA, its interpretation has. Today, the level of restriction is the determining factor, not the severity of the impairment. Further, a substantial limitation in one major life activity need not be limiting in other major life activities in order to be considered a disability, and the determination must be made on a case-by-case basis.
2. Accordingly, the standard for "educational need" is now more flexible under 504 than it is under IDEA. Under 504, educational need or adverse educational impact is *not* the threshold for evaluation; the disability is. (Think disability plus some level of restriction in some area regarding learning, thinking, communicating, and so on, versus the requirement of "adverse educational impact" under IDEA.) The threshold is not the same.

3. As it regards 2e children or bright children who did not previously qualify for special education services, with the new interpretation under 504, a district may *not* use a child's superior or adequate grades as a reason to refuse to evaluate him. *A 504 plan may still be appropriate even in cases where the disability does not impact learning.* Nothing in the ADA or Section 504, or IDEA for that matter, limits eligibility to students who suffer academically. Therefore, a district may not refuse to evaluate a child whose disability has no educational impact *if the child meets the new definition of disability under the ADAA and thus 504.* Thus schools can no longer get away with telling parents that their child doesn't qualify for an evaluation or a 504 plan solely because he is "doing okay without any intervention." To say this is now a violation, says the U.S. Department of Education Office of Civil Rights. Other information about the disability must still be considered. The child may, after a full evaluation, still not qualify for a particular accommodation or service, but he must still be evaluated if he has a physical or mental impairment that materially restricts one or more major life activities, has a record of such an impairment, or is regarded as having such an impairment, regardless of good grades.
4. A "reasonable accommodation" has no definition in educational law and no limit at the moment, other than undue hardship on the part of the district. And the accommodation requested does not need to be directly related to the specific disability. (That does not mean, however, that the sky is the limit in requesting accommodations from the school district. The accommodation request can still be denied if the school district feels it is unreasonable, and then it is up to the hearing officer or judge to decide.)
5. Mitigating measures *cannot* be considered in determining substantial limitation (except for contacts and eyeglasses), and if mitigating measures create an additional impact, there must

also be an accommodation for the issue caused by the mitigating measure. A student must be able to use a mitigating measure independently; if school personnel have to do something, then the disability is not mitigated. When determining whether the disability materially restricts a major life function, school districts must do a ''look back'' evaluation to determine what the child is like when off medication or without the mitigating measure.

6. Perhaps the most important change: kids who have learned to ''self-accommodate'' or adapt — or compensate, as we like to call it — now cannot be penalized for learning to manage the disability on their own. Learned adaptive skills are a mitigation that may *not* be taken into consideration when determining substantial limitation. A child with a reading disability who can learn in other ways is still disabled for the purposes of the new interpretation under Section 504, perhaps even if he is an honor roll student.
7. Clearly, these changes suggest that any child previously refused services under the old interpretation of Section 504 should promptly request an evaluation under the new interpretation. This is especially important for children who did not meet threshold criteria before or who may have had a discipline involvement (or both) and who are now otherwise protected under the ''regarded as'' prong of 504 (for example, already receiving informal accommodations). It is also important for college-bound teens and those seeking accommodations on college boards to be promptly reevaluated under Section 504.
8. Another interesting note: children who are bullied may fall under the ''regarded as'' prong if they are bullied as a result of their perceived disability. And, according to Congress in revising the ADA, that discrimination provides them protection under 504, whether the disability is ''substantially limiting'' or not. This is a very interesting new wrinkle. Conceivably, a child may be entitled to an

accommodation for being bullied if he is discriminated against (bullied because he had a disability), whether or not his disability is materially restricting enough to otherwise qualify for Section 504 protections or accommodations.

9. Evaluations under the new interpretation of Section 504 must be comprehensive and look at all areas of learning: thinking, concentration, communicating, and so on. School districts must meet 504's evaluation and placement procedural requirements when developing the plan. For children with medical conditions who previously had an IHP (health response plan), the IHP may no longer be sufficient to meet 504 procedural requirements, and it may need to be upgraded to a 504 plan.
10. Clinicians who do outside evaluations should also be aware that their evaluations must draw on how the disability materially restricts a major life activity and how it impacts learning (thinking, concentrating, communicating, and so on) and also address any deficits masked by mitigating or self-accommodation measures, and any accommodation required for any effect of a mitigating measure.
11. Accommodations and modifications must actually level the playing field in order to be 504 compliant. Not all actually do what they are intended to do.
12. School districts must have updated their 504 evaluation criteria, procedural requirements, manuals, materials, parent letters, prior written notice letters, and so on, and must have trained personnel not to make statements or policy that violates Section 504. The Office of Civil Rights has said it will enforce Section 504 in a manner consistent with the ADA Amendments Act. Because school districts must create their own evaluation procedures under Section 504, this is particularly challenging. But perhaps the most challenging issue facing school districts is understanding that even children who are doing adequately in school may qualify for Section 504

accommodations and services if they have a disability that materially restricts a major life activity. Parents must be proactive and vigilant in protecting their children's Section 504 rights, even if their school is not.

Disclaimer: Please be advised that this information is not intended to take the place of legal advice. For specific legal questions, seek the advice of a licensed attorney.

(c) Lisa M. LaVardera, Esq.

IDEA 2004: Advancing Awareness of 2e

Gifted education and special education were essentially separate until new regulations under IDEA in 2004 acknowledged for the first time that gifted students may also have disabilities. Although the prevalence of 2e students is unknown, in 2006 the Department of Education estimated that there were approximately 360,000 of these students in U.S. schools; it was also determined that the largest percentage of these students have an SLD.[15] Perhaps the most significant change brought about by IDEA 2004 was in how students with learning disabilities are identified.

Identifying Both Giftedness and Disability in 2e Students

Before IDEA 2004, states identified students as having a learning disability using what is known as the discrepancy model. This approach diagnosed learning disabilities by comparing scores on administered standardized IQ tests and achievement tests to determine areas of weakness.

Unfortunately, this method, coined the "wait and fail approach," often meant that a student would have to fail before being referred for assessment, in part because of the stringent requirements of the original IDEA. It also meant that children in ungraded primary programs were not recommended for testing until fourth or fifth grade. The discrepancy model is an imperfect tool and, according to critics, "has proven at least somewhat ineffective."[16] However, with regard to diagnosing SLDs, the discrepancy model has been the standard for decades in both education and in mental health, and remains the most accurate means of identifying dual exceptionalities of disability and giftedness in a child.

Under this model, a diagnostician individually administers a battery of IQ and achievement tests (usually a combination of some form of Weschler tests and, perhaps, the Stanford-Binet) to discover overall IQ, special abilities, and areas of disability. Contrary to popular belief, the full-scale IQ score is only one part of the picture. The evaluator also looks for notable discrepancies "between scores on different tests; between performance on certain subtests or types of items within a test; between behavior at home and at school; between strong and weak subjects; even between IQ scores of siblings," which are crucial to obtaining a complete picture of the child.[17] The presence of these discrepancies reveals more about the child's particular profile of strengths, weaknesses, and specialized areas of need for educational interventions than does just the overall IQ.

In the field of gifted education, the use of testing has been proven to be reliable in identifying 2e children and their individual learning needs. Educational experts including Susan Baum, Steven Owen, Mary Ruth Coleman, and James Gallagher suggest that separating out scores on IQ tests and subtests is the best way to identify the unique patterns in 2e children, especially because of their out-of-sync development, uneven skills, and inconsistent performance.[18] Likewise, as Baum and Owen explain, the discrepancy model aids in identifying areas of strength that are common in 2e learners—such areas as spatial pattern recognition, verbal comprehension, and abstract conceptualization—as well as common problem areas, such as in processing details and rote memorization.[19]

The continued use of the discrepancy model has allowed experts in 2e education to gain a handle on hallmark characteristics of gifted underachievers. Even though the presence of both high intelligence and inconsistent abilities makes identifying a 2e student difficult, the presence of the following traits indicates the presence of dual exceptionalities:[20]

- Discrepancy between expected and actual achievement
- Evidence of outstanding ability
- Evidence of a processing deficit in one or more areas

Although testing does have drawbacks with regard to cost, time expenditure, and availability of specially trained personnel, it is currently the best option available in education to definitively identify and diagnose the presence of an SLD in a gifted child.

Moving Away from the Discrepancy Model

With IDEA 2004, the door opened to additional means of identifying an SLD so that now, by law, each state

- Must not require the use of a severe discrepancy between intellectual ability and achievement for determining whether a child has a specific learning disability. . . .
- Must permit the use of a process based on the child's response to scientific, research-based intervention; and
- May permit the use of other alternative research-based procedures for determining whether a child has a specific learning disability. . . .[21]

It is important to note that in IDEA 2004, nowhere does it say that the discrepancy model may not be used, just that it must not be required.

An important point to recognize in this legislation is that the emphasis is on *identifying* disability only. As experts Susan G. Assouline, Megan Foley Nicpon, and Claire Whiteman of the Belin Blank International Center for Gifted Education and Talent Development explain, "Despite the IDEA-2004 language, which implies support for alternative ways ... to *identify* an SLD, a comprehensive evaluation is required before a student can be *diagnosed* with an SLD"[22] (emphasis ours). Yet the distinction between these terms is becoming increasingly perplexing for parents and advocates of both gifted and 2e students, especially with the introduction and broadscale promotion of an alternative framework for identifying SLDs known as Response to Intervention or RtI, a framework that affects both identification and diagnosis.

RtI: A Response to IDEA 2004 and a Move Away from the Discrepancy Model

Although all states must generally address the aspects of disability as defined by IDEA 2004, each state is responsible for developing its own set of criteria for students to qualify for special education services. Now each state is given the option of verifying underachievement through "a process that determines if the child responds to scientific, research-based intervention as a part of the evaluation procedures" for an SLD.[23] One such process is RtI, which has been mandated in numerous states and is widely supported at the federal level.

What Is RtI?

RtI is a framework intended to prevent failure by incorporating assessment and intervention to raise student achievement and to reduce behavior problems related to failure.[24] RtI is not a means of *diagnosing* an SLD; instead, it emerged from the field of special education in the mid-2000s as a method of *identifying the learning needs* of low-average and below-average learners.[25] Although RtI programs will vary from state to state, the basic model comprises three tiers, as described here and illustrated in Figure 8.1:[26]

1. Universal assessment and progress monitoring. Teachers use ongoing assessments to monitor student progress and to adapt curriculum to meet individual student needs.
2. Instruction and intervention. Teachers instruct all students in the core curriculum while providing interventions to assist students who struggle to attain proficiency.
3. Collaboration. Teachers, special education specialists, and parents collaborate to decide how to adjust interventions or to determine whether the student should be formally evaluated for an SLD.

According to the National Center on Response to Intervention, RtI allows schools "to identify students *at risk for poor learning outcomes*, monitor student progress, provide evidence-based interventions and adjust the intensity and nature of those interventions depending upon a student's responsiveness, and identify students with learning disabilities" (emphasis ours).[27]

RtI is built on the underlying assumption that the curriculum in a regular classroom is broadly appropriate for *all* learners[28] and that at least 80 to 85 percent of students will be successful with this curriculum.[29] Although proponents of RtI accept that this assumption is valid, we believe that it is a highly questionable and dangerous supposition regarding 2e students, given their varied and complex profiles. In the context of standards-based curriculum, RtI becomes a tool for supporting minimum competency and a means of giving immediate support to students who are struggling in the daily learning activities associated with this curriculum.

Under the RtI model, teachers track students through "frequent *curriculum-based measurement* to assure students are performing at the *expected* level" (emphasis ours) and to determine when to implement mainstream interventions to increase performance.[30] These

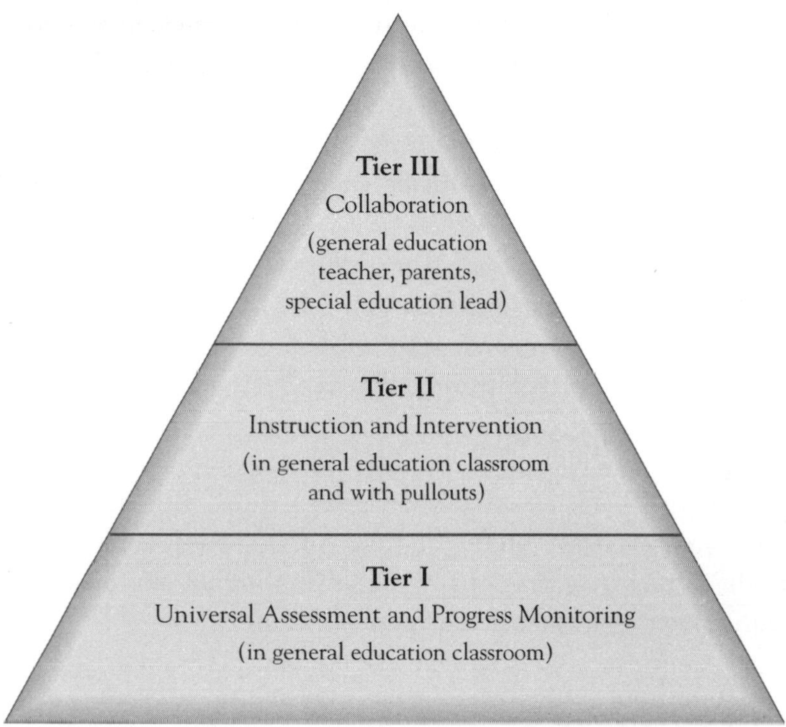

Figure 8.1 RtI Model

Source: Adapted from *The Essential Guide to RtI: An Integrated, Evidence-Based Approach*, by S. L. DeRuvo, 2010, San Francisco: Jossey-Bass.

interventions can take place in the classroom, in small groups, or one-on-one. The classroom teacher modifies instruction, closely monitors student progress, and makes adjustments as necessary; if the interventions do not work, the teacher consults a support team for further guidance and implements its suggestions.[31] If the student's performance does not improve as expected, *then* referral for evaluation for special education services is recommended, the final tier of RtI.

Although RtI is only one possible framework under IDEA 2004, it is the one that the Office of Special Education Programs endorses and that is most widely disseminated and promoted for use in general education classrooms. Once a student enters RtI, parents have the right to request, in writing, a case study evaluation; however, whether the child is actually identified as having an SLD depends not just on actual test results but also on the input of the support team to determine if the child is eligible for services.[32] As educational specialist Barbara Resnick explains, to determine eligibility for special education services, the support team must be able to identify specific areas of school performance that are affected by the learning disability as well as be able to confirm that the child's performance is significantly below that of peers or expected standards despite interventions.[33]

Drawbacks of RtI in Special Education

Although RtI was specifically designed for use with students of low to low-average cognitive abilities, a recent study comparing it to the discrepancy model highlights several significant drawbacks with using the RtI framework for identification:[34]

1. It does not clearly differentiate between students with learning disabilities and pervasive underachievers (which includes many 2e students).
2. It is likely to identify all "slow" learners as having learning disabilities.
3. It does not include any means for formally evaluating cognitive processing or ability.
4. It can be inappropriately influenced by stakeholders who want (or do not want) the child identified for interventions. (Because of this potential abuse, the Office of Special Education Programs recently sent a letter to all state directors of special education stating that it is unlawful for local education agencies to use RtI to delay or deny an evaluation for eligibility under IDEA 2004.)[35]

Although RtI was originally designed to meet the needs of special education students, it has serious limitations in its ability to identify and serve the needs of its intended population, which raises grave concerns about its effectiveness for gifted and 2e children.

RtI for Gifted and 2e Students: A Problem for Our Best and Brightest

A disconcerting development with respect to 2e learners is the rapidity with which gifted education programs are embracing RtI. Of course, any change to gifted education programs affects 2e children too.

Given our country's current economic environment, our federal budget, and funding for education, across the nation special education, general education, and gifted education programs are competing for limited resources, with gifted education, once again, bringing up the rear. In the face of tightening purse strings and increased emphasis on minimum competency standards, school officials recognize that gifted programs "can ill afford to operate on separate agendas if they want to address the need for developing optimal opportunities for their best learners."[36] As a result, schools are looking for ways to streamline the provision of services to best improve learning for all students, including gifted and 2e students.[37] RtI is quickly—perhaps too quickly—becoming the "answer" to this challenge.

RtI: What Does It Mean for Gifted Students?

Recently, major organizations for gifted education professionals have begun endorsing RtI as an effective framework that they hope can be adapted for identifying children's strengths in the general education classroom. The Association for the Gifted and certain special interest groups within NAGC view RtI's tiered approach to supports and services as a viable, effective way to meet the academic needs of the gifted learner.

Like RtI for students with disabilities, RtI for gifted education includes several components to assist with early and ongoing identification of strengths and abilities. At the time of this writing, many of these components are still being developed for gifted learners. In fact, many advocates of RtI, ranging from the Office of Special Education Programs to districts that have implemented it, liken RtI's development to "building a plane while flying it."[38]

Although the proposed RtI model for gifted education closely resembles the framework of RtI in special education, the effectiveness as well as the limitations of RtI for gifted education are speculative at best. To be successfully implemented in gifted education, an RtI framework requires resources, professional development, and curricular materials that are well beyond what is available in most state and local budgets.

Still, to achieve the goal of minimum competency in the face of continuing budget cuts, public schools frequently prefer the option of having gifted students receive differentiated lessons within a general education classroom. Yet a recent study by Jennifer R. Cross of the College of William and Mary; Tracy L. Cross, editor of *Journal for the Education of the Gifted;* and Holmes Finch of Ball State, reliably shows that "classroom teachers lack the knowledge and skills to effectively differentiate curriculum to meet the needs of gifted learners."[39] The authors conclude that for gifted students, especially for those who are twice exceptional, unsuccessful differentiation is not in their best interest.

RtI: More Dangerous for 2e Students

Although the verdict is still out on whether RtI will be effective in identifying strengths and weaknesses in gifted students without disabilities, proponents of RtI claim that it's a very useful framework for assessing gifts in 2e learners, though there is no empirical evidence to support this claim. In our opinion, the limitations of RtI for gifted students become more obvious in the context of 2e education.

In the absence of hard data proving RtI to be effective with gifted students, our nation should proceed slowly and cautiously when implementing this framework for gifted and 2e education. The ideal conditions required for RtI to successfully identify, assess, and meet the needs of gifted students without additional exceptionalities should sound an alarm for parents of 2e students. As 2e expert Baum warns, RtI "has not yet proven itself to be helpful to gifted students and gifted students with academic and behavioral challenges," and with the possibility of widespread adoption of RtI under NCLB law, "attention to the needs of 2e students who may be achieving at grade level will not be a priority."[40]

Under the RtI model, in the context of a general classroom curriculum, the definition of "failure" is the same for a gifted student as it is for a student with average to below-average cognitive abilities,[41] an erroneous (and, we believe, potentially harmful) assumption for 2e students, as the NAGC points out. Consequently, with RtI the same problems with identifying 2e students will remain; their giftedness will most likely go unnoticed because their disabilities make them appear average.[42] Even under RtI, the 2e student receives neither a strengths-based nor a deficits-based education, but will likely spend his academic career in a regular classroom, stuck between the competing needs of his gift and his disability.

The characteristics of the 2e population contribute strongly to these learners' being seen as average or as underachievers. Asynchronous development, uneven skills, exceptional intelligence, discrepant weaknesses, and negative behaviors test the abilities of the most experienced evaluator. How much more are regular education teachers challenged in meeting the responsibility of accurately assessing the 2e student for services?

Other Problems with RtI for 2e Students

Because it rests on data-driven assessments and screening, the RtI framework requires school personnel to focus on the data more than on the student. With regard to disabilities, in the context of RtI, the teacher is placed in a position of becoming a diagnostician.[43] Under this model, classroom teachers become the frontline specialists in terms of assessing or screening to determine the need for interventions so that support for the disabilities is met without testing.[44]

This plan could be problematic for 2e students, however, given that the requirements for teacher training programs vary from state to state. There is currently no consistent program for ensuring that teachers receive thorough instruction on the characteristics of 2e students or on the characteristics of giftedness. Accordingly, "if the teacher does not perceive any problems, as in the potential for higher achievement, or below grade-level performance in an academic subject, the student may never be referred to the problem-solving team."[45] Yet it is commonly recognized that 2e students perform better on individualized tests than on group-administered assessments, so the practice of universal screening may interfere with the 2e child's being properly identified as both disabled and gifted, but especially as gifted.

Finally, for any educational program—whether in general education, gifted and 2e education, or special education—to successfully implement RtI requires the commitment of strong teachers who are willing to be trained in new approaches to differentiating curriculum; managing the classroom; using formative assessment tools to monitor progress; and collaborating with gifted education and special education teachers, parents, and others on a multidisciplinary team to assess, problem-solve, and plan interventions. It also requires the unwavering commitment of administrators to support and assist teachers in the RtI model. However, according to Hughes and colleagues in their article, "Remaining Challenges for the Use of RtI with Gifted Education," such fidelity in implementing this model "is, at best, inconsistent."[46]

Best Practices to Serve 2e Students

In the wake of IDEA 2004, many experts in gifted education agree that the best way to identify and support 2e learners (and all learners, for that matter) is by combining comprehensive assessment with RtI.[47] Using this approach, assessment begins with a comprehensive evaluation based on individualized ability and achievement testing. The comprehensive evaluation "allows for an analysis of the performance discrepancy between the two," which is a strong indicator that the student is twice exceptional—a cognitively gifted student with an SLD.[48] This comprehensive assessment also helps in (1) determining whether a student is twice exceptional, (2) identifying the possibility of psychosocial concerns, and (3) developing educational recommendations.[49] (This first component of the approach is very similar to the discrepancy model.)

When data from this assessment are used along with RtI, "teachers and problem-solving teams can gain a complete picture of the gifted or 2e student and specific recommendations become evident."[50] Once educational recommendations are made, then RtI becomes a wonderful tool for carrying out the recommendations in the classroom. By using the comprehensive evaluation to guide the classroom and schoolwide interventions, teachers and teams can ensure that the emphasis remains on helping the student's exceptional cognitive abilities flourish even while offering remediation for the disability.

A Better Education for 2e Means a Better Education for All

Currently, 2e children are poorly identified by the two major systems intended to help them: the mental health system and the education system. Too frequently, children whose IQs mask their impairments are classified as "emotionally-behaviorally disordered" by the education system, treated with powerful medications, and subjected to interventions that do nothing to help with the hidden impairments that drive the behaviors.

Twice-exceptional students remain stuck in an education system ill equipped to identify and meet their varied, complex needs. On the one hand, federal law requires that schools identify, intervene, and provide services for students with disabilities so that proficiency standards mandated by NCLB are met. On the other hand, educational programs for gifted students are woefully underfunded at the federal, state, and local levels. Teacher education programs poorly prepare teachers to identify and support the characteristics or needs of gifted and disabled learners in the classroom.

Nevertheless, proponents for RtI, including the Office of Special Education Programs, are championing RtI as an alternative to the costly but more precise discrepancy model. Proponents of RtI claim that this framework allows for early identification of disabilities and giftedness so that the needs of all students, including 2e students, can be effectively and collectively met within the regular classroom. However, although RtI was created for special education, its effectiveness in properly identifying low-ability to low-average-ability students is questionable, and for 2e students, highly speculative.[51]

Clearly, America's system of education values equality for all over equity for individual students. Under the current framework of NCLB, the emphasis is on making sure that all students meet proficiency measures through frequent assessment and data collection. This approach emphasizes teaching to the test so that students can demonstrate knowledge rather than teaching children how to think creatively to apply knowledge in real-world contexts to solve problems. Likewise, the current administration's proposed education reform requires that standards-based curricula, accountability, and test scores be used as the broad measures of success for students, teachers, and schools. Unfortunately, this approach plays right into the weaknesses of 2e students, who tend to learn and demonstrate learning much better through project-based tasks that allow them to work in their areas of strength.

As Robinson succinctly states, "Education that transfers data from one brain to another is not education."[52] Yet as our education system continues to emphasize the importance of learned knowledge and preparing for high-stakes tests, our schools continue to fail our students and our future by failing to engage all students, including our best and brightest, in real learning that will ensure their success and ultimately the future success of our nation.

Part III

How to Help Them

9

Diagnosing the Whole Child

Identifying Abilities and Minimizing Deficits

People respect ability, which is why each individual's unique talents must be recognized and developed.

Temple Grandin

Twice-exceptional children are subject to conflicting perspectives and philosophies in identification and treatment. On the one hand, because of their exceptional abilities, these children need to be seen from the whole child perspective, which focuses on their strengths even as it identifies and supports their functional deficits. In the whole child, or dimensional, approach, all aspects of a child's functioning are considered, with giftedness and areas of strengths as a primary focus. At the same time, interventions and treatments for the child are based on a complete picture of all the conditions that affect functioning. Armed with this perspective, parents and professionals can effectively implement therapies that target specific weaknesses, instead of wasting precious time and resources trying to get the "right" label and find the "right" therapies to help the child reach his full potential.

On the other hand, 2e children are all too often trapped in the disabilities world, which is based on the DSM system that identifies them solely by their limitations in functioning. Within the confines of the disabilities perspective, the 2e child's potential languishes, for two critical reasons. First, because the system artificially splits behaviors from impairments and does not recognize the impact of high IQ on functioning, the behaviors accompanying giftedness and ASD are misunderstood and consequently misdiagnosed by treatment professionals, even within the field of autism. The emotional and physical intensities of the 2e child often predispose him to an ADHD diagnosis. However, as we have established, this label offers nothing by way of helping parents and professionals identify and meet the needs of the 2e child. Instead, it often acts as a roadblock to an accurate portrait of the whole child.

Second, because professionals are trained in the DSM system rather than in a whole child approach, they are often restricted in their perspective on diagnosis and identification. The DSM system is designed to lead professionals to a single diagnosis; yet, as we have shown, this single diagnosis is severely limited in its capacity to identify the full range of secondary conditions that also affect the 2e child's ability to function. Further, a single label fails to lead parents to the various therapies and interventions available to address these other conditions. Consequently, the DSM limits our abilities to fully advocate for our 2e children because it limits our options.

The Limitations of Category-Based Tools

Because of the treatment challenges that arise with high rates of comorbidity, clinicians are increasingly recognizing the limitations that the categorical approach imposes on them when trying to help their patients. As we explained, the screening tools tied to the DSM are of limited use in providing a portrait of the whole child. Tied to the diagnostic criteria of each disorder, most category-based diagnostic instruments are more useful in supporting the aims of researchers than the needs of clinicians. When parents suspect that something may be wrong with their child, the process of screening begins to determine whether the child qualifies for a full diagnostic evaluation. Initially, the child is screened for a possible disorder using checklists developed from the DSM system. If the child meets the predetermined criteria, then the process of assessment and diagnosis begins. In each stage of this process, the tools used are all based on the DSM descriptions and criteria (the required number and type of symptoms) of disorders.

In particular, the field of autism relies on two primary diagnostic instruments: the Autism Diagnostic Interview-Revised (ADI-R), an interview schedule intended to gather facts about development and behavior, and the Autism Diagnostic Observation Schedule (ADOS), a structured observational tool to assess a child's social and communicative functioning. Both of these tools are designed more to support research into the various diagnoses than to be helpful to clinicians. According to Catherine Lord, a primary author of the ADI-R and the ADOS, both tools "were developed to operationalize the DSM-IV criteria."[1] She states that these tools were first created for research, but have only recently been adapted for clinical purposes.[2]

Yet in America these screening tools are considered the gold standard for diagnosing autism spectrum disorders, even though their usefulness for diagnosing children with HFA/AS is questionable. Although it is widely recognized that both the ADI-R and ADOS have good validity and reliability with regard to diagnosing *classic* autism, these instruments, even when combined, are less specific in identifying higher-functioning children on the autism spectrum;[3] alone, "the ADI-R has been shown to be insensitive in diagnosing high-functioning children with autism."[4] When the ADI-R is used, high-functioning children are at risk of being overlooked until they are much older and, as a consequence, are less likely to receive interventions.[5]

Because it is so stringently tied to the DSM criteria, the ADI-R is effective in answering the question of whether a child has classic autism, although it is of negligible value when considering the whole child. Despite attempts to make this tool more clinically useful, it remains limited in its capacity to identify the strengths and challenges strongly associated with aspects of autism spectrum disorders that are not part of the autism diagnostic criteria.

The Dimensional Perspective: Seeing the Whole Picture

As we show in Chapter Five, the DSM system is based on a top-down approach to defining disorders, which are established by consensus and opinion. The issue of whether these disorders are indeed discrete, separate entities or "arbitrary distinctions along dimensions of functioning"[6] is a growing concern in psychiatry. Although they indeed may be both (as Spanish psychiatrists Victor Peralta and Manuel J. Cuesta point out),[7] the *dimensional model* is recognized as being more helpful to clinicians because it gives a more complete clinical portrait of the child.

Using the dimensional model, the clinician develops a diagnosis by examining several areas of functioning and naturally occurring symptoms. As personality disorder researchers and experts Widiger and Mullins-Sweatt of the University of Kentucky explain, under the DSM system of using a single diagnostic category, the complete patient profile—symptoms, cognitive level, biochemistry, interpersonal relationships, developmental history—is highly unlikely to be fully described.[8] These researchers believe that a dimensional approach in which various domains of functioning are assessed would be more useful in identifying treatments than the present system of assigning a single diagnostic label. Some of the newer diagnostic tools attempt this more comprehensive approach.

For decades, there has been a strong movement overseas that supports diagnosing autism spectrum disorders dimensionally rather than categorically. The National Autistic Society in the United Kingdom, for example, encourages a dimensional approach to diagnosis using tools that look specifically for areas of strength as well as problems in social interaction, social communication, and social imagination. Because the portrait of autism often changes within the same child over time, and because IQ also affects how it looks from child to child, a dimensional approach that examines "levels of functioning and ability rather than [focusing] upon theoretical diagnostic subgroups"[9] is more effective when diagnosing autism spectrum disorders. In fact, Wing began using a dimensional approach before DSM-III-R. Since then, she and Gould have continued refining it as the understanding of the autism spectrum has grown.

Wing and Gould believe that a dimensional approach is essential for several reasons. Wing states that the "subgroups based on the illogical mix of criteria in ... DSM-IV should be abandoned" in favor of a dimensional approach, which would "facilitate research into genetics, brain pathology, relationships with other conditions" and ways to help individuals within the spectrum.[10] Both Wing and Gould assert that the dimensional approach to describing a child is "far more helpful in prescribing how to help each individual than is assigning a diagnostic category."[11] As they explain, in clinical work, "the primary purpose is to facilitate understanding of the pattern over time of the skills and impairments that underlie the overt behavior." To this end, they have developed the Diagnostic Interview for Social and Communication Disorders (DISCO), an instrument for identifying autism spectrum disorders that cuts through the limitations of category-based tools and provides parents and clinicians a much broader view of a child's social, emotional, and behavioral functioning.

The DISCO

Originally created for clinical use, the DISCO has proven highly reliable in its ability to identify a broad range of disorders and conditions; it has recently been tested and proven highly reliable for research purposes as well.[12] The DISCO covers not only the diagnostic criteria for classic autism but also "has diagnostic algorithms [steps and procedures] for all the commonly used clinical (and research) diagnostic categories in the autism spectrum,"[13] including Asperger's, high-functioning autism, and PDD-NOS. In contrast to the ADI-R, which has "no items designed to identify individuals outside 'core autism,'"[14] the DISCO "diagnoses on levels of ability to elicit a picture of the whole child or adult through the story of their development and behaviour from infancy onwards."[15] The DISCO is useful for any level of IQ from profoundly impaired to highly gifted; for any expression of the autism spectrum; and for identifying conditions frequently associated with the spectrum, including attentional difficulties, disruptive behaviors, and motor skill and sensory processing impairments.[16] As Wing describes it, the DISCO was designed to give a complete clinical portrait of the child:

> Our purpose was to develop a clinical instrument, which didn't ask, does this person have autism?... What problems, what advantages and skills does this person have? Now that is a very different question than "has this person got autism?" It is ever so hard to convey this to people....
>
> What the DISCO tries to do ... is to examine the history right from infancy onwards of the individual concerned, and try to trace the ways in which different aspects of development have gone right or gone wrong or gone differently so that we can see how it is that a person behaves in this way at this particular time. Then, we can work out "This bit's good," "This needs encouraging," "This bit's given the person a lot of difficulty, so what can we do about it?"
>
> We have also built in the capacity for getting computerized diagnoses using the standard criteria as in the ICD 10 system, the DSM-IV system.... We built these in but that is not the main purpose.... What we want

> to know is what makes this person tick in the way they are ticking? It's fascinating … it's a piece of detective work, how this person has reached this point. …
>
> It seems to us from our experience that it is far more important than deciding whether or not someone fits classic criteria. We have come across a lot of people who don't fit any of the classic criteria, but deep down they actually have poor development of their social understanding and their capacity for planning. These two things (they may not have anything else) in life are going to be hellishly difficult for them, and they're going to get into all kinds of silly situations and terrible trouble, even legal trouble as a result. … [T]heir social understanding is very, very poor, and their capacity for planning and imagining the consequences of their actions is very poor. … This to us is what matters.[17]

As you can see, the DISCO is designed to gather a picture of the development of the whole child from infancy onward. Its principal aim is to offer parents and caregivers an accurate picture of the child's strengths and weaknesses, not simply to determine whether a child does or does not qualify for a particular diagnosis of autism or ADHD, among others. Likewise, the DISCO teases out hidden social and executive function difficulties that severely impact the quality of life of so many of the 2e population over the course of a lifetime. Also important is that it creates a portrait of the child that includes the skills and strengths that can and should be developed even as it charts a course for interventions and therapies. Unfortunately, although the DISCO is used internationally, it is largely unavailable in the United States.

Even though the DISCO, ADI-R, and other screening tools do not specifically test for IQ, intelligence is a factor considered in the assessment process. Regardless of the tool used, evaluators of autism understand that to obtain a complete clinical picture, they must count IQ as a factor. Whether IQ is considered in treatment is another matter, especially considering that the disabilities world operates from a deficits-based model instead of a whole child approach when planning interventions. This is why parents must make certain that the treatment professional they select understands and is willing to consider both giftedness and developmental disabilities, and is willing to encourage a variety of concurrent, alternative therapies to minimize deficits and improve behaviors.

Treating the Whole Child

We want to reiterate that used very carefully and conservatively, medication can be an effective tool in a comprehensive therapeutic plan.

In the whole child model, the child's giftedness and areas of strength are the primary focus. These should be a central factor when choosing interventions and treatments for the child. In fact, giftedness should be the first consideration even before the disability, as the disability is so much more obvious and problematic. Understandably, most parents desire alternatives to medication whenever possible and are interested in therapies that enhance a child's development rather than mask symptoms.

With early intervention, many of these therapies have been shown to minimize the deficits, thereby improving the likelihood of positive life outcomes for children. At the same time, the therapies we present are not a cure for the impairments in 2e children. Education is such a major part of the intervention process that we have devoted the next chapter to educational needs and interventions for 2e children. In the Additional Resources section, we list the resources and contact information of organizations, groups, and individuals whose practices support the needs of 2e children.

What follows is an overview of various types of professionals and the services they offer in relation to the impairments and behaviors common in 2e children—for example, social communication deficits, imagination–executive function deficits, and motor skill and sensory processing impairments. When these impairments are effectively supported, their corresponding problematic behaviors, such as inattention, hyperactivity, impulsivity, explosive outbursts, and adherence to routine, may be minimized as well, enabling parents and professionals to focus on developing the real strengths of the 2e child. A recent study shows that "when co-morbidities are addressed, individuals with ASD have improved concentration, benefit from more educational programs, and exhibit fewer challenging behaviors."[18] Some specific areas we address are

- Speech-language therapy
- Occupational therapy and sensory integration
- Diet and nutrition
- Exercise
- Counseling and coaching

When used in conjunction with one another as part of a comprehensive treatment plan to support the child, these therapies have proven effective in enhancing the quality of life for 2e children.

Speech-Language Therapy

With regard to speech and language, 2e children experience several types of difficulties, ranging from the actual use and fluency of language to the social use of language. In children with HFA/AS, language and communication problems are central to the autistic impairment and affect quality of life regardless of the child's level of functioning. Because of the varied range of abilities in 2e children, especially those with HFA/AS, speech-language therapy can enhance intentional communication and help children develop skills in the expression of ideas, social reciprocity, and the verbal and nonverbal aspects of social interaction.[19] In fact,

Agnes Burger-Veltmeijer, a specialist and researcher in dual exceptionalities, states that although 2e children may not show enough characteristics of ASD for a diagnosis, they "are more or less in need of an ASD-like treatment" when it comes to social communication difficulties.[20]

The American Speech-Language-Hearing Association (ASHA) states in its position statement that "due to the pervasive nature of social communication impairment, regardless of age, cognitive abilities, or performance on standardized testing of formal language skills, individuals with ASD should be eligible for speech-language services."[21] On its Web site, ASHA lists several ways that speech-language therapy can assist children with social communication impairments.

According to ASHA guidelines, speech-language therapists are trained to recognize that challenging behaviors are communication and to create therapies that support more positive expressions by developing the child's ability to initiate communication; to comprehend verbal and nonverbal communication at home, school, and other social environments; to communicate for many reasons, including the development of friendships and peer relations; and to develop practical alternatives to challenging behaviors by enhancing social communication abilities. In other words, a good speech-language therapist will assist in alleviating the verbal and nonverbal social communication deficits that affect the whole child's behavior and functioning. (See Chapter Ten for a look at Michelle Garcia Winner's Social Thinking, an excellent curriculum that supports this aim.)

Occupational Therapy and Sensory Integration

Characteristically, 2e children with HFA/AS face a number of motor skill impairments as well as sensory processing deficits. These challenges often result in problem behaviors, which can be alleviated with carefully designed therapeutic programs to assist with the child's functioning in everyday environments. Because the world can be a frightening, painful place for children whose central nervous systems are unable to modulate sensory input, occupational therapy (OT) is essential for 2e children with sensory and physical overexcitabilities. OT minimizes difficulties associated with these oversensitivities and supports the child's ability to pay attention, remain still, coordinate movement and balance, and function in home, academic, and social environments.

Specifically, OT and sensory integration therapies assist with issues of balance, clumsiness, coordination, and fine and gross motor skills. These therapies range from individual sessions to work on specific functional and sensory issues to group therapies and activities, such as swimming, hippotherapy (therapies on horseback), gym time, music and movement, aromatherapy, and others. By retraining the brain and central nervous system to support increased stimulation from the surrounding environment, these activities greatly enhance the 2e child's ability to participate in school and activities where sensory overload is likely to occur.

Some specific sensory integration therapies that have proven effective in reducing challenging behaviors and improving performance are chiropractics and massage.

Chiropractics

Chiropractic therapy can alleviate symptoms of inattentiveness, hyperactivity, anxiety, and stress. This form of treatment is completely natural and can ease symptoms without side effects that normally occur with medications. Chiropractic therapy eases the symptoms of vertebral subluxation, or misalignment, a condition that increases or decreases "the rate at which nerve messages travel from brain to body and back," thereby "affecting the communication between the brain and body."[22] Studies have shown that chiropractic care improves many symptoms associated with sensory and physical overexcitabilities as well as autism spectrum disorders.[23]

Massage Therapy

This alternative therapy has particular benefits for children with ASD. Massage has been shown to ease sleep disturbances, which is particularly important for 2e children with HFA/AS because these children often have difficulties with sleep.[24] Temple, who invented the "squeeze machine," extols the benefits of massage in minimizing many associated symptoms of ASD. Massage therapy has been shown to reduce anxiety, stereotypic behaviors, hyperactivity, and sensory symptoms as well as to improve concentration and aggressive behaviors in children.[25] In short, massage therapy improves inattentiveness, aggression, anxiety, sleep difficulties, and sensory overload; promotes overall well-being; and is widely supported as an effective therapy for all children, but especially those with sensory, emotional, and physical overexcitabilities.

Diet and Nutrition

When discussing diet and nutrition, common sense should be the rule. Throughout childhood, a healthy, balanced diet of whole grains, fresh fruits and vegetables, and hormone-free meats, poultry, dairy, and eggs actually enhances a child's IQ. In fact, a recent study showed that diets which consist mainly of processed foods that are high in fat and sugar *lower* the IQs of children. The study, which appeared in the *Journal of Epidemiology and Community Health*, shows that a diet of predominantly processed foods at the age of three "was associated with a lower IQ at the age of 8.5" and suggests that the diet a child consumes as a toddler impacts IQ at a later age even if dietary habits change.[26] The study concluded that because the brain grows faster during the period from birth to three years, good nutrition during this period can maximize brain growth. Thus it is important that parents provide the healthiest diet possible during the early years.

It almost goes without saying that children with extreme sensitivity and food allergies should avoid certain foods. Literature abounds, some of it of questionable value, on specialized diets and protocols for children on the autism spectrum. Although it is commonly reported that gluten, a protein found in wheat, rye, oats, and barley, as well as casein, a protein in dairy products, contribute to aggression, hyperactivity, and inattentiveness, recent studies are inconclusive when attempting to show the widespread efficacy of a gluten- and casein-free diet for improving symptoms of autism.[27] Still, numerous parents testify to the relief that gluten- and casein-free diets have given their children.

Exercise

Several years ago, the relationship between exercise, brain function, and achievement was still speculative, but increasingly the importance of exercise is being recognized at all levels of our society. Exercise is an essential component of an effective treatment plan, helping improve coordination, motor skills, and one's ability to learn. As Wing explains, regular exercise also helps reduce aggressive behaviors and stereotyped patterns in thinking and movement.[28] Further, group activities such as sports increase social abilities as well as cognition.

John Ratey, associate clinical professor of psychiatry at Harvard Medical School, has studied the benefits of exercise extensively. In his book *A User's Guide to the Brain*, Ratey states that "each person's capacity to master new and remember old information is improved by biological changes in the brain brought on by physical activity."[29] His latest book, *Spark: The Revolutionary New Science of Exercise and the Brain*, builds on this concept and examines how exercise improves cognition and brain performance, helps children control stress and anxiety, improves focus and attention, and improves overall well-being.

Counseling and Coaching

For 2e children, counseling and coaching have both proven effective for supporting areas of strength and weakness.

Counseling

Numerous studies since the early 1980s have shown that counseling can be a very helpful support for 2e children. Counseling assists the 2e child process the awareness that he is different from his peers and learn to embrace his differences rather than resent them. It aids the child in gaining the ability to process social difficulties, and supports alternative approaches and behaviors. Likewise, counseling can help the 2e child process the frustration, self-criticism, and emotional challenges of perfectionism.[30] According to the *2e Twice-Exceptional Newsletter*, both individual and group counseling have been shown to benefit 2e children.[31] Group counseling can be particularly effective in helping the 2e child see that although he is unique, the challenges he faces are common in others with dual exceptionalities. As with any of the suggested therapies, parents must be sure to find a counselor who understands the complex challenges and needs of 2e children.

Life Coaching

Developed within the field of ADHD, coaching is a particularly effective therapy to support 2e children in areas of weakness in executive functioning. According to the American Coaching Association, a life coach helps individuals "set goals, accept limitations and acknowledge strengths, develop social skills, and create strategies that enable them to be more effective in managing their day-to-day lives."[32] In particular, 2e coaches help clients develop "self awareness, self confidence and self efficacy by helping them discover and develop their strengths and using them to overcome their areas of difficulty."[33] They do this by establishing a pattern of frequent communication with clients to make sure they are focused and working steadily toward their goals. Because a life coach works closely with the child, it is critical to choose one whose personality is a good fit and who understands the unique functional, social, and emotional challenges 2e children face.

The Importance of Diagnosing and Treating the Whole Child

Clearly, 2e children stand to benefit significantly from the widest range of treatment options available. Because of their complex profiles, these children need more than a single therapy. In fact, most of them need a variety of interventions to support multiple areas of weakness—areas that remain unidentified and misunderstood by clinicians who must rely on the categorical system for diagnosing disorders.

Although the diagnostic tools designed using DSM criteria are wonderful for supporting research, they are limited in their usefulness at the clinical level, especially with regard to 2e children with HFA/AS. Instead of providing a complete clinical portrait of the child's abilities and impairments, category-based tools narrowly focus on determining whether a child does or does not have enough symptoms to qualify for a diagnosis. When it comes to 2e children with HFA/AS, such diagnostic instruments as the ADI-R and ADOS are limited in their ability to diagnose autism in the higher-functioning population. As a result, these children are either relegated to an ADHD diagnosis with its attending comorbidities and poor understanding of the impairments, or they remain undiagnosed. In both cases, many high-functioning 2e children are ineligible for the therapies and services that would help them attain a better life outcome. In the end, their giftedness and our society suffer.

However, even as new tools emerge, a better, more comprehensive diagnostic tool, the DISCO, has been in use for over thirty years. Because it is dimensionally based, the DISCO assesses children on multiple areas of functioning, leading to a complete picture of the child's strengths and impairments. It has also been proven to effectively diagnose disorders along the entire spectrum from classic autism to HFA/AS, allowing most children whose IQs mask the autistic impairment to receive the diagnosis they need.

Likewise, because it provides a complete clinical portrait of the 2e child, the DISCO allows parents and professionals to develop a treatment plan that incorporates a range of therapies to target the child's unique needs.

In short, once the 2e child's strengths and challenges are identified, therapeutic as well as educational supports can be swiftly implemented to maximize functioning and to minimize deficits. The DISCO has been shown to be more sensitive to the HFA/AS population, especially in its ability to detect social communication impairments, attention difficulties, hyperactivity, motor skill and sensory processing deficits, and executive function impairments. Likewise, because it has algorithms tied to the DSM descriptions of autism and Asperger's syndrome, the DISCO can yield the diagnosis our children need to be eligible for services. It has also been proven to support the needs of researchers. However, as we noted earlier, this valuable instrument remains largely unavailable to clinicians, researchers, and parents in the United States, though efforts are under way to make the DISCO more widely available.

Suggested Resources

What follows is information about several excellent resources for information on the therapies discussed in this chapter. Because parents often need advice on how to adapt therapies to suit their child's needs, we encourage you to join a local or online support group to share ideas, information, and to learn from one another. For more specific information about online support groups, see the Additional Resources section.

Speech-language pathology

American Speech-Language-Hearing Association (www.ASHA.org)

Occupational therapy

American Occupational Therapy Association, Inc. (www.AOTA.org)

Sensory integration

Sensory Processing Disorder Foundation (www.SPDfoundation.net)

The Out-of-Sync Child—Carol Kranowitz (http://out-of-sync-child.com/)

Chiropractic and massage therapy

American Chiropractic Association (www.acatoday.org)

International Chiropractic Pediatric Association (www.icpa4kids.org)

American Massage Therapy Association (www.amtamassage.org)

Life coaching

International Coach Federation (www.coachfederation.org)

10

Educating the Whole Child

Nurturing Abilities and Supporting Challenges

True happiness involves the full use of one's power and talents.

John W. Gardiner

I've noticed an alarming trend. Ten-year-olds come up to me and want to talk about their autism, not about what they've done at the science fair. They're fixated on their autism instead of their special interests. We've developed a handicapped mentality where the focus is on the disability. So Temple believes, and we agree. Too much emphasis is placed on the deficits instead of on the talents of 2e children.

Lost in the complicated interplay between the diagnostic and education systems, too many of our 2e students' talents remain unrecognized and undeveloped. Instead, these students are more likely to be labeled as behaviorally disordered, oppositional and defiant, emotionally disordered, developmentally delayed, learning disabled, or some combination of these, rather than as gifted. Sadly, teachers are ill-prepared to meet the unique blend of strengths and challenges that characterize 2e students.

In an era when teacher accountability and academic achievement continues to be emphasized in public education because of NCLB, teachers recognize that academic achievement and effective behavior management are inextricably bound together. Yet these same teachers are frustrated and confused by the chronic behavioral problems they face from students diagnosed with social, emotional, and behavioral disorders. Statistically, the number of students identified as emotionally disturbed has more than doubled since 1976, and the number of those receiving educational supports for autism has increased tenfold since 1994; at the same time, the numbers of students receiving services for other health impairments (OHI) (the category that includes ADHD) as well as learning disabilities continue to grow.[1]

Unfortunately, the DSM system creates and promotes the idea that giftedness and such disorders as ADHD and ASD are distinct and unrelated; therefore, many teachers are unaware of *why* 2e students struggle with chronic behavioral problems. Teachers receive only cursory treatment of giftedness, ASD, ADHD, and related disorders in their college special education programs, and this information is based on the DSM explanations of ADHD and autism. As a result, teachers must daily deal with challenging behaviors without ever understanding how behaviors identified and understood as ADHD are often fueled by the identical deficits and hidden impairments in autism or by traits of giftedness.

A new understanding of the relatedness and similarities of these conditions would help educators serve 2e children much more sensitively and effectively. IEP teams could develop more individually specialized plans to target the identified impairments and reduce challenging behaviors. More individualized and specific IEPs also ensure student progress and emotional well-being by making certain that all members of the educational team—especially general education teachers—"get" that the presence of challenging behaviors likely indicates the presence of one or more of these associated impairments as well as the possibility of giftedness. (Such "consciousness raising" might also have the long-term benefit of increasing the possibility that more of the hidden 2e population will be identified.)

There are dimensional forms of screening that readily identify the presence and relative impact of these hidden impairments on a child's functioning. These forms of assessment move beyond the diagnosis of a particular condition and examine all areas of functioning (strengths and weaknesses) to assess the needs of the whole child. The value of such assessment is that safe and proven therapies and interventions that have been shown to improve a child's functioning and minimize these deficits can be employed, reducing reliance on dangerous and powerful medications. By approaching these disorders differently, educators, other professionals, and parents can develop a toolbox of interventions from which to effectively design an IEP and implement instruction that will truly benefit the 2e child.

In business, an owner needs to have an accurate inventory of goods and staff to chart a direction for growth; similarly, parents and teachers also need a proper inventory based on a clear understanding of the 2e child's skills and deficits to select the most effective interventions and therapies. In the whole of educational programming, but especially in the realm of giftedness and 2e, there needs to be a shift to dimensional assessment tools and strengths-based programming in order to create an environment where 2e learners receive rigorous instruction along with individual accommodations and adaptations to ensure that their needs are met. One such tool, the DISCO, bridges the mental health and education systems. We are working to make it, along with other forms of dimensional assessments, more widely available in the United States.

This chapter examines several considerations for educators who wish to design a classroom and curriculum appropriate for 2e students, and for parents who need to understand what to look for in schools claiming to meet the needs of 2e children.

Identifying 2e Students: Intellectual Ability, Achievement, and Creativity

The first step to developing an effective program is to properly identify the 2e learner—a difficult feat in an education system that generally favors children with learning disabilities or giftedness, but rarely both.

Although 2e students share many similarities with learning-disabled and gifted populations, they also have their own unique profile as a population: their performance is inconsistent; their development is asynchronous; and their skills are uneven.[2] At the same time, this population also includes some of our most extraordinarily gifted individuals. To accurately identify and educate the whole child, parents and professionals must understand the dichotomous and seemingly contradictory nature of dual exceptionalities.

The whole child model rests on an accurate psychological portrait of a child's giftedness and disabilities. Too often parents are under the assumption that most treatment professionals and educational professionals—counselors, psychologists, psychiatrists—understand the unique educational, creative, social, emotional, and behavioral profiles of 2e children. However, this assumption is unfounded. In fact, Johns Hopkins University has conducted an ongoing survey since 2000 which shows that although a majority of school districts nationwide have expressed interest in identifying and meeting the needs of 2e students, they have no procedures in place.[3] Instead, parents must be painstaking in their pursuit of professionals who are qualified to identify and support the complex needs of the gifted and learning-disabled child.

In particular, there are four areas that must be examined when assessing a child for giftedness and learning disabilities: intellectual ability, achievement and performance, and creativity.

Intellectual Ability

In the general education classroom, proficiency does not always equal accomplishment for 2e students, nor is it an accurate indicator of teacher competency. A student who is labeled with a learning disorder or other disability and who consistently scores as proficient on standardized assessments in one or more content areas may be gifted as well. Early assessment is vital with regard to future life outcomes, because once giftedness is recognized and nurtured, the child's strengths can become the focus of educational planning and programming.

When looking at the 2e learner, the whole child perspective becomes even more important in identifying areas of potential giftedness, especially with regard to early identification for appropriate educational programming. As Linda Silverman, director of the Gifted Development Center in Colorado, explains, "superior abilities should be recognized as a sign of giftedness and developed to the fullest extent possible, regardless of indications that the child is less advanced in other areas."[4]

When considering IQ testing, Silverman explained in an interview with us why a professional assessment is preferable over testing offered through public school systems, especially with regard to 2e children:

> Limited funding for the identification of gifted children in schools generally confines gifted assessment to IQ screeners administered by teachers or gifted program personnel. Screeners are used for accepting or rejecting children from gifted programs, but lack in-depth diagnostic capability.... They also tend to average the strengths and weaknesses of twice-exceptional children (gifted with learning deficits), yielding scores too low for gifted program admission. They rarely reveal that a child might be highly gifted. Screeners fail to provide

the in-depth information needed to guide educational planning.

In short, widespread screening in schools, such as that proposed by supporters of RtI (discussed in Chapter Eight), will miss a significant portion of the 2e population.

In contrast, a professional assessment, though costlier, identifies areas of superior ability and "provides objective verification of the child's needs and prescribes accommodations, relieving some of the parent's burden."[5] Individual assessment by a professional identifies the true extent of a child's abilities as well as the presence of learning disabilities. A professional assessment also yields an educational intervention plan that addresses both strengths and weaknesses, thereby meeting the needs of the whole child.[6]

Typically, a professional assessment includes IQ assessment and the administration of achievement tests to measure discrepancies between ability and achievement. Common IQ tests include the Wechsler Preschool and Primary Scale of Intelligence-III (WPPSI-III) for children ages two years, six months, to seven years, three months; the Wechsler Intelligence Scale for Children (WISC-IV) for children ages six to sixteen years, and the Stanford-Binet, which is the oldest. At the Gifted Development Center, the Stanford-Binet is given only if a child reaches the highest score on two or more subtests on the WISC that are rich in abstract thinking. Discrepancies in scores indicate areas that warrant further testing to determine the presence of learning disabilities. Many professionals use the Ravens Progressive Matrices, which are similar to the performance subtest on WISC-IV. The Ravens is used to measure abstract thinking ability, though this assessment will underpredict IQ in children who have problems with visual memory or directionality.[7] The best IQ assessments are those that rely on multiple types and sources of information.

Achievement and Performance

IQ assessments are often paired with achievement testing and creativity tests to determine areas of giftedness. One widely used achievement test is the Woodcock-Johnson Test of Achievement, which shows how well a student is performing in a particular subject area. Likewise, all states administer some form of achievement tests, which are often used as part of the body of evidence for a student's inclusion in gifted programming. IQ and achievement tests are also sometimes paired with portfolios that include journal entries, writing pieces, teachers' comments, and other works to reveal and assess the student's thought process and original ideas for evidence of distinguished performance, especially when students do not test well.

Creativity

Although underachievement and lack of motivation are common in 2e students, high motivation in one or more areas of interest is an indication of creative potential and possible giftedness. A highly valuable and recommended form of assessment for identifying 2e students is creativity testing. This form of testing yields valuable and reliable insights into a student's creative potential over the course of his lifetime. The standard is the Torrance Test of Creative Thinking, which measures divergent thinking, fluency, flexibility, originality, and elaboration.[8] Other aspects of creativity are generally measured by the following tests, most of which can be administered by teachers:[9]

- *Divergent thinking:* Guilford's Alternative Uses Task
- *Convergent thinking:* Insight Problems; Remote Associations Task
- *Artistic thinking:* Barron-Welsh Art Scale
- *Self-assessment:* Khatena-Torrance Creative Perception Inventory; the Creativity Behavior Inventory; Gough Personality Style
- *Early assessment:* Preschool and Kindergarten Interests Descriptors

Finally, with respect to giftedness, experts often recommend that assessment also include the Scales for Rating the Behavioral

Characteristics of Superior Students (SRBCSS). Originally developed in the 1970s by several gifted-2e experts, including Joseph S. Renzulli, these scales have been updated over the past thirty years. They measure the following characteristics of gifted learners and can be administered in the classroom:[10]

- Learning
- Creativity
- Motivation
- Leadership
- Artistic
- Musical
- Dramatics
- Communication (precision and expression)
- Planning
- Mathematics
- Reading
- Science
- Technology

Moving Beyond Identification: The IEP

Once a student has been identified as twice exceptional, a highly specific individualized education plan (IEP) is created to ensure that the student receives the accommodations, supports, and adaptations necessary to achieve success. Education specialists, special education teachers, parents, and, sometimes, outside advocacy experts design the content of the IEP, although it is the regular education teacher's legal and professional responsibility to ensure and prove that the instructional requirements are consistently met in the classroom. Thus it is crucial that the IEP be effectively written so that teachers can offer appropriate instruction and support to 2e students.

An effective IEP, according to Diane Twachtman-Cullen—a speech-language pathologist whose work with students labeled with HFA/AS, ADHD, and disorders of communication is respected globally—must be based on a proper understanding of the hidden deficits common to these disorders. In their new book titled *The IEP from A to Z,* Twachtman-Cullen and her daughter Jennifer Twachtman-Bassett explain that these conditions share common educational needs "in the areas of cognitive and social-cognitive functioning ... communication and language," but the invisible nature of these conditions often keeps students from being identified.[11] Instead, as we have shown, many of these students "don't present with obvious signs of disability but rather with certain behaviors" that are misconstrued as "willful or volitional, or as reflecting a lack of motivation or laziness." As a result, educators often misperceive the expressions of these hidden deficits as "bad behavior," and the student's educational and emotional needs are unmet in the classroom.

To enable classroom teachers to deliver quality instruction, an effective IEP must be based on an accurate understanding of the underlying deficits common to HFA/AS and ADHD. The IEP must specifically state the goals, conditions, and methodologies classroom teachers are to use in designing instruction for students.[12] According to Twachtman-Cullen and Twachtman-Bassett, an effective IEP for students with these conditions must reflect an inherent understanding of the common impairments and behaviors in order (1) to ensure progress by establishing clear goals and appropriate methodologies that are educationally beneficial to the child, and (2) to ensure the student's emotional well-being and social development within the general education classroom.

At the same time, *all* rank-and-file teachers and school personnel must be educated in the underlying deficits and their concurrent behavioral manifestations as well as in the highly specialized educational needs of 2e students in order for them to design an instructional environment that supports the social-emotional needs, offers a strength-based focus, and provides learning supports necessary to deliver a quality education to 2e students.

Best Practices for 2e Students

In the general education classroom, the teacher is responsible for creating a climate and designing instruction that supports learning for all students. With regard to 2e students, however, there is the added responsibility of meeting the legally mandated requirements of the IEP.

Best practices for 2e students are rooted in dually differentiated instruction that fosters areas of strength and interest while providing supports for areas of weakness. In general, best practices for 2e students include the following:[13]

- Gifted instruction in areas of strength
- Instruction in skills and strategies for areas affected by disabilities
- Differentiated programs that include individualized adaptations, accommodations, and modifications
- Programming to support social-emotional development
- Comprehensive case management to ensure coordination of all aspects of the IEP and to review student progress

These are all elements that parents should look for when considering an educational program for the 2e student.

Educating 2e Students: Meeting the Needs of the Whole Child

General education teachers can safely assume that they will have one or more 2e students in their classroom at some point, whether or not these students have been formally identified. This being said, many of the following suggestions for developing a classroom that supports 2e learners are widely appropriate, except where specified, for students who are mildly to moderately impaired as well as for students with the multiple conditions embodied by this book's description of dual exceptionalities.

Classroom Climate

A classroom that successfully meets the needs of 2e learners will meet the needs of all students. Creating and maintaining a safe, nurturing, yet challenging environment is fundamental to supporting the needs of 2e learners. Characteristically, teachers create this climate through programming that includes strategies for supporting the academic and social-emotional challenges of students in a variety of ways, including the following:[14]

Academic	Social-Emotional
Is aware of students' strengths and needs	Teaches social curriculum
Accommodates multiple learning styles and intelligences	Respects everyone
Creates a visually supportive and stimulating environment	Encourages open exchange of ideas
Posts standards and expectations for performance	Connects students through shared interests and strengths
Encourages self-advocacy	Teaches self-advocacy
Uses flexible groupings	Teaches students ways to handle frustrations
Creates an interactive classroom	Offers choices
Centers on individualized programming	Offers enrichment activities
Encourages active listening	Teaches planning and goal setting
Teaches strategies for managing conflict	Is structured yet flexible

(*continued*)

Academic	Social-Emotional
Incorporates multimedia resources	Is organized
Incorporates technological supports: calculators, word processors, spell checkers	Encourages attitude of self-efficacy
Offers multiple means of assessment	

Most literature on 2e students addresses two central components that are integral to a successful educational program: (1) social and emotional supports and (2) strengths and interest-based accommodations. Both of these areas are essential parts of a complete system of instructional delivery and support for 2e students. For the purposes of this book, we have focused on ways to integrate these three areas at the classroom level, though to fully meet 2e students' needs, these components would be part of a schoolwide approach to learning.

Social and Emotional Supports

Social and emotional supports are an aspect of educational programming that is essential to helping 2e students experience success in the classroom. Teachers need to be aware of the social and emotional challenges 2e students face and should provide explicit instruction in social thinking as well as create an environment that is safe and supportive.

Supporting Social Thinking

One crucial area of functioning that frequently leads educators to misperceive the 2e student is social thinking. *Social thinking*, or social cognition, is a critical part of our intelligence frequently taken for granted. As world-renowned speech-language pathologist Michelle Garcia Winner explains, "Social thinking develops from birth, much like walking; it is intuitively 'hard wired' into most people to work at learning how the social world works."[15] We use social thinking in everyday activities, such as watching television or reading a novel, and anytime we consider another's perspective. Clearly, social thinking has a significant impact on academic performance and success.

Winner, creator of the internationally acclaimed Social Thinking curriculum, explains that 2e students typically exhibit weaknesses in one or more of the following areas of social knowledge and skills:[16]

- Recognition and understanding of the "hidden rules" of social situations
- Perspective taking (along with language processing)
- Visual interpretation of the social context and cues
- The ability to formulate a related response (verbal or nonverbal) in a very short period of time (from milliseconds up to three seconds)

Perspective taking, more formally known as theory of mind (which we also discussed in Chapter Four), is an ability that allows individuals "to consider the points of view, emotions, thoughts, beliefs, prior knowledge and intentions of others"[17] and to use this information when interacting with the world around them. As Winner explains,

> [T]he ability to take perspective is vital to relate to others, not only for the purpose of socialization, but also to interpret meaning that is critical for academic work and personal problem solving skills critical for living independently as an adult.[18]

Students with social deficits are also usually students who struggle academically. Deficiencies in social thinking often become apparent in the classroom during more abstract academic activities, such as writing, reading for comprehension in literature, organizing and planning assignments, and working word problems in math. Commonly, students who have been identified as exceptionally bright are able to "hold it together" academically and emotionally—that is, until the demands of abstract thinking in the classroom along with the increased demands of social thinking exceed their abilities to compensate for the social thinking deficits.

Deficits in social thinking must be taken seriously in education. They affect not only academic performance but also how students view themselves and others. Because most education systems are just starting to understand, acknowledge, and address social learning disabilities, students who are weak in social thinking are often "perceived as having behavior problems or even being emotionally disturbed."[19] Students with average to above-average IQs are often diagnosed with anxiety, depression, and OCD in early adolescence, or even in childhood.[20] Bright children with social thinking deficits may become overwhelmed to the point that they experience suicidal thoughts or rages in response to the emotional side effects of being different socially.[21]

Unfortunately, the standardized tests used to assess for IQ and achievement are inadequate when attempting to identify the full impact of a social learning disability. Few students with social thinking deficits have an IEP for helping them learn more vital abstract concepts and associated skills, such as group participation, reading comprehension, written expression, flexible thinking and problem solving, and organization. Further, teachers are inadequately trained in recognizing, understanding, and supporting these deficits in students, though such deficits have a dramatic impact on academic and, ultimately, life outcomes.

A variety of supports have been adapted by autism treatment professionals and are appropriate for parents with children who have social deficits. In particular, we recommend literature by Michelle Garcia Winner, Diane Twachtman-Cullen, Brenda Smith Myles, Barry Prizant, and Carol Gray.

Supporting Emotional Needs

Emotional needs in the classroom are inextricably tied to our children's hidden impairments. Just as social thinking deficits threaten the mental and emotional stability of many 2e students, so do misdiagnosed or undiagnosed anxiety, OCD, sensory processing difficulties, depression, and perfectionism. The explosive behaviors that arise from these unrecognized and unmet needs also threaten stability at school and at home.

An emotionally safe, supportive environment begins with the teacher and extends to each individual student. Here are some strategies teachers can use to establish and maintain a safe environment for everyone:

1. *Have a positive attitude*. Show concern for and interest in each student through individual conversations. Model appropriate behavior by staying calm in the face of conflict. Include books, activities, and themes that reflect the individual interests of students when appropriate.
2. *Support diversity in the classroom*. Encourage students to recognize and value all kinds of diversity—physical, cultural, and educational. Focus on the strengths of each student and draw from these during instruction to allow the individual to be valued for his contributions to the class. Encourage the child to "own" his giftedness.[22] Encourage students to give their best, but avoid unreasonable expectations or demands.
3. *Support social development through carefully designed and implemented group work*. Provide opportunities for monitored peer involvement. Ask students to share some aspect of themselves through art, music, or a special area of interest. Encourage students to advocate for themselves.

4. *Have a zero-tolerance policy when it comes to teasing, bullying, verbal violence, and physical altercations.*
5. *Consider the sensory needs of 2e children in the classroom.* Use visual supports to communicate due dates, schedules, and important information. Monitor noise levels. Avoid clutter. Keep the temperature moderate. Avoid fluorescent lighting if possible. Establish and maintain predictable routines.[23]

Creating a socially predictable climate of tolerance and respect within a well-organized environment supports the emotional needs of 2e children.

Strengths- and Interest-Based Instruction in the Classroom

Undoubtedly, the most important aspects of the 2e profile are the student's exceptional abilities and areas of interest. These strengths hold the key to the student's future because this is how he will be able to fulfill his unique purpose. An effective educational program must center on utilizing and developing these strengths to keep the student engaged in the learning process.

For the purpose of this discussion, we present a broad overview of strategies that are appropriate for all content areas, with the idea that interested readers will apply these to the best of their abilities within the confines of more specific requirements within the larger school system.

The following list is a set of characteristics of strengths-based instruction gleaned from a handful of public school districts and schools that truly "get" 2e students and their educational needs.[24] These programs understand the importance of remediating academic difficulties in the context of a strengths-based program.

Characteristics of Strengths-Based Programming

- Incorporates activities and tasks that fit students' learning styles, preferences, and individual strengths
- Allows student choice
- Utilizes multimodal instruction

- Involves students in designing criteria for assessment
- Offers multiple means of demonstrating knowledge
- Offers accelerated content
- Allows students to "go deeper" in areas of interests
- Provides hands-on learning experiences
- Grounds learning in real life tasks

Susan Winebrenner, 2e advocate, author, and international education consultant, advises that teachers in general education classes follow these principles for teaching 2e students:[25]

- In areas of strength, differentiate and compact curriculum as for gifted students.
- During instructional time devoted to areas of strength, avoid the temptation to remediate in areas of weakness.
- In areas of weakness, teach the specific strategies needed to increase success.

In order to support the whole child approach in instruction, teachers must honor the area of giftedness by allowing the child to explore and to grow. At the same time, the child may need targeted instruction in specific strategies to support areas of challenge.

Beyond this principle, here are some other approaches to assist 2e students in their areas of challenge and of strength. These strategies have been adapted from Winebrenner's article "Teaching Strategies for Twice-Exceptional Students."[26]

Challenges

- *Use multimodal instruction*. Incorporate visual supports, movement, rhythm, and hands-on approaches to meet the varied learning needs and styles of students. Keep in mind the visual-spatial learner, the kinesthetic learner, and the auditory-sequential learner when developing lesson plans.
- *Give students the whole picture first*. Teach concepts first, specifics second. Keep in mind that students need to see the

big picture before they can understand how each piece contributes to it.

- *Scaffold learning*. Use the old information ⇒ new information pattern for teaching new concepts. Activate students' prior knowledge before introducing new material. Use visual supports, such as graphic organizers, charts, and graphs, to help students visualize relationships within lessons.
- *Help students develop manageable goals and the skills to support these*. Show students ways to set attainable goals, break them down into smaller ones, and celebrate success with each accomplishment. Model a variety of strategies for time management, including the use of planners, schedules, and calendars.
- *Help students get and stay organized*. Establish and maintain an organized classroom. Model and teach the use of color-coding to organize space, materials, and ideas. Encourage students to develop their own routines for remembering materials and assignments and have them share these with the class. Develop a system that students can use to monitor and adjust their organization routines.
- *Accommodate needs to support success*. Encourage the use of technology. Use ability groupings to provide extra support. Use preferential seating. Allow students to read aloud to one another. Read instructions and test questions aloud to the class. Use direct instruction and reteach when necessary.

Strengths

- *Allow students to demonstrate mastery*. Use pretests as well as other forms of assessment to allow students to "show what they know." (Remember, 2e students often perform poorly on standardized or more formal measures of knowledge.)

Compact instruction to focus only on content that is not known and use extra time for enrichment activities. Use flexible groupings to allow students to move through content faster.

- *Differentiate instruction*. Accelerate curriculum in areas such as reading or mathematics. Allow students to engage in project-based learning beyond the scope of the general curriculum. Offer independent study options tied to some aspect of the curriculum. When appropriate, allow group investigations of real-world problems.
- *Maintain rigor*. Create and maintain high expectations for student achievement. Insist that students consistently work to their level. Insist that students engaged in enrichment activities and independent projects take the same assessments at the same time as the rest of the class to monitor progress and to ensure mastery.

Considering the emphasis on inclusion in our classrooms, the onus is on teachers to adequately identify and support 2e students' weaknesses while recognizing and developing their strengths (assuming that the teacher has been able to identify the 2e students). Educators interested in more content-specific techniques will find resources for ways to support giftedness, specific learning styles, and disabilities in the Additional Resources section.

Educating Beyond the Classroom: Meeting the Social, Emotional, and Learning Needs of 2e Children

Many trends in our culture and in our education system are actually detrimental to the social, emotional, and academic well-being of 2e children. Because our education system is so focused on performance and proficiency, little time or opportunity is left for creativity and real-world learning to take place within the classroom. At the same time, because of curricular constraints arising from mandated testing, 2e children do not get their academic needs met within the classroom. Often the content they are required to learn appears to have little to do with their interests, passions, and strengths. As a result, many 2e students remain unchallenged and unmotivated, and their gifts remain undeveloped.

It falls primarily on parents, caregivers, and interested educators to extend learning beyond the classroom. Although it is rare, there are a few private schools across the nation that understand the full scope of 2e students' social, emotional, and academic needs, and offer alternatives to the customary drills-and-skills approach found in most schools. Unfortunately, for the majority of families, educational options to foster their 2e children are unavailable or too costly; as a result, many parents opt to homeschool their 2e children.

The educational movement toward performance and achievement as opposed to playful learning[27] has robbed our children of opportunities for developing creativity, social skills and behaviors, and vitally constructive relationships with peers who share the same interests and are at the same skill level.[28] Instead, as Temple and countless gifted experts recognize, 2e children need opportunities to work with mentors not only to develop their areas of interest but also to gain essential skills for employment. Recommendations for helping 2e children identify, cultivate, and develop their areas of giftedness fall into three broad categories:

- Discovering areas of interest
- Nurturing areas of interest
- Developing talents

Discovering Areas of Interest

Discovery begins with play, and as Thomas Armstrong, author of *Awakening Your Child's Natural Genius*, notes, imaginative play allows children to develop theories and resolve conflicts in creative ways.[29] Encouraging children to explore their world and offering them a wide variety of options to engage in playful activities allow parents to identify areas of potential giftedness. Because children are naturally curious, parents' exposing them to nature and to a variety of art, literature, science, music, mathematics, and dance will help them discover their areas of interest.

So where do parents begin? The safest place for children to begin exploring their world is at home. Parents can provide numerous opportunities for play and engagement through toys, nature walks, art, music and dance, singing, pretend play, and games.

If the child's behavior permits, taking trips to various playgrounds, parks, museums, science centers, plays, musical productions, and community events allows the child to explore a wide range of interests and absorb an abundance of knowledge at the same time. Ideally, activities should allow for hands-on exploration and movement to ensure engagement. However, parents need to be prepared to leave should the child become overstimulated.

Temple advises parents to encourage and support the child in areas of interest. *Look for areas or activities the child is drawn to and start there. For instance, my mother always encouraged my drawing and art. The fact that as a little kid I produced really good art was something to show that there was something I could do, something that I was talented at. I loved to draw horses. My mother always encouraged me to try drawing different things. I was given books on perspective. I had really nice watercolors. I was given art supplies that were better than the ''kiddie'' stuff.*

In other words, observe what the child is drawn to, what excites and energizes him, and use this as a starting point for discovering the child's natural talents.

Nurturing Areas of Interest

As children develop, the importance of nurturing their interests becomes ever more critical to social functioning and positive life outcomes. Strengthening areas of giftedness and talent gives

2e children a platform for belonging socially. Celebrating their talents shows children that they are accepted for who they are. As Sharon Lind shares in her article "Overexcitability and the Gifted," allowing children the opportunity to explore their passions "shows respect for their abilities and intensities and allows time for them to 'wallow' in what they love, to be validated for who they are."[30] The confidence they gain from having abilities they can share with others will help mediate feelings of isolation and uniqueness (an emotional need common in 2e children, which is often addressed through counseling). Likewise, the attending social and life skills that 2e children gain while engaged in nurturing their talents will serve them throughout their lives.

Once parents identify potential areas of giftedness, fostering their growth allows 2e children to develop a foundation for future careers. As learning specialist Priscilla Vail explains, "Talent withers without nurture."[31] Temple believes that a child's fixations and special interests can be channeled and broadened out into activities that can turn into careers. *If a child draws airplanes all the time, a parent should then ask him to draw the airport and then different parts of the airport, such as the coffee shop or the ticket counter. The child will stay interested because the parts of the airport are linked to his fixation with airplanes.* Although Temple speaks mainly about children who are visual thinkers, her advice holds true for discovering the strengths of all types of minds: begin with the child's special interests.

As Temple stated earlier, she is seeing too much evidence that our culture has developed a "handicapped mentality," one of diminished expectations because a child has been diagnosed with a developmental or learning disability. Because the tendency is to remediate the disability instead of to focus on the strength, 2e children frequently grow up without the necessary experience and skill set to become productive members of our society. In her speaking and consulting for autism, Temple sees too many smart kids with various labels who graduate from high school with absolutely no work skills. She believes that when children get to middle school (eighth and ninth grade), parents and teachers need to engage the child in work activities.

At the same time, Temple underscores the importance of choice when engaging a child in activities to nurture abilities and develop life skills. She describes how her mother made sure she had many opportunities for such learning throughout childhood and even into young adulthood. Her mother even arranged for Temple to work in a research lab while in college.

Mother was always pushing me to try new things. She let me have choices. I had the choice of trying something new for a short time or doing it for a longer time. When she had me start a sewing job two afternoons a week, I found I liked it and did it all summer. I also liked the money I earned.

Of course, getting 2e children to attempt new activities can be extremely challenging, which is why Temple insists that parents keep the focus on the child's special areas of interest. Even though the child may balk, Temple explains that a good parent or teacher has to have an instinct to know how hard to push.

Obviously one cannot push a child to do something he is totally incapable of, but the comfort zone has to be stretched. Mother was always getting me to try new things. One word of caution: NO SURPRISES. When I was fifteen, I was afraid to go to my aunt's ranch. The choice was one week or all summer. Months before going to the ranch, I was shown pictures of the ranch, and I talked on the phone to my aunt at the ranch.

Because of their sensory, social, and executive function difficulties, 2e children have a myriad of reasons to avoid new experiences. Their need for sameness and routine makes it imperative for parents to prepare the child well in advance of the experience. (See Brenda Smith Myles in the Additional Resources section for some excellent suggestions for ways to prepare a child for future experiences.)

Temple's experiences also taught her valuable social skills within the context of work. Although she was nonverbal until the age of four, Temple developed excellent language skills and even served as a freelance writer for a cattle magazine. She explains that through her early work experiences, she learned valuable social and communication skills, including following social rules and manners, initiating conversations, and asking for help. When she had her sewing job, she would have to ask her customers what they wanted and then deliver the product and collect the money. These skills are fundamental to doing business in today's world.

Throughout Temple's childhood, her mother also coached her in the basics of social etiquette, teaching her the fundamental social skills expected in school and the workplace. As Temple describes it, in the 1950s, all children were expected to learn table manners and say "please" and "thank you." When she made a social mistake, her mother instructed her in how to behave. If Temple forgot to say "please," her mother would say, "You forgot to say ..." When Temple then said "please," her mother praised her. Decades later, these social skills still help Temple as she navigates all levels of society and interacts with a wide variety of people.

In short, nurturing a child's giftedness through a variety of experiences also lays the foundation for the development of important social and life skills. This foundation is critical for developing the talents necessary for success.

Developing Gifts and Talents

Perhaps Temple's strongest advice for helping 2e teens discover their unique place in society is to provide project-based learning opportunities and mentoring. Project-based learning allows 2e children an opportunity for hands-on educational experiences while helping them find out the vocational areas best suited to their abilities.

At the same time, project-based learning allows 2e children to demonstrate their knowledge in ways other than through testing and culminates in a portfolio of work that can eventually be used for job interviews. In fact, it was Temple's portfolio of drawings that helped her establish her livestock facilities design business:

> When I first started, I could get few others in that industry to take me seriously. What the engineers and designers saw was a woman (bad enough) with odd, off-putting mannerisms trying to talk with them about her ideas. They only would talk with me and take me seriously after I showed them my portfolio, a collection of drawings and designs.[32]

Likewise, autism expert Stephen Shore rode his "portfolio" to job interviews. Excellent at bicycle repair, Shore obtained a job by showing off his handiwork to the shop owners. Armed with portfolios and projects, 2e teens and adults can minimize any social and personality differences by keeping the focus on their gifts and abilities.[33]

Finally, Temple's strongest recommendation for helping the 2e child overcome the stigma of being different while also discovering and nurturing his unique talents is mentorship. Mentoring is a proven means of developing the 2e child's talents. An effective mentor is matched with the child's interest and personality, has an interest in inspiring confidence and shaping the child's character, and is willing to advocate for him. Mentors help the child use his fixations in a productive, powerful way that affirms the child's identity as a valuable individual. They guide children and teens in discovering their talents, serve as social coaches in social situations and in decision making, and encourage them to persevere. This is particularly important for the underachieving 2e student, who needs success and encouragement to remain motivated and engaged. Mentors come from all areas of life: teachers in areas of specialized interest, professionals in vocational areas, and volunteers and even friends with special interests can all guide and encourage the 2e child to develop his special talents—talents that can lead to successful vocations and positive life outcomes.

Moving Beyond Blame to Success

What is responsible for our children's talents languishing? Our culture? Our schools? According to Temple, both factors hinder 2e children from reaching their full potential. *Our culture doesn't feed the imagination. Kids play video games that show real violence in real time; there's nothing left for them to imagine. Whereas when we would listen to fairy tales, we had to imagine castles, and princesses, and pirates, and the violence. Similarly, the classes that have been removed from many public school curricula employed the type of education 2e children need: hands-on classes where they can be introduced to areas they might be interested in.*

Despite these trends, parents and educators can support the creative, social, emotional, and educational needs of 2e children, but doing so requires considerable creativity, effort, and commitment to put in place the supports needed to foster the strengths of 2e learners. In this era of inclusion, educators must deliberately create and maintain classrooms and design instructional materials with the 2e student in mind. Given the 2e student's range of needs, educators who create a classroom suited to support success for these students will likely have a classroom that supports learning for *all* students.

Likewise, parents charged with the awesome responsibility of raising a 2e child have to deliberately plan ways to meet this child's educational and developmental needs outside the classroom. Parents must provide opportunities for play and exploration to help the child discover his talents. Once they see areas of interest, parents can become more deliberate in their approaches to developing talents, social skills, and life skills by creating safe opportunities for the child to take risks in trying new things in new situations. With the help of mentors and an emphasis on project-based learning, 2e children can flourish in their areas of strength, become highly productive members of society, and discover their identity through their gifts.

Conclusion

Ensuring the Best Future for Our Brightest Minds

Neglect not the gift that is in thee.

1 Timothy 4:14

When we set out to find answers to help 2e children find a way to embrace their strengths in the face of challenges, we never imagined that our journey would lead us through the intricacies of two of the largest systems in America: the DSM and the education system. Yet as we examined the ways that these systems trap our children, we recognized that we had to share what we discovered, regardless of how complicated and controversial it is.

One goal in this book is to help you avoid the pitfalls of losing sight of the gifts because of the disabilities—in short, to develop a whole child perspective. Only when you see the giftedness as the first and most important variable can you fully embrace the whole child approach. Unfortunately, giftedness—as most people understand it and as our educational system still applies it—is equated with achievement, performance, and academic success. Likewise, HFA/AS is often stigmatized because it is commonly associated with the more severe expressions of autism.

Another goal, one that the three of us share with Lorna Wing, is to facilitate communication between the gifted and autism communities. In a recent correspondence, Wing stated that although she has heard of gifted education, until our conversations she was unfamiliar with the expression "2e." She added that "The concept seems quite appropriate, as in the course of our clinical work, my colleagues and I have met many children and adults who have this mixture of disability and one or more remarkable skills." She agrees that it would be "highly beneficial for these communities to share information." Temple also expresses her sincere desire to bring the fields of autism, giftedness, and related disabilities together, especially because she sees so many children and young adults with different labels but very similar symptoms. We all believe that giftedness accompanied by disabilities is an area that remains underserved in both fields. By helping the public understand who these children are, why they're stuck, and how to help them, we hope to advance research into the mental health system and to increase awareness of the varied needs of 2e students in the educational system. In the next sections, we review the major themes of this book.

Who Are They?

> *My most major challenge that causes me endless grief is also a phenomenal ability that has enabled me to achieve a great deal.*
>
> *2e individual on wrongplanet.com*

The field of dual exceptionalities offers a nontraditional portrait of giftedness, one that more fully accounts for the variations along the gifted spectrum. The understanding of intelligence has recently expanded to include multiple intelligences so that more areas of giftedness are recognized. Experts in dual exceptionalities now recognize that gifted children are asynchronous in their development and uneven in their performance, and they experience the world in ways that differ markedly from the experience of typical children. Gifted children embody a range of overexcitabilities that predispose them to behaviors, impressions, and expressions that are often diagnosed as disabilities. Parents and professionals are just beginning to understand how the complicated interplay between gifts and disabilities causes these children to be misunderstood, misdiagnosed, and missed altogether by the mental health and education systems. Unfortunately, because the focus remains on the disability, parents of 2e children are often unaware of the rich, important information contained within the field of giftedness.

Why Are They Stuck?

> *We believe our evidence is sufficiently robust to argue that we need a diagnostic paradigm shift.*
>
> *Dr. Matthew Thompson*

With regard to mental health, there is one main reason why our 2e children are trapped in misdiagnosis: the DSM system. Considering the criticisms of this system on the part of leading experts in the field of psychiatry, this system, which is mired in controversy over its usefulness and validity, appears to be fundamentally flawed. The categorical system has come under fire from clinicians and top-level psychiatrists alike because of its structure and design, which is based on categories of disorders that rely on narrowly defined sets of symptoms to separate those categories from one another.

The DSM

When the system was developed, the symptom sets to define each disorder were derived from consensus and opinion rather than from naturally occurring clusters of symptoms that are found in broader syndromes. In other words, the disorders in the DSM are defined by artificially defined sets of symptoms that may or may not be separate from those of another disorder. As a result, children receive multiple labels, making it seem that they suffer from multiple, unrelated disorders. Instead of helping guide clinicians to the presence of a single disorder that would account for all of the symptoms, the DSM leads to excessive comorbidity in the child, confusion for clinicians and parents, and missed opportunities for effective therapies and interventions.

ADHD

Comorbidity often arises with an ADHD diagnosis. According to researchers in ADHD, this disorder has the highest comorbidity rate possible—60 to 100 percent. The symptom set labeled ADHD is very generic, so much so that its symptoms arise as a result of characteristics of giftedness as well as from the impairments in HFA/AS. In the case of 2e children, the ADHD label is particularly problematic, then, because it obscures more than it clarifies, especially with regard to the hidden impairments in autism. Because ADHD is usually diagnosed with ODD, this mix of labels leads to the use of dangerous combinations of stimulants and antipsychotics to help control children as young as preschool age who are believed to be behaviorally disordered. We decry this practice, especially given the unpredictable effects these medications have on developing brains.

There are also serious questions regarding the validity of ADHD. Debates continue about whether it is a distinct disorder exclusively defined by a specific set of symptoms, especially considering that its symptoms have been shown to result from a myriad of other conditions. Yet ADHD continues to receive a large share of government and private funding for disability research, even though many of these studies duplicate prior studies and findings conducted in the fields of autism and related disorders. Despite the controversy surrounding ADHD, it remains the most commonly diagnosed psychiatric disorder of childhood.[1]

Autism

Although the field of autism has solid explanations for the hidden impairments that can cause "ADHD-like" behaviors, the DSM stands in the way of many 2e children who might receive an autism spectrum diagnosis. The field of autism offers a comprehensive understanding of impairments that can cause hyperactivity, inattention, impulsivity, explosive behaviors, anxiety, and social difficulties. Yet the current paradigm of autism focuses primarily on classic (severe) autism, which is estimated to affect approximately one-third of the total autism population. The remaining two-thirds are the high-functioning individuals, who continue to be poorly identified and frequently misdiagnosed; and as Wing, Temple, and others show, they are often gifted.

These population ratios are extremely significant but, unfortunately, sorely misunderstood, especially considering that the spectra of HFA/AS and giftedness intersect at many points, often making it difficult to distinguish the two groups from one another. Also unfortunate, the stigma attached to the autism label leads parents to believe that an ADHD diagnosis is a better alternative. However, as we hope we have shown, an HFA/AS diagnosis holds more answers for many of the symptoms and challenges, and as a result can help parents discover more effective therapies and interventions for the 2e child.

The Education System

The second system that traps our 2e children is, unfortunately, the system that bridges giftedness with disability, the education system. Within the confines of the regular classroom, our 2e students are likely to fall through the cracks. With the education system's continued emphasis on equality and proficiency rather than on creativity and equity for gifted learners, 2e students are denied the rich learning experiences afforded by project-based learning. Instead of recognizing the presence of untapped potential, many educators tend to view these students as lazy, unmotivated, defiant, and behaviorally disordered rather than as impaired in the ability to interact because of social deficits—a view that arises from the conditioning brought about by the DSM system.

Likewise, with regard to identifying and helping our 2e children, the education system is a perfect storm for these students. In the wake of NCLB and budgetary considerations, our education system is concerned with helping America's lowest-performing students achieve proficiency within the context of a general-level classroom. Consequently, 2e students whose disability and giftedness mask one another are likely to remain unidentified either as gifted or as disabled because proficiency is the gold standard. Those 2e students whose disabilities more obviously affect performance are likely to be identified as disabled. In either situation, the giftedness will probably remain unrecognized and undeveloped, at the expense not only of the individual student but of society as a whole.

How Can We Help Them?

Success is achieved by developing our strengths, not by eliminating our weaknesses.

Marilyn vos Savant

As 2e students remain stuck in two systems that define them as broken rather than as bright, it is our obligation as parents, advocates, and educators to make a strong stand within our communities for a paradigm shift in both of these systems. Parents and professionals must examine their assumptions about the meaning of giftedness and disability, and consider the possibility that giftedness may, perhaps, embrace both exceptionalities.

We encourage the use of dimensional assessment tools that identify the whole child rather than screen only for the presence of a disability; such tools help parents quickly secure targeted, appropriate interventions and therapies to support their children's weaknesses and strengths. We also urge parents to be highly discerning when selecting a school for their 2e children, and to examine the programming to make sure it offers adequate social, emotional, and academic support for their children's needs.

Further, we highly recommend that parents carefully consider how to develop their children's talents and giftedness outside of school through mentors and selected activities.

A Call to Action

When spider webs unite, they can tie up a lion.
Ethiopian proverb

Professionals from nearly all levels of psychiatry are acknowledging that the DSM system is flawed and seriously limited in its ability to meet the needs of clinicians. Although its categorical approach may serve the needs of researchers, clinicians and parents require a more useful and effective approach to diagnosis, one that yields a complete portrait of a child's strengths and weaknesses and how these affect his ability to function. While DSM committees for years have discussed the idea of a dimensional approach, with the encroaching publication of DSM-5 the conversation has become more public. However, it appears that without pressure from parents and private organizations, a shift to a truly dimensional system is unlikely to occur for many years.

Likewise, as concerned parents as well as citizens, we must seriously examine how effectively our present system of education meets the needs of all students and consider its potential impact on the future of our nation.

There are several movements under way to challenge the current emphasis on proficiency and achievement in our education system, even as President Obama's Blueprint for Reform and Race to the Top incentives are being instituted. However, both NCLB and Race to the Top mandate that schools use data collection through standards-based assessments to evaluate the effectiveness of teachers, administrators, and schools—an approach that has proven largely ineffective in encouraging creativity, supporting learning differences, and challenging 2e students to achieve their full potential.

The recent push for RtI also places our 2e students in danger of remaining underidentified or unidentified. Given the limitations to RtI's ability to identify either special needs or gifted students within a general population, it is likely that 2e students will continue to remain largely unidentified in our schools. If our education system falls short of identifying and cultivating the creative potential, unique talents, and analytical thinking abilities of our brightest, most challenged students, then we must question how well it is preparing our next generation of inventors, artists, and leaders for the future. As responsible citizens, we must insist on an education system that is grounded in nurturing the creative potential of each student, especially our best and brightest.

Sir Ken Robinson, renowned innovation consultant and creativity expert, recognizes that we must change the paradigm of our education system if our nation is to compete and survive in a global economy:

> [G]iven the challenges we face, education doesn't need to be reformed—it needs to be transformed. The key to this transformation is not to standardize education, but to personalize it, to build achievement on discovering the individual talents of each child, to put students in an environment where they want to learn and where they can naturally discover their true passions.[2]

Although there are several excellent groups, including Race to Nowhere, working diligently to reform our broken education system, there has been little organized effort at the grassroots level to target reform of the DSM system.

We encourage you to join us in forming a grassroots effort to petition for a postponement of the publication of the proposed version of DSM-5, scheduled for release in 2013. This request is to allow ample time for review of the merits of switching paradigms from a categorical to a dimensional system. Ideally, a neutral council with no vested interest in the current paradigm should coordinate this review. With the goal of evaluating the usefulness of a dimensional approach, the review should include a comprehensive, cross-categorical survey of clinical data, one that compares symptoms, patterns of comorbidities, and epidemiologies and gathers other information relevant to the presence of giftedness and how it affects individual functioning. To this end, we are currently working to make dimensional assessment tools more widely available in the United States in order to generate clinical data necessary to support research into a dimensional system.

We urge you to share the information in this book with others in your community, your treatment professionals, and your educators, with the goal of banding together to reform the two systems that limit the innate potential of our 2e children, who deserve to be seen as bright not broken.

Additional Resources

Many of the resources listed here and others can be found at www.brightnotbroken.com.

Books

Armstrong, Thomas. *Neurodiversity*. Cambridge, MA: Da Capo Press, 2010.

Bashe, Patricia Romanowski, and Barbara L. Kirby. *The Oasis Guide to Asperger Syndrome: Advice, Support, Insight, and Inspiration* (Rev. ed.). New York: Crown, 2005.

Baum, Susan M., and Steven V. Owen. *To Be Gifted and Learning Disabled: Strategies for Helping Bright Students with LD, ADHD, and More*. Mansfield Center, CT: Creative Learning Press, 2004.

Baum, Susan M., and Sally M. Reis. *Twice-Exceptional and Special Populations of Gifted Students*. Thousand Oaks, CA: Corwin Press, 2004.

Baum, Susan M., Julie Viens, and Barbara Slatin. *Multiple Intelligences in the Elementary Classroom: A Teacher's Toolkit*. New York: Teachers College Press, 2005.

Carlat, Daniel. *Unhinged: The Trouble with Psychiatry*. New York: Free Press, 2010.

Daniels, Susan, and Michael M. Piechowski. (Eds.). *Living with Intensity: Understanding the Sensitivity, Excitability, and the Emotional Development of Gifted Children, Adolescents, and Adults*. Scottsdale, AZ: Great Potential Press, 2009.

Davidson, Bob, and Jan Davidson. *Genius Denied: How to Stop Wasting Our Brightest Young Minds*. New York: Simon & Schuster, 2004.

Eide, Brock, and Fernette Eide. *The Mislabeled Child*. New York: Hyperion, 2006.

Frith, Uta. *Autism and Asperger Syndrome*. Cambridge, England: Cambridge University Press, 1991.

Frith, Uta. *Autism: Explaining the Enigma*. Malden, MA: Wiley-Blackwell, 2003.

Gilman, Barbara Jackson. *Academic Advocacy for Gifted Children: A Parent's Complete Guide*. Scottsdale, AZ: Great Potential Press, 2008.

Grandin, Temple. *Thinking in Pictures*. New York: Vintage, 2010.

Grandin, Temple. *The Way I See It, Revised and Expanded 2nd Edition: A Personal Look at Autism and Asperger's*. Texas: Future Horizons, Inc. 2011.

Grandin, Temple, and Kate Duffy. *Developing Talents*. Shawnee Mission, KS: Autism Asperger Publishing, 2004.

Jacobsen, Mary-Elaine. *The Gifted Adult: A Revolutionary Guide for Liberating Everyday Genius*. New York: Ballantine Books, 1999.

Kennedy, Diane M., and Rebecca S. Banks. *The ADHD-Autism Connection: A Step Toward More Accurate Diagnosis and Effective Treatment*. Colorado Springs, CO: WaterBrook Press, 2002.

Ratey, John J. *Spark: The Revolutionary New Science of Exercise and the Brain*. New York: Little, Brown, 2008.

Robinson, Ken, with Lou Aronica. *The Element: How Finding Your Passion Changes Everything*. New York: Viking Penguin, 2009.

Robinson, Ken. *Out of Our Minds: Learning to be Creative* (2nd ed.). Chichester, England: Capstone, 2011.

Silverman, Linda. *Upside-Down Brilliance: The Visual-Spatial Learner*. Glendale, CO: DeLean, 2002.

Smith Myles, Brenda. *Simple Strategies That Work! Helpful Hints for All Educators of Students with Asperger Syndrome, High-Functioning Autism, and Related Disabilities*. Shawnee Mission, KS: Autism Asperger Publishing, 2006.

Twachtman-Cullen, Diane, and Jennifer Twachtman-Bassett. *The IEP from A to Z: How to Create Meaningful and Measurable Goals and Objectives*. San Francisco: Jossey-Bass, 2011.

Webb, James T., Edward R. Amend, N. E. Webb, J. Goerss, P. Beljan, and F. R. Olenchak. *Misdiagnosis and Dual Diagnoses of Gifted Children and Adults*. Scottsdale, AZ: Great Potential Press, 2005.

Wing, Lorna. *The Autistic Spectrum*. Berkeley, CA: Ulysses Press, 2001.

Winner, Michelle Garcia. *Think Social! A Social Thinking Curriculum for School-Age Students*. San Jose, CA: Think Social Publishing, 2005.

Winner, Michelle Garcia. *Thinking About YOU Thinking About ME* (2nd ed.). San Jose, CA: Think Social Publishing, 2007.

Winner, Michelle Garcia. *A Politically Incorrect Look at Evidence-Based Practices and Teaching Social Skills*. San Jose, CA: Think Social Publishing, 2008.

Winner, Michelle Garcia, and Pamela Crooke. *Newly Updated! Socially Curious and Curiously Social: A Social Thinking Guidebook for Bright Teens & Young Adults*. San Jose, CA: Think Social Publishing, 2011.

Wolf, Lorraine E., Jane Thierfeld Brown, and G. Ruth Kukiela Bork. *Students with Asperger Syndrome: A Guide for College Personnel.* Shawnee Mission, KS: Autism Asperger Publishing, 2009.

Web Sites, Support Groups, Newsletters, and Additional Information

The following resources offer a rich variety of information, resources, and support for parents and professionals.

Gifted and Twice Exceptional

2e Twice-Exceptional Newsletter (www.2enewsletter.com/welcome page.htm)

Association for the Education of Gifted Underachieving Students (AEGUS) (www.aegus1.org)

Association for the Gifted (www.cectag.org)

Connie Belin & Jacqueline N. Blank International Center for Gifted Education and Talent Development at the University of Iowa (www.education.uiowa.edu/belinblank)

Davidson Institute for Talent Development (www.davidsongifted.org)

Gifted Child Quarterly (publication of NAGC) (http://gcq.sagepub.com/)

Gifted Child Today (http://journals.prufrock.com/IJP/b/gifted-child-today)

Gifted Development Center (www.gifteddevelopment.com)

Hoagies' Gifted Education Page (www.hoagiesgifted.org)

International Center for Talent Development (http://internationalcenterfortalentdevelopment.com)

Journal for the Education of the Gifted (publication of TAG) (http://journals.prufrock.com/IJP/b/journal-for-the-education-of-the-gifted)

National Association for Gifted Children (NAGC) (www.nagc.org)

National Institute for Twice-Exceptionality (NITE) (www.education.uiowa.edu/belinblank/clinic/nite.aspx)

Neag Center for Gifted Education and Talent Development (www.gifted.uconn.edu)

PROJECT2EXCEL: A Study of Twice-Exceptionality (www.stthomas.edu/project2excel)

Roeper Review (www.roeper.org/Roeperinstitute/roeperReview)

The SENG Vine (newsletter) (www.sengifted.org)

Sir Ken Robinson, PhD (www.sirkenrobinson.com)

Supporting Emotional Needs of the Gifted (SENG) (www.SENGifted.org)

Uniquely Gifted (www.uniquelygifted.org)

Autism and Asperger's

Autism Asperger Publishing (AAPC) (www.aapcpublishing.net)

Autism Asperger's Digest Magazine (publication of Future Horizons) (www.autismdigest.com)

Autism Society of America (ASA) (www.autism-society.org)

Autism Spectrum Quarterly (www.asquarterly.com)

Center for Social Thinking (www.socialthinking.com)

Exceptional Parent (EP) (www.eparent.com)

Exceptional Parent (publication of EP) (www.eparent.com)

Families of Adults Affected by Asperger's Syndrome (FAAAS) (www.faaas.org)

Future Horizons (www.fhautism.com)

NAS Lorna Wing Centre for Autism (division of NAS) (www.autism.org.uk/en-gb/our-services/diagnosing-complex-needs/about-the-nas-lorna-wing-centre-for-autism)

National Autistic Society (www.autism.org.uk)

Online Asperger Syndrome Information and Support and MAAP Services (Oasis@MAAP) (www.aspergersyndrome.org)

Wales Autism Research Centre (WARC) (www.walesautismresearchcentre.com)

Notes

Introduction

1. Grandin, T. (2011). *The Way I See It: Revised and Expanded 2nd Edition: A Personal Look at Autism and Asperger's*. Arlington, TX: Future Horizons.

2. Poland, J. (2002, February 25). [Review of the book *DSM-IV Sourcebook*]. www.mentalhelp.net/poc/view_doc.php?type=book&id=996&cn=88.

3. Fizgerald, M. (2005). *The genesis of artistic creativity: Asperger syndrome and the arts*. London: Jessica Kingsley, p. 105.

4. Armstrong, T. (2010). *Neurodiversity*. Cambridge, MA: Da Capo Press, p. viii.

5. Quoted in National Association for Gifted Children. (2009). *State of the nation in gifted education*. www.nagc.org/uploadedFiles/Information_and_Resources/State_of_the_States_2008-2009/2008-09%20State%20of%20the%20Nation%20overview.pdf.

Chapter 1: Twice Exceptional

1. National Association for Gifted Children. (2010). What is giftedness? www.nagc.org/index.aspx?id=574.

2. Silverman, L. (2008). Characteristics of giftedness. Gifted Development Center. www. gifteddevelopment.com.

3. Glen Ellyn Media. (2010, June 1). What is 2e? *2e Twice-Exceptional Newsletter*. www.2eNewsletter.com/What_is_twice-exceptional.htm.
4. Baum, S. (1990). *Gifted but learning disabled: A puzzling paradox*. ERIC. www.education.com/reference/article/Ref_Gifted_but_Learning/; Webb, J. T. (1993). Nurturing social-emotional development of gifted children. In F.J.K.A. Heller (Ed.), *International handbook of research and development of giftedness and talent* (pp. 525–538). Oxford: Pergamon Press.
5. National Association for Gifted Children, What is giftedness?
6. Novelli, C. (2010, June 25). Gifted underachievement: Part IV—twice exceptionality. *Examiner.com*. www.examiner.com/gifted-education-in-fort-collins/gifted-underachievement-part-iv-twice-exceptionality#ixzz1DEbl05t3.
7. Wing, L. (2001). *The autistic spectrum: A parents' guide to understanding and helping your child*. Berkeley, CA: Ulysses Press; Frith, U. (1994). *Autism and Asperger syndrome*. Cambridge, England: Cambridge University Press.
8. Webb, J. T., Amend, E. R., Webb, N. E., Goerss, J., Beljan, P., & Olenchak, F. R. (2005). *Misdiagnosis and dual diagnoses of gifted children and adults*. Scottsdale, AZ: Great Potential Press; Kennedy, D. M., & Banks, R. S. (2002). *The ADHD-autism connection: A step toward more accurate diagnosis and effective treatment*. Colorado Springs, CO: WaterBrook Press.
9. Silverman, L. (2007, March). What is giftedness? Gifted Development Center. www.gifteddevelopment.com/What_is_Gifted/whatis.htm.
10. Ibid.
11. Busi, K. (n.d.). Twice exceptional kids: Exceptional because they are gifted & exceptional because they learn differently. *Parent Guide News*. www. parentguidenews.com; Idaho State Department of Education. (2010, January). *Twice-exceptional: Students with both gifts*

and challenges or disabilities. www.sde.idaho.gov/site/gifted_talented/twice-exceptional/docs/2E Manual.pdf; Montgomery County Public Schools. (2010, January). *Twice exceptional students: A guidebook for supporting the achievement of gifted students with special needs*. www.montgomeryschoolsmd.org/curriculum/enriched/mcpsprograms/gtld/docs1/2010 Twice Exceptional.pdf; Silverman, Characteristics of giftedness.

12. ADHD compared to ADHD/Asperger? (2010, May 17). PsychForums. www.psychforums.com/asperger-syndrome/topic50006.html.

13. Child Behavior [forum]. (2010, May 27). MedHelp. www.medhelp.org/posts/Child-Behavior/Correct-Diagnosis-such-as-ADHD--PDD--Aspergers--ODD--OCD/show/277980.

14. Child Behavior [forum]. (2007, October 15). MedHelp. www.medhelp.org/posts/Child-Behavior/Too-many-issues-Please-help/show/323343.

15. Gardner, H. E. (2006). *Multiple intelligences: New horizons in theory and practice*. New York: Basic Books, pp. 8–13.

16. Armstrong, T. (1994). *Multiple intelligences in the classroom*. Alexandria, VA: Association for Supervision and Curriculum Development.

17. Silverman, What is giftedness?

18. Webb, Nurturing social-emotional development of gifted children; Silverman, L. (2010, June 14). Strengths and problems of gifted learners. Mesa Supporters of the Gifted and Talented. www.msgt.org/generalinfo.htm.

19. Silverman, L. (1999). Perfectionism: The crucible of giftedness. *Advanced Development Journal*, 8, 47–61.

20. Silverman, What is giftedness?

21. Daniels, S., & Piechowski, M. M. (Eds.). (2009). *Living with intensity: Understanding the sensitivity, excitability, and emotional*

development of gifted children, adolescents, and adults. Scottsdale, AZ: Great Potential Press.

22. Lind, S. (2001). Overexcitability and the gifted. *Supporting Emotional Needs of the Gifted Newsletter, 1*(1), 3–6.
23. Daniels & Piechowski, *Living with intensity*, p. 15.

Chapter 2: Recognizing 2e

1. Webb, J. T., Amend, E. R., Webb, N. E., Goerss, J., Beljan, P., & Olenchak, F. R. (2005). *Misdiagnosis and dual diagnoses of gifted children and adults*. Scottsdale, AZ: Great Potential Press.
2. Winner, E. (1996). *Gifted children: Myths and realities*. New York: Basic Books, p. 4.
3. Brown, T. E. (2005). *Attention deficit disorder: The unfocused mind in children and adults*. New Haven, CT: Yale University Press, p. 33.
4. Frith, U. (2003). *Autism: Explaining the enigma*. Malden, MA: Blackwell, p. 171.
5. Quoted in Frith, *Autism*, p. 173.
6. Rogers, quoted in Webb et al., *Misdiagnosis and dual diagnoses*, p. 41.
7. Barkley, R. A. (n.d.). ADHD fact sheet. Dr. Russell A. Barkley, Ph.D.: The Official Site. www.russellbarkley.org/content/adhd-facts.pdf.
8. Webb et al., *Misdiagnosis and dual diagnoses*.
9. Barkley, R. A. (2010, July 1). Child behavior management tips from Dr. Barkley. Attention Deficit Disorder Resources. www.addresources.org/article_behavior_barkley.php; Robin, A. L. (1998). *ADHD in adolescents*. New York: Guilford Press.
10. Klein, B. (2007). *Raising gifted kids: Everything you need to know to help your exceptional child thrive*. New York: AMACOM, p. 16.
11. Silverman, L. (1995, August). *The universal experience of being out-of-sync*. Keynote address at the World Conference on Gifted and Talented Children, Hong Kong.

12. Eide, B., & Eide, F. (2006). *The mislabeled child: Looking beyond behavior to find the true sources and solutions for children's learning challenges*. New York: Hyperion.
13. Barkley, R. A. (2000). *Taking charge of ADHD: The complete authoritative guide for parents*. New York: Guilford Press, p. 200.
14. Hallowell, E. M., & Ratey, J. J. (2006). *Delivered from distraction*. New York: Ballantine Books.
15. Frith, *Autism;* Winner, M. G. (2011, January 6). What is social thinking? Social Thinking. www.socialthinking.com/what-is-social-thinking/social-thinking-challenges.
16. Frith, *Autism*, p. 222.
17. Silverman, L. (2009, October 13). The two-edged sword of compensation: How the gifted cope with learning disabilities. WePapers. www.wepapers.com/Papers/61940/The_two-edged_sword_of_compensation-_How_thegifted_cope_with_learning_disabilities.
18. Webb et al., *Misdiagnosis and dual diagnoses*, p. 38.
19. American Academy of Pediatrics. (2000, May). Clinical practice guideline: Diagnosis and evaluation of the child with attention-deficit/hyperactivity disorder. *Pediatrics, 105*, 1158–1170. http://aappolicy.aappublications.org/cgi/reprint/pediatrics;105/5/1158.pdf.
20. Webb, L.-H. (2005). *The gift of ADHD: How to transform your child's problems into strengths*. Oakland, CA: New Harbinger, p. 200.
21. Hallowell & Ratey, *Delivered from distraction*, p. 13.
22. Armstrong, T. (2010). *Neurodiversity*. Cambridge, MA: Da Capo Press, p. viii.
23. Barkley, R. A. (2010, April 12). ADHD is not a gift. *YouTube*. Toronto: Centre for ADHD Awareness, Canada. www.youtube.com/watch?v=4xpEBE9VDWw. (DVD can be purchased on CADDAC Web site: www.caddac.ca/cms/page.php?2)
24. Barkley, Child behavior management tips.
25. Ibid.

26. Brown, *Attention deficit disorder*, p. 176.

27. Brown, *Attention deficit disorder*.

Chapter 3: 2e, ADHD, and Labels

1. Kendrick, T.-B. (2010, December). Finding the right mental health provider for your gifted/talented child. SENG: Supporting the Emotional Needs of the Gifted. www.sengifted.org/articles_directorscorner/kendrick_december10.shtml.

2. Seattle Country Day School. (2010, Fall). A visit with James Webb. *Kinetics*. www.seattlecountryday.org/_literature_77256/James_Webb_Article.

3. American Psychiatric Association. (2000). *Diagnostic and statistical manual of mental disorders* (4th ed., text rev.). Arlington, VA: Author, p. 93.

4. Centers for Disease Control and Prevention. (2010, May 25). Facts about ADHD. www.cdc.gov/ncbddd/adhd/facts.html.

5. MedHelp. (2008, September 21). ADD/ADHD Community: Discussion. www.medhelp.org/forums/ADD---ADHD/show/175. (*Note:* The three statements quoted here without notes are from unattributable postings on Facebook, 2009 and 2010.)

6. Ridenour, C. (2010, April 25). Autism: questions. AllExperts. http://en.allexperts.com/q/Autism-1010/2009/2/ASpergers-versus-Gifted.

7. Wolraich, M. L., Wibbelsman, C. J., Brown, T. E., Evans, S. W., Gotlieb, E. M., Knight, J. R., et al. (2005, June 1). Attention deficit/hyperactivity disorder among adolescents: A review of the diagnosis, treatment, and clinical implications. *Pediatrics, 115*, 1734–1746. http://pediatrics.aappublications.org.

8. Ibid.

9. Ibid.

10. Gillberg, C. (2010, December 1). *A new concept in mental health: What is ESSENCE?* DocStoc. www.docstoc.com/docs/69854703/Child-mental-health-problems-in-preschool-epilepsy.

11. Barkely, R. (2010, July 12). Russell Barkley - ADHD co-morbidity. [Excerpt from a lecture to the Centre for ADHD Awareness, Canada (CADDAC).] *YouTube*. www.youtube.com/watch?v=415QYaQcICQ.

12. Hallowell, E. M., & Ratey, J. J. (2006). *Delivered from distraction*. New York: Ballantine Books, p. 24.

13. American Academy of Child and Adolescent Psychiatry. (2007, January). Practice parameter for the assessment and treatment of children and adolescents with bipolar disorder. *Journal of the American Academy of Child and Adolescent Psychiatry*, 46, 107–125. www.aacap.org/galleries/PracticeParameters/JAACAP_Bipolar_2007.pdf; Compton, K., Taylor, L., Carlozzi, N., & Fortson, B. (2006, December 1). Distinguishing ADHD from juvenile bipolar disorder: A guide for primary care PAs. *Journal of American Academy of Physician Assistants*. www.jaapa.com/distinguishing-adhd-from-juvenile-bipolar-disorder-a-guide-for-primary-care-pas/article/139524/.

14. Greenspan, S., & Glovinsky, I. (2002). *Bipolar patterns in children*. Bethesda, MD: Interdisciplinary Council on Developmental and Learning Disorders.

15. Webb, J. T., Amend, E. R., Webb, N. E., Goerss, J., Beljan, P., & Olenchak, F. R. (2005). *Misdiagnosis and dual diagnoses of gifted children and adults*. Scottsdale, AZ: Great Potential Press.

16. American Academy of Child and Adolescent Psychiatry, Practice parameter for the assessment and treatment of children and adolescents with bipolar disorder.

17. National Institute of Mental Health. (2006, April 1). Clinical Antipsychotic Trials of Intervention Effectiveness. www.nimh.nih.gov/trials/practical/catie/index.shtml.

18. Elliott, C. (2010, September/October). The deadly corruption of clinical trials. *Mother Jones*. http://motherjones.com/environment/2010/09/dan-markingson-drug-trial-astrazeneca.

19. Carey, B. (2006, June 6). Use of antipsychotics by the young rose fivefold. *New York Times*. www.nytimes.com/2006/06/06/health/06psych.html.

20. Libby, J. L. (2006). *Handbook of preschool mental health*. New York: Guilford Press, p. 323.

21. American Academy of Child and Adolescent Psychiatry. (2007, January). Practice parameter for the assessment and treatment of children and adolescents with oppositional defiant disorder. *Journal of the American Academy of Child and Adolescent Psychiatry*, 46, 126–141; Barkley, R. A. (2006). *Attention-deficit hyperactivity disorder: A handbook for diagnosis and treatment* (Vol. 1). New York: Guilford Press, pp. 672, 674; Biederman, J., Mick, E., Wozniak, J., Aleardi, M., Spencer, T., & Faraone, S. V. (2005). An open-label trial of risperdone in children and adolescents with bipolar disorder. *Journal of Child and Adolescent Psychopharmacology*, *15*, 311–317; Goldstein, S., & Ingersoll, B. (2001). Lonely, sad, and angry. PDFCast.org. http://pdfcast.org/pdf/lonely-sad-and-angry.

22. Zito, J. M., Derivan, A. T., Kratochvil, C. J., Safer, D. J., Fegert, J. M., & Grennhill, L. L. (2008). Off-label psychopharmacologic prescribing for children: History supports close clinical monitoring. *Child and Adolescent Psychiatry and Mental Health*, *2*(24). doi: 10.1186/1753-2000-2-24.

23. Edwards, J. (2009, March 29). Biederman's finances: He names his own price and it's $550 an hour. BNET. www.bnet.com/blog/drug-business/biederman-8217s-finances-he-names-his-own-price-and-it-8217s-550-an-hour/103727.

24. Edwards, J. (2008, November 19). FDA: J&J's Risperdal and Lilly's Zyprex are over-used in kids. BNET. www.bnet.com/blog/drug-business/fda-j-j-8217s-risperdal-and-lilly-8217s-zyprexa-are-over-used-in-kids/218.

25. Use of antipsychotics by the young rose fivefold.

26. Olfson, M. et al. (2006). National trends in the outpatient treatment of children and adolescents with antipsychotic drugs. *Archives of General Psychiatry*, 63, 679–685. http://archpsych.ama-assn.org/cgi/content/short/63/6/679.

27. Libby, *Handbook of preschool mental health*, p. 313.
28. Ibid.
29. Ibid.
30. Barkley, R. A. (2010, May 30). Deficient emotional self-regulation is a core component of ADHD: Evidence and treatment implications. http://ccf.buffalo.edu/pdf/BarkleySlides_CCFSpeakerSeries0910.pdf.
31. Faraone, S. K., & Kunwar, A. R. (2007, May 1). *ADHD in children with comorbid conditions: ADHD and disruptive behavior disorders*. Medscape Education. www.medscape.org/viewarticle/555748_2.
32. American Academy of Child and Adolescent Psychiatry, Practice parameter for the assessment and treatment of children and adolescents with oppositional defiant disorder.
33. Hamilton, S. S., & Armando, J. (2008, October 1). Oppositional defiant disorder. *American Family Physician, 78*, 861–866. www.aafp.org/afp/2008/1001/p861.html.
34. American Psychiatric Association, *Diagnostic and statistical manual of mental disorders* (4th ed., text rev.), pp. 100–101.
35. American Academy of Child and Adolescent Psychiatry, Practice parameter for the assessment and treatment of children and adolescents with oppositional defiant disorder; Hamilton & Armando, Oppositional defiant disorder.
36. Breen, M. J., & Altepeter, T. S. (1990). *Disruptive behavior disorders in children: Treatment-focused assessment*. New York: Guilford Press, p. 23.
37. American Psychiatric Association, *Diagnostic and statistical manual of mental disorders* (4th ed., text rev.), pp. 101–102.
38. Lovecky, D. V. (2004). *Different minds: Gifted children with AD/HD, Asperger syndrome, and other learning deficits*. London: Jessica Kingsley, p. 392.
39. Ibid., p. 394.
40. Barkley, R. A. (2008, October 9). Management of ADHD. *YouTube*. www.youtube.com/watch?v=q3d1SwUXMc0.

Chapter 4: Autism and 2e

1. Quoted in Hughes, B.G.R. (2003, August). Understanding our gifted and complex minds: Intelligence, Asperger's syndrome, and learning disabilities at MIT. *Infinite Connection*. www.alum.mit.edu/news/WhatMatters/Archive/200308.

2. Goin-Kochel, R. P., Mackintosh, V. H., & Myers, B. (2006). How many doctors does it take to make an autism spectrum diagnosis? *Autism, 10*, 439–451.

3. Centers for Disease Control and Prevention. (n.d.). Facts about ASDs. www.cdc.gov/ncbddd/autism/facts.html.

4. American Psychiatric Association. (2000). *Diagnostic and statistical manual of mental disorders* (4th ed., text rev.). Arlington, VA: Author, p. 81.

5. Wing, L., & Gould, J. (1979). Severe impairments of social interaction and associated abnormalities in children: Epidemiology and classification. *Journal of Autism and Childhood Schizophrenia*, 9, 11–29.

6. American Psychiatric Association, *Diagnostic and statistical manual of mental disorders* (4th ed., text rev.), p. 72.

7. Asperger, H. (1991). "Autistic psychopathy" in childhood. In U. Frith (Ed.), *Autism and Asperger syndrome* (pp. 37–92). Cambridge, England: Cambridge University Press; Bernardi, S., Anagnostou, E., Shen, J., Kolevzon, A., Buxbaum, J., Hollander, E., et al. (2010, December 23). In vivo (1) H-magnetic resonance spectroscopy study of the attentional networks in autism. *Brain Research*, 198–205.

8. Palmer, J. (2006, March 11). Regarding social issues in high school [e-mail]. Outside the Box! http://adhd.kids.tripod.com.

9. Blair, R. (2008). Fine cuts of empathy and the amygdala: Dissociable deficits in psychopathy and autism. *Quarterly Journal of Experimental Psychology*, *61*(1), 157–170.

10. Mrug, S., Hoza, B., Gerdes A. C., Hinshaw, S., Arnold, L. E., Hechtman, L., & Pelham, W. E. (2009, January). Discriminating

between children with ADHD and classmates using peer variables. *Journal of Attention Disorders, 12*, 372–380.

11. Ibid.

12. Barkley, R. A. (2010, October 11). *Attention-deficit/hyperactivity disorder: Nature, course, outcomes, and comorbidity*. ContinuingEdCourses.net. www.continuingedcourses.net/active/courses/course003.php.

13. Hupp, S. D., LeBlanc, M., Jewell, J. D., & Warnes, E. (2009). History and overview. In J. L. Matson (Ed.), *Social behavior and skills in children*. New York: Springer, p. 3.

14. Goldstein, S. (2003). The catalytic role of ADHD. *ADDult ADDvice*. www.addresources.org/files/summer_2003.pdf.

15. Brown, T. E. (2005). *The Brown model of ADD syndrome*. Dr. ThomasEBrown.com. www.drthomasebrown.com/brown_model/index.html.

16. MediaLink. (2006, September 13). Medialink features: Back to school with ADHD: Facing the challenges of one of the most common childhood disorders. BNET. http://findarticles.com/p/articles/mi_m0EIN/is_2006_Sept_13/ai_n26985414/.

17. Meyer, R. N. (2000, December 8). Oppositional defiant disorder? Just how inappropriate a co-morbid diagnosis can be. www.rogernmeyer.com/children_and_parents_odd.html.

18. Wing, L., Gould, J., & Gillberg, C. (2011). Autism spectrum disorders in the DSM-V: Better or worse than the DSM-IV? *Research in Developmental Disabilities, 32*, 768–773.

19. Frith, U. (2003). *Autism: Explaining the enigma*. Malden, MA: Blackwell.

20. Ibid., p. 111.

21. Blair, Fine cuts of empathy and the amygdala.

22. Frith, *Autism*, p. 114.

23. Vaquerizo-Madrid, J., Estevez-Diaz, F., & Diaz-Maillo, I. (2006). A review of the alert and psycholinguistic intervention model in

attention deficit hyperactivity disorder. *Journal of Neurology*, *42*, S53–S61.

24. Ellis, A. (2003). ADHD and intimate relationships. ADDers.org. www.adders.org/partners5.pdf.

25. Brown, T. E. (2005). *Attention deficit disorder: The unfocused mind in children and adults*. New Haven, CT: Yale University Press.

26. Barkley, R. A. (2010, May 30). Deficient emotional self-regulation is a core impairment of ADHD: Evidence and treatment implications. http://ccf.buffalo.edu/pdf/BarkleySlides_CCFSpeakerSeries0910.pdf.

27. Jordan, R., & Jones, G. (1999). *Meeting the Needs of children with autistic spectrum disorders*. London: David Fulton, p. 112.

28. Jackson, S. (2002). *Autism, challenging behaviour and communication*. Sheffield Hallam University. www.shu.ac.uk/faculties/ds/education/theautismcentre/docs/behaviour.doc.

29. Koegel, R., & Koegel, K. (2006). *Pivotal response treatments for autism*. Koegel Autism Center. http://education.ucsb.edu/autism/PRTbook.htm.

30. Brown, T. E. (2005). *The Brown model of ADD syndrome*. Dr. ThomasEBrown.com: www.drthomasebrown.com/brown_model/index.html; Barkley, R. A. (2008, November 10). *Advances in the Understanding and Management of ADHD*. University of California Television.
www.uctv.tv/search-details.aspx?showID=14660.

31. Ibid.

32. Wing et al., Autism spectrum disorders in the DSM-V.

33. Ibid.

34. Corbett, B. A., Constantine, L. J., Hendren, R., Rocke, D., & Ozonoff, S. (2009). Examining executive functioning in children with autism spectrum disorder, attention deficit hyperactivity disorder and typical development. *Psychiatry Research, 166*, 210–222; Soorya, L. V., & Halpern, D. (2009). Psychosocial interventions for motor coordination, executive functions, and

socialization deficits in ADHD and ASD. *Primary Psychiatry*, *16*(1), 48–54.

35. Sinzig, J., Morsch, D., Bruning, N., Schmidt, M. H., & Lehmkuhl, G. (2008). Inhibitions, flexibility, working memory and planning in autism spectrum disorders with and without ADHD-symptoms. *Child and Adolescent Psychiatry and Mental Health*, *2*(4), 1–12.
36. Tantam, D. (2003). The challenge of adolescents and adults with Asperger syndromes. *Child and Adolescent Psychiatric Clinics of North America*, *12*(1), 143–163.
37. Ashburner, J., Ziviani, J., & Rodger, S. (2010). Surviving in the mainstream: Capacity of children with autism spectrum disorders to perform academically and regulate their emotions and behavior at school. *Research in Autism Spectrum Disorders*, *4*(1), 18–27.
38. Sacks, O. (1995). *An anthropologist on Mars*. New York: Vintage Books, p. 245.
39. Cash, A. B. (1999, September 1). A profile of gifted individuals with autism: The twice-exceptional learner. BNET. http://findarticles.com/p/articles/mi_hb6470/is_1_22/ai_n28742221.
40. Rimland, cited in Cash, A profile of gifted individuals with autism.
41. Quoted in Sacks, O. (1993, December). An anthropologist on Mars. *New Yorker*, pp. 106–125.
42. Glen Ellyn Media. (2010, June 1). What is 2e? *2e Twice-Exceptional Newsletter*. www.2eNewsletter.com/What_is_twice-exceptional.htm.

Chapter 5: A Layman's Guide to the DSM

1. Psychiatrists call for overhaul of unwieldy DSM. (2001, October 1). BNET. http://findarticles.com/p/articles/mi_hb4345/is_10_29/ai_n28870188/.
2. Maj, M. (2005). "Psychiatric comorbidity": An artefact of current diagnostic systems? *British Journal of Psychiatry*, *186*, 182–184.
3. Mayes, R., & Horwitz, A. V. (2005). DSM-III and the revolution in the classification of mental illness. *Journal of the History of the Behavioral Sciences*, *41*, 249–267.

4. Ibid.
5. Ibid., p. 261.
6. American Psychiatric Association. (2000). *Diagnostic and statistical manual of mental disorders* (4th ed., text rev.). Arlington, VA: Author.
7. Mayes & Horwitz, DSM-III and the revolution in the classification of mental illness, p. 249.
8. American Psychiatric Association. (1994). *Diagnostic and statistical manual of mental disorders* (4th ed.). Arlington, VA: Author, p. xviii.
9. Ibid., p. xxiii.
10. Spitzer, R. L., & Fleiss, J. L. (1974). A re-analysis of the reliability of psychiatric diagnosis. *British Journal of Psychiatry, 135*, 241–247.
11. Ibid.
12. Ibid.
13. Spiegel, A. (2005, January 3). The dictionary of disorder: How one man revolutionized psychiatry. *New Yorker*. www.newyorker.com/archive/2005/01/03/050103fa_fact.
14. Kirk, S. A., & Kutchins, H. (1994). *The myth of the reliability of DSM*. Academy for the Study of the Psychoanalytic Arts. www.academyanalyticarts.org/kirk&kutchins.htm.
15. Williams, Gibbon, First, Spitzer, Davies, & Borus, cited in Kirk & Kutchins, *The myth of the reliability of DSM*; Spiegel, Dictionary of disorder; Kirk & Kutchins, *The myth of the reliability of DSM*; Mayes, & Horwitz, DSM-III and the revolution in the classification of mental illness.
16. Frances, A., Mack, A. H., Ross, R., & First, M. B. (2000). *The DSM-IV classification and psychopharmacology*. American College of Neuropsychopharmacology. www.acnp.org/g4/GN401000082/CH081.html.
17. Ibid.
18. Quoted in Spiegel, Dictionary of disorder.
19. Spitzer & Fleiss, Re-analysis.

20. Quoted in Spiegel, Dictionary of disorder.
21. Kendell, R., & Jablensky, A. (2003, January). Distinguishing between the validity and utility of psychiatric diagnoses. *American Journal of Psychiatry*, *160*, 4–12.
22. Charney, D. S., Barlow, D. H., Botteron, K., Cohen, J. D., & Goldman, D. (2002). Neuroscience research agenda to guide development of a pathophysiologically based classification system. In D. J. Kupfer, M. B. First, & D. A. Regier (Eds.), *A research agenda for DSM-V* (pp. 31–83). Arlington, VA: American Psychiatric Association.
23. Kendell & Jablensky, Distinguishing between the validity and utility of psychiatric diagnoses, p. 4.
24. Quoted in Carlat, D. J. (2010). *Unhinged: The trouble with psychiatry—a doctor's revelations about a profession in crisis*. New York: Free Press, p. 53.
25. Ibid.
26. Ibid.
27. American Psychiatric Association. (2000). *Diagnostic and statistical manual of mental disorders* (4th ed., text rev.). Arlington, VA: Author, p. xxxi.
28. Frances et al., *DSM-IV classification and psychopharmacology*.
29. Maj, "Psychiatric comorbidity."
30. Ibid., p. 182.
31. Widiger, T. A., & Mullins-Sweatt, S. (2007). Mental disorders as discrete clinical conditions: Dimensional versus categorical classification. In M. Hersen, S. M. Turner, & D. C. Beidel (Eds.), *Adult psychopathology* (5th ed., pp. 3–13). Hoboken, NJ: Wiley.
32. Hyman, S. E. (2010, September 28). Slipping the "cognitive straitjacket" of psychiatric diagnosis. *Scientific American*, pp. 1–3.
33. Widiger & Mullins-Sweatt, Mental disorders as discrete clinical conditions.

34. First, M. (2005). Mutually exclusive versus co-occurring diagnostic categories: The challenge of diagnostic comorbidity. *Psychopathology*, *38*, 206–210.

35. Kendell & Jablensky, Distinguishing between the validity and utility of psychiatric diagnoses.

36. Ibid.

37. Connor, M. G. (2004). Criticism of America's diagnostic bible—the DSM. OregonCounseling.org. http://oregoncounseling.org/diagnosis/criticismofdsm.htm.

38. Wing, L. (2005). Problems of categorical classification systems. In F. R. Volkmar (Ed.), *Handbook of autism and pervasive developmental disorders* (pp. 583–605). Hoboken, NJ: Wiley.

39. Phillips, J. (2010, July 1). The DSMs: Useful for whom? *Psychiatric Times*. www.psychiatrictimes.com/display-old/article/10168/1601688.

40. Ibid.

41. Quoted in Franklin, K. (2010, February 20). DSM-V: Will shoddy manual implode years before launch date? [Blog post]. http://forensicpsychologist.blogspot.com/search?updated-max=2010-04-29T10%3A00%3A00-07%3A00&max-results=50&reverse-paginate=true.

42. Kupfer et al., *Research agenda for DSM-V*, p. xix.

43. Rounsaville, B. J., Alarcon, R. D., Andrews, G., Jackson, J. S., Kendell, R. E., & Kendler, K. (2002). Basic nomenclature issues for DSM-V. In Kupfer et al., *Research agenda for DSM-V* (pp. 1–30).

44. Rounsaville et al., Basic nomenclature issues for DSM-V, p. 11.

45. Quoted in The DSM-V cometh: How will it change things for us? (n.d.). [Blog post]. BrainTalk. www. brain.hastypastry.net.

46. Poland, J. (2002, February 25). [Review of the book *DSM-IV Sourcebook*]. www.mentalhelp.net/poc/view_doc.php?type=book&id=996&cn=88.

47. King, M. (1964, October 22). *The future of integration*. [Address at Oberlin College]. www.oberlin.edu/external/EOG/BlackHistoryMonth/MLK/MLKmainpage.html.

48. Lincoln, A. (n.d.). www.abrahamlincolninfo.com/abrahamlincolnquotes/.

Chapter 6: Fact or Fallacy

1. Barkley, R. A. (2000). *Taking charge of ADHD: The complete and authoritative guide for parents*. New York: Guilford Press, pp. 12–13.

2. American Academy of Child and Adolescent Psychiatry. (2007, July). Practice parameter for the assessment and treatment of children and adolescents with attention-deficit/hyperactivity disorder. *Journal of the American Academy of Child and Adolescent Psychiatry*, 46, 894–921. www.aacap.org/galleries/PracticeParameters/JAACAP_ADHD_2007.pdf.

3. American Academy of Pediatrics. (2000, May). Clinical practice guideline: Diagnosis and evaluation of the child with attention-deficit/hyperactivity disorder. *Pediatrics*, *105*, 1158–1170. http://aappolicy.aappublications.org/cgi/reprint/pediatrics;105/5/1158.pdf.

4. Barkley, R. A. (2006). The nature of ADHD. In R. A. Barkley, *Attention-Deficit Hyperactivity Disorder: A Handbook for Diagnosis and Treatment* (3rd ed.). New York: Guilford Press.

5. Three-quarters of ADHD diagnoses wrong. (2004, November 10). *ABC News Online*. www.abc.net.au/news/newsitems/200411/s1240127.htm.

6. Gray area exists in diagnosis of ADHD. (2005, September 18). *Arizona Republic*. www.azcentral.com/arizonarepublic/local/articles/0918edADHDintro.html.

7. Wasowicz, L. (2006, January 27). Pedmed: The ADHD quandary. Access My Library. www.accessmylibrary.com/coms2/summary_0286-12483401_ITM.

8. Carey, W. B. (2003, Autumn). What to do about the ADHD epidemic. *American Academy of Pediatrics, Section on Developmental*

and Behavioral Pediatrics Newsletter. www.ahrp.org/children/CareyADHD0603.php.

9. Fix the diagnosis, not the children. (2006, March 7). Alliance for Human Research Protection. www.ahrp.org/cms/index2.php?option=com_content&do_pdf=1&id=98.

10. Nearly one million children in U.S. potentially misdiagnosed with ADHD, study finds. (2010, August 17). *ScienceDaily*. www.sciencedaily.com/releases/2010/08/100817103342.htm.

11. Healthtree. (2011, January 4). Is ADHD overdiagnosed? www.healthtree.com/articles/adhd/diagnosing/overdiagnosis/.

12. American Professional Society of ADHD and Related Disorders. (2009, June 1). International experts in attention deficit hyperactivity disorder (ADHD) take charge of expanding necessary professional education. www.apsard.org/APSARD/APSARD/AboutUs1/News/APSARDLaunch/Default.aspx; Cincinnati Children's. (2010, December 5). Mental health conditions and diagnoses: Attention deficit hyperactivity disorder/ADHD. www.cincinnatichildrens.org/health/info/mental/diagnose/adhd.htm.

13. National Institutes of Health. (1998, November 18). Diagnosis and treatment of attention deficit hyperactivity disorder. *NIH Consensus Statement Online*, *16*(2), 1–37. http://consensus.nih.gov/1998/1998AttentionDeficitHyperactivityDisorder110html.htm.

14. Timimi, S., Moncrieff, J., Jureidini, J., Leo, J., Cohen, D., Whitfield, C., et al. (2004, March.) A critique of the International Consensus Statement on ADHD. *Clinical Child and Family Psychology Review*, *7*(1), 59–63; discussion, 65–69. www.critpsynet.freeuk.com/Acritiqueofconsensus.htm.

15. American Professional Society of ADHD and Related Disorders, International experts.

16. Wasowicz, L. (2006, February 10). Ped med: Diagnosing attention deficits. RedOrbit. www.redorbit.com/news/health/386028/ped_med_diagnosing_attention_deficits/index.html.

17. National Institutes of Health, Diagnosis and treatment of attention deficit hyperactivity disorder.

18. Thurber, S., Sheehan, W., & Roberts, R. J. (2009). Attention deficit hyperactivity disorder and scientific epistemology. *Dialogues in Philosophy, Mental and Neuro Sciences, 2*(2), 33–39.

19. Ibid.

20. Thurber et al., Attention deficit hyperactivity disorder and scientific epistemology; Visser, J., & Jehan, Z. (2009, June). ADHD: A scientific fact or a factual opinion? A critique of the veracity of attention deficit hyperactivity disorder. *Emotional and Behavioural Difficulties, 14*(2), 127–140. http://pdfserve.informaworld.com/492040_912284663.pdf; Furman, L., & Berman, B. W. (2004). Rethinking the AAP attention deficit/hyperactivity disorder guidelines. *Clinical Pediatrics, 43*, 601–603; Timimi et al., A critique of the International Consensus Statement on ADHD; Carey, W. B. (1998, November 16–18). *Is attention deficit hyperactivity disorder a valid disorder?* Presentation to the NIH Consensus Development Conference on Diagnosis and Treatment of Attention Deficit Hyperactivity Disorder, National Institutes of Health. (Abstract available at http://user.cybrzn.com/kenyonck/add/nih/19981118b.htm)

21. Thurber et al., Attention deficit hyperactivity disorder and scientific epistemology.

22. Ibid.

23. Ibid.

24. Johnson, K. A., Wiersema, J. R., & Kuntsi, J. (2009). What would Karl Popper say? Are current psychological theories of ADHD falsifiable? *Behavioral and Brain Functions*, 5(15). doi:10.1186/1744-9081-5-15. www.behavioralandbrainfunctions.com/content/5/1/15.

25. Lurie, K. (2005, January 20). ADHD brain scan. *ScienCentral Archive*. www.sciencentral.com/articles/view.php3?article_id=218392460; Silk, T. J., Rinehart, N., Bradshaw, J. L., Tonge, B., Egan, G., O'Boyle, M., & Cunnington, R. (2006,

August). Visuospatial processing and the function of prefrontal-parietal networks in autism spectrum disorders: A functional MRI study. *American Journal of Psychiatry, 160,* 1440–1443.

26. Corbett, B. A., Constantine, L. J., Hendren, R., Rocke, D., & Ozonoff, S. (2009). Examining executive functioning in children with autism spectrum disorder, attention deficit hyperactivity disorder and typical development. *Psychiatry Research, 166,* 210–222; Pennington, B. F., & Ozonoff, S. (1996, January). Executive functions and developmental psychopathology. *Journal of Child Psychology and Psychiatry, 37*(1), 51–87.
27. Rommelse, N. N., Geurts, H. M., Franke, B., Buitelaar, J. K., & Hartman, C. A. (2011, May). A review on cognitive and brain endophenotypes that may be common in autism spectrum disorder and attention-deficit/hyperactivity disorder and facilitate the search for pleiotropic genes. *Neuroscience Biobehavioral Reviews, 35,* 1363–1396; Anderson, A. (2010, April 22). Researchers probe genetic overlap between ADHD, autism. Simons Foundation Autism Research Initiative (SFARI). https://sfari.org/news/-/asset_publisher/6Tog/content/researchers-probe-genetic-overlap-between-adhd-autism?redirect=%2Fnews; Rommelse, N. N., Franke, B., Geurts, H. M., Martman, C. A., & Buitelaar, J. K. (2010, March). Shared heritability of attention-deficit/hyperactivity disorder and autism spectrum disorder. *European Child and Adolescent Psychiatry, 19,* 281–295; Ronald, A., Simonoff, E., Kuntsi, J., Asherson, P., & Plomin, R. (2008, May). Evidence for overlapping genetic influences on autistic and ADHD behaviours in a community twin sample. *Journal of Child Psychology and Psychiatry, 49,* 535–542; Franke, B., Neale, B. M., & Faraone, S. V. (2009, July). Genome-wide association studies in ADHD. *Human Genetics, 126*(1), 13–50; Smalley, S. L., Kustanovich, V., Minassian, S. L., Stone, J. L., Ogdie, M. N., McGough, J. J., et al. (2002). Genetic linkage of attention-deficit/hyperactivity disorder on chromosome 16p13, in region implicated in autism. *American Journal of Human Genetics, 71,* 959–963. www.ncbi.nlm.nih.gov/pmc/articles/PMC378550/; Ogdie, M. N., Macphie, I. L., Minassian, S. L.,

Yang, M., Fisher, S. E., Francks, C., et al. (2003). A genomewide scan for attention deficit/hyperactivity disorder in an extended sample: Suggestive linkage on 17p11. *American Journal of Human Genetics*, *72*, 1268–1279. www.ncbi.nlm.nih.gov/pmc/articles/PMC1180278/; Ogdie, M. N., Fisher, S. E., Yang, M., Ishii, J., Francks, C., Loo, S. K., et al. (2004). Attention-deficit/hyperactivity disorder: Fine mapping supports linkages to 5p13, 6q12, 16 p13, and 17p11. *American Journal of Human Genetics*, *75*, 661–668. www.ncbi.nlm.nih.gov/pmc/articles/PMC1182053/; Bakker, S. C., van der Meulen, E. M., Buitelaar, J. K., Sandkuijl, L. A., Pauls, D. L., Monsuur, A. J., et al. (2003). A whole-genome scan in 164 Dutch sib pairs with attention-deficit/hyperactivity disorder: Suggestive evidence for linkage on chromosomes 7p and 15q. *American Journal of Human Genetics*, *72*, 1251–1260. www.ncbi.nlm.nih.gov/pmc/articles/PMC1180276/.

28. Tait, G. (2009). The logic of ADHD: A brief review of fallacious reasoning. *Studies in Philosophy and Education*, *28*, 239–254.

29. Rappaport, cited in Furman, L. (2005). What is attention-deficit hyperactivity disorder (ADHD)? *Journal of Child Neurology*, *20*, 994–1002; Rie, cited in Furman; Rappaport et al., cited in Furman.

30. Furman, What is attention-deficit hyperactivity disorder (ADHD)?

31. Furman, L. (2008). Attention-deficit hyperactivity disorder (ADHD): Does new research support old concepts? *Journal of Child Neurology*, *23*, 775–784.

32. Furman, What is attention-deficit hyperactivity disorder (ADHD)?

33. Carey, W. B. (2002). Is ADHD a valid disorder? In P. S. Jensen & J. R. Cooper, (Eds.), *Attention deficit hyperactivity disorder: State of science best practices* (pp. 3.1–3.14). Kingston, NJ: Civic Research Institute.

34. Ibid.

35. Furman, What is attention-deficit hyperactivity disorder (ADHD)?

36. Rommelse, N. N., Altink, M. E., Fliers, E. A., Martin, N. C., Buschgens, C. J., Hartman, C. A., et al. (2009). Comorbid problems in ADHD: Degree of association, shared endophenotypes, and

formation of distinct subtypes: Implications for a future DSM. *Journal of Abnormal Child Psychology, 37*, 793–804.

37. Ajmone, C. (2010, April 7). Pseudo ADHD: Pathologies and conditions mimicking ADHD. http://adhd.altervista.org/en/.
38. Victoroff, J. (2000, September 1). Calling attention to ADHD: Is the disorder real? *WebMD*. www.webmd.com/add-adhd/news/20000901/calling-attention-to-adhd-is-disorder-real.
39. U.S. Department of Health and Human Services. (2011, February 14). *Estimates of funding for various research, condition, and disease categories (RCDC)*. National Institutes of Health: Research Portfolio Online Reporting Tools. www.report.nih.gov/rcdc/categories/.

Chapter 7: Misunderstanding the Spectrum of Autism

1. Brown, K. (2004, July 27). Submit a question: School related medical issues [topic area]. Ask a Specialist. www.askaspecialist.ca.gov/archives/2003/medical.
2. Barkley, R. A. (2005). *ADHD and the nature of self-control*. New York: Guilford Press.
3. Biederman, J. (2005). Breaking news: The social and economic impact of ADHD. *Medscape Psychiatry, 10*(1). www.medscape.com/viewarticle/502480_3.
4. Centers for Disease Control and Prevention. (2010, May 25). Facts about ADHD. www.cdc.gov/ncbddd/adhd/facts.html.
5. "Lance." (2011, January 28 and 31). [Comments on the blog post "Proposed revisions to autism diagnosis in DSM-V"]. www.starkravingmadmommy.com/2011/01/proposed-revisions-to-autism-diagnosis.html.
6. University of Michigan Autism and Communication Disorders Center. (2009, September). ADOS/ADI-R FAQs. www.umaccweb.com/education/faqs.html.
7. Rutter, M., & Schopler, E. (1987). Autism and pervasive developmental disorders: Concepts and diagnostic issues. *Journal of Autism and Developmental Disorders, 17*(2), 159–186; Wing, L.

(2001). *The autistic spectrum: A parents' guide to understanding and helping your child*. Berkeley, CA: Ulysses Press.

8. K., C. (2010, December 5). *Gifted 102: The next steps ...* Hoagies' Gifted Education Page. www.hoagiesgifted.org/gifted_102.htm.
9. Cash, A. B. (1999, September 1). A profile of gifted individuals with autism: The twice-exceptional learner. BNET. http://findarticles.com/p/articles/mi_hb6470/is_1_22/ai_n28742221.
10. Grandin, T. (1995). *Thinking in pictures and other reports from my life with autism*. New York: Doubleday, p. 271.
11. Rimland, cited in Cash, A profile of gifted individuals with autism.
12. Grandin, T. (2005, March 1). Genius may be an abnormality. *Autism Today*. www.autismtoday.com/articles/Genius_May_Be_Abnormality.htm.
13. Kanner, L. (1943). Autistic disturbances of affective contact. *Nervous Child, 2*, 217–250.
14. Asperger, H. (1991). "Autistic psychopathy" in childhood. In U. Frith (Ed.), *Autism and Asperger syndrome* (pp. 37–92). Cambridge, England: Cambridge University Press.
15. Wing, L. (1981). Asperger's syndrome: A clinical account. *Psychological Medicine, 11*(1), 115–129.
16. Wing, L. (1991). The relationship between Asperger's syndrome and Kanner's autism. In Frith (Ed.), *Autism and Asperger syndrome* (pp. 93–121).
17. Wing, Asperger's syndrome.
18. Wing, L. (1996). *The history of ideas on autism: Legends, myths and reality*. From 5th Congress Autism–Europe: Articulos/Proceeding. www.autismo-br.com.br/home/Artig089.htm.
19. Snyder, A. (2004, April). Books and arts: Autistic genius. *Nature*. www.nature.com/nature/journal/v428/n6982/full/428470a.html.
20. Random House. (n.d.). Imagination. *Random House Webster's Unabridged Dictionary Version 3.0 and 2.2* [CD-ROM].

21. Wing, L., Gould, J., & Gillberg, C. (2011). Autism spectrum disorders in the DSM-V: Better or worse than the DSM-IV? *Research in Developmental Disabilities, 32*, 768–773.

22. Ibid.

23. Wing et al., Autism spectrum disorders in the DSM-V.

24. Ibid.

25. Matson, J. L. (2008). *Clinical assessment and intervention for autism spectrum disorder*. London: Academic Press.

26. Wing, *Autistic spectrum*.

27. Ruta, L. (2010, January 19). Obsessive-compulsive traits in children and adolescents with Asperger syndrome. *PubMed*. www.ncbi.nlm.nih.gov/pubmed/19557496.

28. Kamp-Becker I, G. M. (2008, October 21). Dimensional structure of the autism phenotype: Relations between early development and current presentation. *PubMed*. www.ncbi.nlm.nih.gov/pubmed/18941880.

29. Tantam, D. (2003). The challenge of adolescents and adults with Asperger syndromes. *Child and Adolescent Psychiatric Clinics of North America, 12*(1), 143–163.

30. Wing, Asperger's syndrome.

31. Ibid.

32. Asperger, "Autistic psychopathy" in childhood, p. 63.

33. Quoted in Sacks, O. (1995). *An anthropologist on Mars*. New York: Vintage Books, p. 252.

34. Twachtman-Cullen, D. (1995). Blinded by their strengths: The topsy-turvy world of Asperger's syndrome. OASIS @ MAAP. www.aspergersyndrome.org/Articles/Blinded-By-Their-Strengths--The-Topsy-Turvy-World-.aspx.

35. Kennedy Krieger Institute. (2008, May 20). IAN research findings: Issues of attention and mood in children with ASDs, their siblings, and parents. IAN Community. www.iancommunity.org/cs/ian_research_reports/cooccurring_conditions_minireport_.

36. Asperger, "Autistic psychopathy" in childhood, p. 38.

37. Ibid., p. 39.

38. Ibid.

39. Wing et al., Autism spectrum disorders in the DSM-V.

40. Wing, L. (2007). Editorial. *Autism, 10*(1), 7–10.

41. Associated Press. (2009, October 5). Higher autism rates detected: Now 1 in 100 kids. Mental Health on msnbc.com. www.msnbc.msn.com/id/33165127/ns/health-mental_health.

42. Wallis, C. (2009, November 3). A powerful identity, a vanishing diagnosis. *New York Times*. www.nytimes.com/2009/11/03/health/03asperger.html.

43. Bialik, C. (2006, November 30). The numbers guy: How many children have autism? *Wall Street Journal*. http://online.wsj.com/article/SB116481159830835726.html.

44. Centers for Disease Control and Prevention. (n.d.). Facts about ASDs. www.cdc.gov/ncbddd/autism/facts.html.

45. Ozonoff, S., Dawson, G., & McPartland, J. (2002). *A parent's guide to Asperger syndrome and high-functioning autism*. New York: Guilford Press.

46. Grinker, R. R. (2007). *Unstrange minds: Remapping the world of autism*. Cambridge, MA: Perseus Press.

47. Cited in Spiegel, A. (2010, December 29). What's a mental disorder? Even experts can't agree. *All Things Considered*. www.npr.org/2010/12/29/132407384/whats-a-mental-disorder-even-experts-cant-agree.

48. Wing et al., Autism spectrum disorders in the DSM-V.

49. Cash, A profile of gifted individuals with autism.

50. Bashe, P. R., Kirby, B. L., & Attwood, T. (2001). *The OASIS guide to Asperger's syndrome: Advice, support, insight, and inspiration*. New York: Random House, p. 27.

51. Lord, C., & Somer, B. L. (2010). Autism spectrum disorders: Diagnosis, prevalence, and services for children and families. *Social Policy Report, 24*(2), 1–21.

52. American Psychiatric Association. (2011, January 26). 299.00 autistic disorder. www.dsm5.org/ProposedRevisions/Pages/proposedrevision.aspx?rid=94#.
53. Volkmar, F. (2010). Autism and Social policy: Issues, needs, and directions for the future. *Social Policy Report, 24*(2), 25.
54. Wallis, A powerful identity, a vanishing diagnosis.
55. American Psychiatric Association. (2011, January 26). Social communication disorder. www.dsm5.org/ProposedRevisions/Pages/proposedrevision.aspx?rid=489.

Chapter 8: 2e Students and Education

1. Kentucky Department of Education. (2010–2011). *Jefferson County Public Schools: Southern high school school leadership assessment report*. www.education.ky.gov/kde/administrative+resources/school+improvement/leadership+assessment/leadership+assessment+reports+2010-2011.htm.
2. Huckabee - Sir Ken Robinson, author of *The Element* (01-31-2009). (2009, January 31). *YouTube*. www.youtube.com/watch?v=f9OoSHZbBHQ.
3. Quoted in Blog: Race to Nowhere on NPR's On Point (2010, December 18). Race to Nowhere. www.racetonowhere.com/news/blog-race-nowhere-nprs-point-0.
4. Huckabee - Sir Ken Robinson, author of *The Element* (01-31-2009).
5. Quoted in Nielson, L. (2011, February 22). Empowered parents are the solution to ending this race to nowhere. Huffpost Education. www.huffingtonpost.com/lisa-nielsen/parents-are-the-key-to-ge_b_825540.html.
6. Plucker, J. A., Burroughs, N., & Song, R. (2010, February 4). *Mind the (other) gap! The growing excellence gap in K-12 education*. Center for Evaluation and Education Policy. www.iub.edu/~ceep/Gap/excellence/ExcellenceGapBrief.pdf.
7. Brown, E. F. (2008, Summer). Excellence versus equity: Political forces in the education of gifted students. *Digest of Gifted Research*. Duke TIP. www.tip.duke.edu/node/903.

8. Coleman & Gallagher, cited in Rizza, M. G., & Morrison, W. F. (2007). Identifying twice exceptional students: A toolkit for success. *Teaching Exceptional Children Plus*, *3*(3). http://escholarship.bc.edu/cgi/viewcontent.cgi?article=1284&context=education/tecplus.

9. Nicpon, M. (2007). *Tips for parents: Meeting the diverse needs of twice-exceptional students*. Davidson Institute for Talent Development. www.davidsongifted.org/db/Articles_id_10428.aspx.

10. Brown, Excellence versus equity.

11. National Association for Gifted Children. (n.d.). *State of the nation in gifted education*. www.nagc.org/uploadedFiles/Information_and_Resources/State_of_the_States_2008–2009/2008–09 State of the Nation overview.pdf.

12. Ibid.

13. Reis, S. M. (2008, September 14). Brightness at risk. *Washington Times*. www.washingtontimes.com/news/2008/sep/14/brightness-at-risk/?page=all#pagebreak.

14. Office of Special Education Programs. (2010, January 13). Letter to Anonymous. 110 LRP 52277. www.sst5.k12.oh.us/OSEP_Letter_Re_Gifted_ADD.pdf.

15. Cited in National Association for Gifted Children. (2009, March). *NAGC position statement: Twice-exceptionality*. www.nagc.org/index.aspx?id=5094.

16. LDinfo. (n.d.). *Response to Intervention (RTI) vs the discrepancy model*. www.ldinfo.com/rti.htm.

17. Silverman, L. K. (1989). Invisible gifts, invisible handicaps. *Roeper Review*, *12*, 37–42.

18. Baum, S., & Owen, S. V. (2004). *To be gifted and learning disabled: Strategies for helping bright students with LD, ADHD, and more*. Mansfield Center, CT: Creative Learning Press; Coleman, M. R., Gallagher, J., & Foster, A. (1998). *Updated report on state policies related to the identification of gifted students*. Chapel Hill: University of North Carolina Press.

19. Baum & Owen, cited in Bracamonte, M. (2010, March). Twice-exceptional students: Who are they and what do they need?

2e Twice-Exceptional Newsletter. www.2enewsletter.com/arch_Bracamonte_2e_Students_pubarea_3-10. htm.

20. Silverman, Invisible gifts, invisible handicaps.
21. U.S. Department of Education. (2006, October 10). Topic: Identification of specific learning disabilities. ED.gov. http://idea.ed.gov/explore/view/p/%2Croot%2Cdynamic%2CTopicalBrief%2C23%2C.
22. Assouline, S. G., Nicpon, M. F., & Whiteman, C. (2010). Cognitive and psychosocial characteristics of gifted students with written language disability. *Gifted Child Quarterly*, 54(2), 102–115.
23. Quoted in LDinfo, *Response to Intervention (RTI)*.
24. National Center on Response to Intervention. (2011, March). What is RtI? www.rti4success.org/whatisrti.
25. National Association of State Directors of Special Education. (2011, January 12). Response to Intervention (RtI) project. www.nasdse.org/Projects/ResponsetoInterventionRtIProject/tabid/411/Default.aspx.
26. UNC FPG Child Development Center. (2010, December). What is RTI? http://randr.fpg.unc.edu/origins-rr-response-intervention-rti.
27. National Center on Response to Intervention, What is RtI?
28. National Association for Gifted Children, NAGC *position statement*.
29. National Association of State Directors of Special Education and the Council of Administrators of Special Education. (2006, May). *Response to Intervention*. www.casecec.org/pdf/rti/RtI An Administrator's Perspective 1-061.pdf.
30. Resnick, B. (2009). What is Response to Intervention (RTI)? Rush NeuroBehavioral Center. www.rnbc.org/2009/10/what-is-response-to-intervention-rti/.
31. Ibid.
32. Ibid.
33. Ibid.
34. LDinfo, *Response to Intervention (RTI)*.

35. Office of Special Education and Rehabilitative Services. (2010, January 21). Memorandum: A response to intervention (RtI) process cannot be used to delay-deny an evaluation for eligibility under the Individuals with Disabilities Education Act (IDEA). www2.ed.gov/about/offices/list/osers/index.html.

36. Brown, E. F., & Abernathy, S. H. (2009). Policy implications at the state and district level with RtI for gifted students. *Gifted Child Today*, *32*(3), 52–57.

37. Ibid.

38. Doolittle, J. (2007, December 17). *Response to intervention: Implementation considerations*. Office of Special Education Programs. http://docs.google.com/viewer?a=v&q=cache:lWgFTJCv0VYJ:www.pbismaryland.org/documents/Coaches122007/12-13-07%2520Response%2520to%2520Intervention.ppt+RtI+building+an+airplane+while&hl=en&gl=us&pid=bl&srcid=ADGEESgG0uqVUiBiYAkU2_ei78sA1gGZxCILN-aEkx2wGpFEXn5dTvQlbC4N5Rj30cUjG51TlD4cvlgZEK9jUQhPzVPqjHtQWkbRBndSQPy1To_0qa0c0RXA3WTrJCskOhtsLOXrJLSg&sig=AHIEtbSoEvlQlJTLWavjWSqeY2AVbnIcdg.

39. Cross, J. R., Cross, T. L., & Finch, H. (2010). Maximizing student potential versus building community. *Roeper Review*, *32*, 235–248.

40. Baum, S. (2009, January). 2e experts look ahead at 2009. *2e Twice-Exceptional Newsletter*, no. 32, p. 22.

41. National Association for Gifted Children, *NAGC position statement*.

42. Ibid.

43. L. Silverman, interview with the authors, November 17, 2010.

44. Silverman interview; National Association for Gifted Children, *NAGC position statement*.

45. Hughes, C. E., Rollins, K., Johnsen, S. K., Pereles, D. A., Omdal, S., Baldwin, L., et al. (2009, Summer). Remaining challenges for the use of RtI with gifted education. *Gifted Child Today*, *32*(3), 58–68.

46. Ibid.

47. Baum, 2e experts look ahead at 2009; Assouline et al., Cognitive and psychosocial characteristics; McKenzie, R. G. (2010). The insufficiency of Response to Intervention in identifying gifted students with learning disabilities. *Learning Disabilities Research & Practice*, *25*(3), 161–168.
48. Assouline et al., Cognitive and psychosocial characteristics.
49. Ibid
50. Ibid.
51. Silverman interview; B. Gilman, interview with the authors, November 17, 2010.
52. Huckabee - Sir Ken Robinson, author of *The Element* (01-31-2009).

Chapter 9: Diagnosing the Whole Child

1. Risi, S., Lord, C., Gotham, K., Corsello, C., Chrysler, C., Szatmari, P., et al. (2006). Combining information from multiple sources in the diagnosis of autism spectrum disorders. *Journal of American Academy of Child and Adolescent Psychiatry*, *45*, 1094–1103.
2. University of Michigan Autism and Communication Disorders Center. (2009, September). ADOS/ADI-R FAQs. www.umaccweb.com/education/faqs.html.
3. Jordan, R., Howlin, P., & Bowler, D. (2006). Editorial. *Autism*, *10*, 227–228; Nygren, G., Hagberg, B., Billstedt, E., Skoglund, A., Gillberg, C., & Johansson, M. (2009). The Swedish version of the Diagnostic Interview for Social and Communication Disorders (DISCO-10). Psychometric properties. *Journal of Autism and Developmental Disorders*, *39*, 730–741.
4. Yirimiay, Sigman, & Freeman, cited in Nygren et al., Swedish version of the Diagnostic Interview for Social and Communication Disorders.
5. Jordan et al., Editorial.
6. Widiger, T. A., & Mullins-Sweatt, S. (2007). Mental disorders as discrete clinical conditions: Dimensional versus categorical classification. In M. Hersen, S. M. Turner, & D. C. Beidel (Eds.), *Adult psychopathology* (5th ed., pp. 3–33.). Hoboken, NJ: Wiley.

7. Peralta, V., & Cuesta, M. J. (2007, June). A dimensional and categorical architecture for the classification of psychotic disorders. *World Psychiatry*. www.ncbi.nlm.nih.gov/pmc/articles/PMC2219908/.

8. Widiger & Mullins-Sweatt, Mental disorders as discrete clinical conditions.

9. National Autistic Society. (n.d.). *Diagnostic options: A guide for health professionals*. www.autism.org.uk/en-gb/working-with/health/screening-and-diagnosis/diagnostic-options-a-guide-for-health-professionals.aspx.

10. Wing, L. (2005). Introduction. *Plenary presentations, National Autistic Society International Conference 2005*. London: National Autistic Society. www.autism.org.uk/en-gb/news-and-events/nas-conferences/our-previous-conferences/international-conference-2005/plenary-presentations.aspx.

11. DISCO. (n.d.). Diagnostic Interview for Social and Communication Disorders (DISCO): A brief description. www.autism.org.uk/our-services/diagnosing-complex-needs.aspx.

12. Wing et al., Swedish version of the Diagnostic Interview for Social and Communication Disorders; Wing, L., Leekam, S. R., Libby, S. J., Gould, J., & Larcombe, M. (2002). The Diagnostic Interview for Social and Communication Disorders: Background, inter-rater reliability and clinical use. *Journal of Child Psychology and Psychiatry*, *43*(3), 307–325.

13. Nygren et al. (2009). The Swedish version of the Diagnostic Interview for Social and Communication Disorders (DISCO-10) Psychometric properties. *Journal of Autism and Developmental Disorders*, *39*(5), 730–741.

14. Ibid.

15. DISCO, Diagnostic Interview for Social and Communication Disorders.

16. Ibid.

17. Wing, L. (2006, January 16). DISCO and the triad of impairments. (E. Hopkins, Interviewer). Autism Connect. www.autismconnect.org.uk/interviews.asp?section=000100040001&id=4092.

18. Coury, cited in Dawson, G. (2010). The changing face of autism requires rethinking policy needs. *Social Policy Report*, *24*(2), 22–23.

19. American Speech-Language Hearing Association. (2006). *Roles and responsibilities of speech-language pathologists in diagnosis, assessment, and treatment of autism spectrum disorders across the life span.* www.asha.org/docs/html/PS2006-00105.html.

20. Burger-Veltmeijer, A. (n.d.). *Gifted or autistic? The "grey zone."* www.agnesburger.nl/images/uploads/Gifted_or_autistic.pdf.

21. American Speech-Language Hearing Association, *Roles and responsibilities*.

22. Bruhl, W. (2000, Spring). Pediatric chiropractic for developmental delays. *New Developments*, *5(4)*. Developmental Delay Resources. www.devdelay.org/newsletter/articles/html/149-pediatric-chiropractic.html.

23. Aguilar, A. L., Grostic, J. D., & Pfleger, B. (2000.). Chiropractic care and behaviour in autistic children. *Journal of Clinical Chiropractic Pediatrics*, 293–304; Sandefur, R., & Adams, E. (1987, December). The effect of chiropractic adjustments on the behaviour of autistic children: A case review. *Journal of Chiropractic*, *24*(12), 21–25.

24. Field, T., Morrow, C., Valdeon, C., Larson, S., Kuhn, C., & Schanberg, S. (1992). Massage reduces anxiety in child and adolescent psychiatric patients. *Journal of the American Child and Adolescent Psychiatry*, *31*, 125–131.

25. Escalona, A., Field, T., Singer-Strunk, R., Cullen, C., & Hartshorn, K. (2010). Brief report: Improvements in the behavior of children with autism following massage therapy. *Journal of Autism and Developmental Disorders*, *31*, 513–516.

26. Processed food diet in early childhood may lower subsequent IQ. (2011, February 7). *British Medical Journal*. e! Science News.

http://esciencenews.com/articles/2011/02/07/processed.food.diet.early.childhood.may.lower.subsequent.iq.

27. Whiteley, P., Haracopos, D., Knivsberg, A-M., Reichelt, K. L., Parlar, S., Jacobsen, J., et al. (2010, April). The ScanBrit randomized, controlled, single-blind study of a gluten- and casein-free dietary intervention for children with autism spectrum disorders. *Nutritional Neuroscience, 13*(2), 87–100.
28. Wing, L. (2001). *The autistic spectrum: A parents' guide to understanding and helping your child*. Berkeley, CA: Ulysses Press.
29. Ratey, J. (2000). *A user's guide to the brain*. New York: Pantheon, p. 178.
30. Bracamonte, M. (2010, March). Twice-exceptional students: Who are they and what do they need? *2e Twice-Exceptional Newsletter*. www.2enewsletter.com/arch_Bracamonte_2e_Students_pubarea_3-10.htm.
31. Ibid.
32. American Coaching Association. (2010, February 19). www.americoach.org/.
33. An interview with two coaches: Coaching for gifted children with attention and other issues. (2011, January/February). *2e Twice-Exceptional Newsletter*. www.cognitivesolutionslc.com/2e.pdf.

Chapter 10: Educating the Whole Child

1. Otten, K., & Tuttle, J. (2011). *How to reach and teach children with challenging behavior*. San Francisco: Jossey-Bass.
2. Bracamonte, M. (2010, March). Twice-exceptional students: Who are they and what do they need? *2e Twice-Exceptional Newsletter*. www.2enewsletter.com/arch_Bracamonte_2e_Students_pubarea_3-10.htm.
3. Ibid.
4. Silverman, L. (2009, Oct. 13). The two-edged sword of compensation: How the gifted cope with learning disabilities. WePapers. www.wepapers.com/Papers/61940/The_two-edged_

sword_of_compensation-_How_the_gifted_cope_with_learning_disabilities.

5. Gifted Development Center. (2010, December 28). Assessment. www.gifteddevelopment.com/About_GDC/assessment.htm.
6. Ibid.
7. Coleman, M. R. (2010, October 30). Raven Intelligence Test. Family Education. http://school.familyeducation.com/gifted-education/educational-testing/41838.html?detoured=1.
8. Beckley, D. (1998, Spring). Gifted and learning disabled: Twice exceptional students. *NRC/GT Newsletter*. Neag Center for Gifted Education and Talent Development. www.gifted.uconn.edu/nrcgt/newsletter/spring98/sprng984.html.
9. Bonk, C. J. (2011, January). Instructional strategies for thinking, collaboration, and motivation. www.indiana.edu/~bobweb/r546/index.html.
10. Renzulli, J. S., Reis, S. M., Gavin, M. K., Siegle, D., & Sytsma, R. (2003). *Four new scales for rating the behavior characteristics of superior students*. Neag Center for Gifted Education and Talent Development. www.gifted.uconn.edu/siegle/Conferences/SRBCSSNAGC2003Handout.pdf; Beckley, Gifted and learning disabled.
11. Twachtman-Cullen, D., & Twachtman-Bassett, J. (2011). *The IEP from A to Z: How to create meaningful and measurable goals and objectives*. San Francisco: Jossey-Bass, p. 2.
12. Ibid, p. 3.
13. Montgomery County Public Schools. (2010, January). *Twice exceptional students: A guidebook for supporting the achievement of gifted students with special needs*. www.montgomeryschoolsmd.org/curriculum/enriched/mcpsprograms/gtld/docs1/2010 Twice Exceptional.pdf; Colorado Department of Education. (2005). *Twice exceptional students: Gifted students with disabilities: An introductory resource book*. Denver: Colorado Department of Education; Bracamonte, Twice-exceptional students.

14. Colorado Department of Education, *Twice exceptional students;* Montgomery County Public Schools, *Twice exceptional students;* Virginia Department of Education. (2010, September). *Supporting the identification and achievement of the twice-exceptional student.* www.doe.virginia.gov/instruction/gifted_ed/twice_exceptional.pdf.

15. Winner, M. G. (2010, November 13). Introduction to social thinking. Social Thinking. www.socialthinking.com/what-is-social-thinking/introduction.

16. Ibid.

17. Winner, M. G. (n.d.). Perspective taking across the school and adult years for persons with social cognitive deficits. Fairfield Special Education PTA. www.fairfieldsepta.org/documents/PerspectiveTakingSpectrum.pdf.

18. Ibid.

19. Winner, M. G. (2010, December 17). Social thinking and academics. Social Thinking. www.socialthinking.com/what-is-social-thinking/academic-issues.

20. Ibid.

21. Ibid.

22. Buescher, T. M., & Higham, S. (2003, November). Helping adolescents adjust to giftedness. SENG: Supporting Emotional Needs of the Gifted. www.sengifted.org/articles_social/BuescherHigham_HelpingAdolescentsAdjust.shtml.

23. Smith Myles, B. (2005). *Children and youth with Asperger syndrome.* Thousand Oaks, CA: Corwin Press.

24. Montgomery County Public Schools, *Twice exceptional students;* Colorado Department of Education, *Twice exceptional students;* Virginia Department of Education, *Supporting the identification and achievement of the twice-exceptional student.*

25. Winebrenner, S. (2003). Teaching strategies for twice-exceptional students. *Intervention in School and Clinic, 38,* 131–137.

26. Ibid.

27. Armstrong, T. (1991). *Awakening your child's natural genius.* New York: Penguin Putnam.

28. Webb, J., Amend, E. R., Webb, N. E., Goerss, J., Beljan, P., & Olenchak, F. R. (2005). *Misdiagnosis and dual diagnoses of gifted children and adults*. Scottsdale, AZ: Great Potential Press, p. 23.
29. Armstrong, *Awakening your child's natural genius*.
30. Lind, S. (2001). Overexcitability and the gifted. *Supporting Emotional Needs of the Gifted Newsletter*, *1*(1), 3–6.
31. Vail, P. L. (1989). *Smart kids with school problems*. New York: Penguin Plume, p. 32.
32. Grandin, T., & Duffy, K. (2004). *Developing talents: Careers for individuals with Asperger syndrome and high-functioning autism*. Shawnee Mission, KS: Autism Asperger Publishing, p. 46.
33. Ibid.

Conclusion

1. National Resource Center on AD/HD. Real science defines ADHD as real disorder. www.help4adhd.org/en/about/science.
2. Robinson, S. K. (2009). *The element: How finding your passion changes everything*. New York: Viking Press, p. 238.

Acknowledgments

Since the publication of our previous book, we have continued to search for answers to better understand our children and their challenges, but mostly for ways to help them embrace their individual gifts and talents. Along this journey, we have been strengthened and emboldened by the love of our Lord, and by the many parents who have shared their stories, struggles, and triumphs with us. Our work is for you.

Thanks to the enthusiastic support and encouragement of our editor Marjorie McAneny at Jossey-Bass, a vision has become a reality. Her dedication to this project has been invaluable at every stage of development, and her passion to serve parents and teachers of twice-exceptional children is remarkable. Our thanks also go to the president of Jossey-Bass, Debra Hunter, whose belief in this project allowed it to be born. We are also grateful for the wonderful Jossey-Bass team, especially Carol Hartland, Michele Jones, and Tracy Gallagher. Michele, in particular, we thank you for your hard work, keen eye, and unwavering commitment to excellence.

Because of the encouragement of gifted, pioneering women such as Temple Grandin, Lorna Wing, and Judith Gould, who have dedicated their lives to helping children such as ours, we had the courage to address many of the controversies in mental health and education that so profoundly affect twice-exceptional children.

Through the years, Temple has mentored us in our quest to see our children as bright not broken and has been a driving force behind our efforts to bring the gifted and disabled communities together. We are deeply grateful for her willingness to share her experience, strength, and hope with us as well as for her passion and dedication to helping others. She has given generously of herself, helping us reason through controversial subjects and encouraging us to take a strong stand rooted firmly in science and research. Thank you, Temple, for being an example of unwavering courage and commitment.

We are also deeply indebted to Dr. Lorna Wing and Dr. Judith Gould for their contributions and comments. Years ago, as we discussed the problems we saw with the DSM system, ADHD, and the autism spectrum, Lorna encouraged us, saying that "there is nothing like the steely determination of two moms" to promote change within the current system. As we consulted with her and her colleague Judith, their passionate enthusiasm for our work and their input into this manuscript have been invaluable. We are especially grateful for permission to reprint excerpts from their many insightful works. Bless you both.

In our quest to learn about the gifted community, we have been fortunate to meet many enthusiastic, dedicated professionals. We are especially grateful to Dr. Linda Silverman, who has encouraged us personally and professionally. Her work has been foundational in helping the world understand the true nature of giftedness and in seeing the importance of uniting the gifted and disabled communities. We also thank Bobbie Gilman for her comments on the challenges of identifying twice-exceptional children in the classroom. We are grateful to you both for sharing your time and knowledge with us.

We are extremely thankful for Dr. Lydia Furman's candid and objective examinations of ADHD. Her support and advice proved invaluable as we tackled the highly controversial subject of the validity of ADHD as a distinct disorder.

Lisa LaVardera's insightful commentary and guidance into the legal implications of 504 have helped us as well as countless others for whom she serves as an advocate. A mother of two twice-exceptional children, she has given generously of her time to review the manuscript. Her comments have been invaluable, as have her encouragement and friendship throughout the years. We also thank Carl Daisy for his insightful comments and perspective.

Our gratitude also extends to the three highly dedicated professionals whose work has blazed the trail for understanding how giftedness and disabilities impact children and families. First and foremost, we thank Michelle Garcia Winner for her unwavering support throughout the years. Her dedication and tireless efforts to help individuals develop the social thinking skills necessary for success is truly admirable. Likewise, we are indebted to Diane Twachtman-Cullen and Brenda Smith Myles for their continued encouragement in our work and their ongoing efforts in helping those with autism spectrum disorders and related conditions.

We also thank the many other professionals whose work has proven invaluable in our quest to understand and embrace giftedness and disabilities. These include Drs. Uta Frith, James Webb, Edward Amend, Sally Reis, Susan Baum, Maureen Neihart, Megan Nicpon, Susan Assouline, Thomas Armstrong, and John Ratey.

Finally, we come to our prayer warriors, without whom none of this would have been possible. Their prayers sustained us when the pressures of family, deadlines, and work overwhelmed us. Just as this project and we have been in your hearts, so you are in ours. Thank you Chris Jolly, Teresa Knittle, Debra Miller, Connie White, Brenda Houghton, and Ruth Collins.

Rebecca S. Banks

When we embarked on this journey over a decade ago, neither Diane nor I had a clue that our work was as much about understanding ourselves as it was about understanding our children.

Through the years, as we have grown deeply in friendship, knowledge, and awareness, Diane has taught me much about patience, perseverance, and determination. It has been a joy to watch as she grew in her awareness of her own giftedness and to share in her journey of discovery. Her painstaking commitment to excellence and perfectionism has compelled me to grow both personally and professionally. At the same time, I have learned so much from her, especially about staying dedicated to a vision. Thank you, Diane, for inviting me on this most exciting voyage, for encouraging me to embrace my own giftedness, and for our continued friendship.

On a more personal level, I want to thank those closest to me who made this book possible. My husband, Andrew, whose love has been a constant in my life, encourages me daily. Throughout this project, he graciously kept the household going. For all of his delicious dinners, the clean laundry, his loving support, and his faithful prayers, I am deeply grateful.

I also want to thank my two children who put their needs on hold and gave me the necessary space to complete this book. Although I was in the trenches, so to speak, while writing this book, my children's constant encouragement freed me to focus on this important work. Both of them have worked hard to see themselves as bright not broken. I am extremely proud of my son, Graham, whose courageous determination has allowed him to embrace his gifts and become a successful young adult. And, throughout her life, my daughter Erin's persistence and resilience have inspired me as I have watched her squarely face her challenges and grow in her gifts. I am proud of the young woman she is becoming.

I also must thank the one woman who encouraged me to rise above my circumstances and to pursue my dreams: my late grandmother, Helen Banks. Her love sustained me when it seemed nothing else could, and she believed in me when no one else would. Her loving care and support are why I am alive today.

Diane M. Kennedy

First and foremost I would like to thank my coauthor and best friend of over ten years, Rebecca Banks. Through this project we have discovered and learned exciting new things not only about our work but about ourselves. Once again I am in awe of her ability to take the most difficult subjects and controversial issues and make sense of them both in my head and on paper. Writing, organizing, and editing are all part of Becky's gifts and abilities. I am grateful for them and I was more than willing to let her take the lead using them. This project definitely grew into a much bigger challenge than either of us had ever imagined. Rebecca's determination and dedication to excellence are also two qualities I admire and deeply respect. I am especially thankful for the friendship we have shared through the years and look forward to our continued work together helping to serve those we believe are bright not broken.

Our inspirational office space became a second home to me as the months turned into years. I am especially grateful to Andrew Cull for all of the coffee, meals, prayers, and assistance. We consider you a very important member of our team! Bless you and thank you for all your encouragement along the way. Erin Cull, I am thankful for your willingness to share your mom so much and especially for your help with technology issues! You are a very gifted young lady; your desire to serve twice-exceptional kids is moving. You will make a wonderful and welcome advocate!

I am grateful for the love and support of my own family as I became consumed with the challenges of such an intense book project. To my husband, Tom, thank you for your help and support. Without you I would not have the wonderful children who have given my life such purpose and joy. This book has taught me how blessed I am to have such a big family full of wonderful gifts and talents. To my sister Debbie, who is my rock of support and always there, thank you for your belief in me and helping me see I just may be a little smart too.

My children are the reason I began this work so many years ago. I am excited about the many ways they have all learned to embrace their talents and abilities.

Jeff, your dedication to excellence and determination to consistently challenge yourself has earned you the highest of honors as a Marine officer. I couldn't be more proud of you and your service to our country. You are a wonderful husband, father, and son. I cherish our friendship and am so happy Melisa found her way into our lives; she is a treasure.

Ben, you have always shined with your intellectual abilities and dedication to serving others. When you embraced your exceptional skills and talents and devoted your career as a Marine to serving our nation at the highest levels, I knew it would be a perfect fit, and it was. At the same time, you are a dedicated husband and father whom I truly admire. Becky and your family are especially near and dear to my heart.

Sam, you are probably the main reason this book has been so important to me. Your gifts and talents have always been crystal clear to me, but it has been a long road of ups and downs. The resilience you have repeatedly shown as you faced the challenges and struggles of being twice exceptional is nothing short of remarkable. You have tackled each defeat with a renewed sense of determination and enthusiasm. Your sense of humor, your compassion and deep sense of moral justice are all qualities I cherish about you. I know Kara Beth does too! I am very thankful for her being in both of our lives! It is in your gifts and talents that you will find both peace and potential to help others as I know in your heart you desire to do. I sincerely hope this work has helped bring an understanding to what you wanted to embrace: being bright not broken.

Index

Page reference followed by *fig* indicates an illustrated diagram; followed by *t* indicates a table.

I